BIOGRAPHY OF A HACIENDA

Biography of a Hacienda

Work and Revolution in Rural Mexico

ELIZABETH TERESE NEWMAN

THE UNIVERSITY OF
ARIZONA PRESS

TUCSON

The University of Arizona Press
© 2014 The Arizona Board of Regents
All rights reserved

www.uapress.arizona.edu

Library of Congress Cataloging-in-Publication data are available from the Library of Congress.

Publication of this book was made possible in part by a grant from The Reed Foundation.

Manufactured in the United States of America on acid-free, archival-quality paper containing a minimum of 30% post-consumer waste and processed chlorine free.

19 18 17 16 15 14   6 5 4 3 2 1

for my grandmother Wilma Denser
who always knew I was a teacher

and

for Jane Theodoropoulos
who introduced me to the field of anthropology over a cup of tea

Contents

Illustrations

Acknowledgments

Dr. Harold Juli began the Acocotla project more than a decade ago. While in graduate school and searching for a dissertation project, I stopped in Puebla to visit him in June 2004. When I stepped off the bus in Puebla, I was not expecting to toss aside carefully laid plans to work elsewhere in favor of joining his project. But Harold's dedication to teaching, his intellectual generosity, his enthusiasm for the project, and his love of Mexico won me over immediately. I spent many happy hours working and talking with Harold and his wife, Harriet, both in Mexico and at home. Harold was diagnosed with cancer the week he was due to join me in Mexico for our 2006 summer field season, and he passed away eight months later. Somehow, before his passing, he found the time and energy to spare a thought for this project that he loved so much, requesting that all his research materials make it into my hands for inclusion here. Even more incredible, following Harold's death, Harriet found the time and energy to go through his office and make sure every potentially relevant scrap of paper made it into my hands. I have done my best to honor Harold's wishes and Harriet's work, and I hope that he would be pleased with and proud of the final product.

This research would not have been possible without the support and permission of a number of organizations and funders. The people of La Soledad Morelos allowed me to conduct the excavations, assisted in my work with enthusiasm and interest, and welcomed me into their town and homes. The National Institute of Anthropology and History of Mexico gave permission for the archaeological excavations. Archaeological, ethno-historic, and ethnoarchaeological investigations were made possible through the generous support of The Reed Foundation, New York; the FAHSS Fund, Stony Brook University; the Foundation for the Advancement of Mesoamerican Studies, Inc.; the Agrarian Studies Program, Yale University; the MacMillin Center, Yale University; the John F. Enders Fund, Yale University; the Augusta Hazard Fund, Department of Anthropology, Yale University; the Josef Albers Traveling Fellowship, Department of Anthropology, Yale University; and two anonymous donors. Archival work in Mexico City and the state of Puebla was made possible by the generous permission and support of the following people: at the Archivo General de la Nación, Jorge Ruiz Dueñas, director; at the Archivo General del Estado de Puebla, Pilar Pacheco Zamudio, director, and Guadalupe Farfán; at the Archivo General de Notarías de Puebla, Ana Rosa Freda Holguín, director; and at the Archivo Historico Municipal de Atlixco, Natalia Pacheco Pérez. In the United States, Patricia Kervick of Harvard's Peabody Museum Archives generously donated her time, scanning and e-mailing me a copy of a one-of-a-kind manuscript. At the University of Arizona Press, Allyson Carter and her colleagues shepherded this book (and me) through the publication process with great patience. The input of anonymous reviewers proved invaluable. Rani Alexander's generosity to a scholar new to the field cannot be overstated.

Because this research began as a dissertation project, former teachers have played a central role in shaping the way I thought about and presented the material in this book. Judith Zeitlin lured me to Mexico when I was still an undergraduate. Though I stopped being her "responsibility" many years ago, she has continued to be generous with her time and advice. I hope this book is at least a partial repayment for her kindness and support. In Mexico, Patricia Plunket Nagoda stepped into the gap left by Harold's death and assumed the role of project adviser and mentor. This book would have been impossible without her hours of advice. At Yale University, my adviser Marcello Canuto introduced perspectives to my work that would have otherwise escaped me. Richard Burger gave me the opportunity to think outside of Mesoamerica by sharing his extensive knowledge of and love for all things Andean. Mary Miller taught me to think creatively about architecture and about my writing. At the University of Massachusetts, Boston, Ann Blum set the foundations for my understandings of Mexican history and, like the great teacher she is, pushed me to be better than I knew I could be. Stephen Mrozowski, who enticed me out of the history department and into the field of historical archaeology with his engaging lectures, did much to form the way I interpret the past.

At Stony Brook University, the history department has given me a warm and supportive academic home, and my colleagues, always ready to celebrate another milestone, have lent many sympathetic ears to the highs and lows of bringing this book to publication. Special thanks to Brooke Larson, who insisted I stay true the voice I found writing this book when I was overwhelmed with doubt. The archaeologists in the anthropology department also welcomed me warmly, including me in their lectures and great parties. Elsewhere, Melissa Forbis offered comments on the manuscript, excellent coffee, and empathy. Ginny Clancy read and commented on the manuscript and, when I needed a break, lent me novels that had nothing to do with my research. My students, both in history and in the environmental humanities program, have taught me much about what I needed to say and how best to say it. Their questions and comments forced me to rethink my assumptions and reconsider how I frame my explanations. Angelica Leigh Whitehorne edited early drafts with the eye of both student and writer and harassed me from her seat in the front row of my classroom on days when I had not written anything new.

In Mexico, faculty and students at the Universidad de las Américas, Puebla, played a central role in the development and completion of this project. Gabriela Uruñuela Ladrón de Guevara provided oft-consulted, sage advice about the archaeology of the region. Maria Teresa Salomón Salazar provided support and assistance in the lab. Timothy Knab shared his books and knowledge of Puebla's ethnographic literature. Students from the Universidad de las Américas, Puebla, assisted in both the field and the lab with enthusiasm and goodwill. MaryCarmen Romano spent years working in the field and archives, collecting oral histories and researching the documentary history of the hacienda. Su Lin Casanova of the National School of Anthropology and History, Mexico, assisted during the 2007 field season and was responsible for project photography during those months. Karime Castillo Cardenas provided invaluable assistance in the lab and archives; without her, this book would have taken many more years to write. Back in the United States, Estefany Molina edited my many images and prepared them for publication.

I have been lucky to have a number of friends and colleagues willing to read and reread the manuscript and share their thoughts and advice. The assistance and input of friends and family have not just made this book possible, but made the process of writing it a joy. Trina Waldron read and commented on numerous drafts, but her most important contribution was her enthusiasm for the project. Her inescapable insistence on knowing "what happened to Rafaela next" pushed me to write a more accessible book. Like Trina's, Zee Green's enthusiasm for "my little stories" pushed me to write more and better just to answer her questions. Along with her enthusiasm came great knowledge of the archaeology of the Cholula region and life in Mexico. She taught me to navigate both with kindness and with patience. Catherine Timura lent the eye of a cultural anthropologist, finding time at the very last minute for "one more read." Her comments were just the most recent contribution to years of ongoing discussion and debate, all of which have made me a better anthropologist. Katherine Lee Priddy found time to comment on multiple drafts, using her many years of training and experience in the field to make sure the archaeological details were clear. Always generous with her time and never one to turn something in late, she did not even stop reading when she went into labor with her son William, getting me comments from the hospital so I could make my deadlines even while her own, much larger "deadline" loomed. Lew Stevens made many of the beautiful architectural drawings found in the following pages and, more important, made sure I never lost my sense of humor. On days when I felt like I wouldn't (or couldn't) finish this project, he found the time to take me to lunch and make sure I knew I could. Finally, thanks go to my family, who taught me to pursue my passions above all else and to laugh while doing it.

BIOGRAPHY OF A HACIENDA

Introduction

This book captures the experience of doing historical archaeology for anyone who is curious about the hows and whys of such work. The following
pages are a mosaic of academic prose, memoir, and fiction. Together, the
three distinct narratives sum up the essence of archaeology—technical
analysis, hard work, and a bit of imagination. As you read, you may note a
tension between the prose, memoir, and fiction. It is a tension that archaeologists confront daily. We balance what we can know and what we want
to know as we struggle with the reality of doing the work.

The academic prose is much like you would find in books, articles, or
reports about archaeology. These sections are not at all unusual for a traditional, academic text and may be of the most interest to a specialist.
Grounded in factual events, the sections of memoir are often idealized
compilations of experiences my colleagues, students, and I had in the archives, lab, and field. These sections are intended to illustrate the me-
chanics of doing historical, archaeological, and ethnographic research—
specialists will likely find these texts to be very familiar—and they highlight
the ways in which we collected the data for students and others not ac-
quainted with the sort of research presented in this book. In these sections
of memoir, and in all sections dealing with ethnographic research, the
names used are pseudonyms (with the exception of my research assistants).
I mask the identity of informants and former students to protect their
privacy.

Though the fiction is just that, it is as much a part of the scientific process as any other aspect of inquiry presented in this book. It is this creative

side of research that often drives a scholar, regardless of field, to explore a particular question. The fiction represents my informed imaginings of what someone living during the time under study would have thought and experienced, and my choice of characters and storylines reflects the personal interests that drive my research.

The characters that appear in these narratives were ghosts who wandered in and out of my dreams when I was working too much and sleeping too little. In a few cases, I have woven in glimpses from the archival sources. Whenever I have done so, I identify the kernels of truth and applicable sources in the text. For example, in chapter 3, you meet Lucas Pérez Maldonado and María Catarina. After you read about the characters, you will learn which of their experiences represent actual historical moments.

Often, pieces of the archaeological record find their way into the stories, just as they found their way into my dreams—look for Rafaela's earrings in a few chapters. Most of the time, we do not know who owned artifacts like the earrings, and we can never truly understand the context in which the owners use them. Yet the seemingly physical link of holding these "things" often makes us imagine the life of the unknown person to whom we are connected. With each artifact we unearth, a mystery unfolds.

But why investigate these mysteries? The artifacts and the archives make the stories I tell in the following pages feel like "history." For many, history is something in the past, something to be argued about by academics and memorized by schoolchildren. For the peoples of ancient Mesoamerica, history was past, present, and future. Time was cyclic; events in the past would come to pass again. When I began the research described in the following pages, I, like most Americans, was thinking about the past as something over and done. Since then, I have found myself reconsidering my understanding of history; maybe the people of Mesoamerica were right. The questions I stumbled across in the classroom while studying events like the Mexican Revolution, an event that began more than one hundred years ago, became contemporary, even urgently relevant, when I walked into the central Mexican villages I was studying.

The story that I had learned in the classroom, the "master narrative" of the Mexican Revolution and the resulting agrarian reforms, provided the foundation for my original research design.[1] Ultimately, the results of the research challenged me to think differently about that research design, and about Mexican history and Mexico today. In this book, I share that challenge. The Mexican Revolution is the axis around which the stories told here revolve; this book is about the smallest and most common moments that move people toward revolt rather than about daily life during the Revolution. How did the Hacienda Acocotla's humble workers end up on the national revolutionary stage one hundred years ago? This book explores answers to that question and, using the tools of historical archaeology, shifts the master narrative's focus on men to one that includes women and families. As we will see in the coming pages, historical research suggests that an attack on men's patriarchal roles pushed rural peoples into rebellion. This study suggests that the attack was one that also affected women and children by reconstructing the lives of people who rarely made it into the written record or, when they did, made it there on someone else's terms. It is about the conditions of daily life, and the manipulation of those conditions, that destabilized Atlixco's countryside in the early years of the twentieth century. It is about what that destabilization did, and did not, do for the people who live in the valley today. Though many points may be applicable elsewhere, this is a case study of a single community.

The first two chapters of this book provide the context necessary to understand the research that follows. I begin in chapter 1 with an overview of Mexico in the nineteenth century to orient those with no prior knowledge of this period. It was an extraordinary century bookended by two wars, one of independence and one of internal revolution; it is a complex period in Mexican history during which there were more than forty changes in government and multiple foreign interventions. Films have been made, novels have been written, and historians have produced thousands of pages of historical analysis about each change of regime. The chapter presents what might be considered the "master narrative," and, for the sake of brevity, many of the more nuanced historiographical arguments are ignored. These more nuanced arguments are, however, revisited in much greater depth later in the text if they are relevant to the material being presented. Chapter 2 continues by establishing the geographical and theoretical context of my study and discusses the research design used to address the questions I have presented here. It explains how I went about studying the history of a community in central Mexico because of—and in spite of—the master narrative described in chapter 1.

Chapters 3, 4, and 5 comprise the data section of the book and make transparent the methods used to collect the data. Beginning with what is perhaps the most obvious source of information, chapter 3 surveys the available archival records, exploring what historical research can and cannot tell us about the Hacienda San Miguel Acocotla and its many, diverse inhabitants. This chapter examines the history of the hacienda from its

1577 founding through the early years of the twentieth century, introducing Acocotla's *hacendados* (owners), their families, *mayordomos* (managers), and *peones* (workers). We also look at the complicated relationship between the Hacienda Acocotla and its neighboring villages, upon which the hacienda owners and managers depended and to which workers returned following the dissolution of the haciendas during the first half of the twentieth century. These data show, unsurprisingly, that the elite members of the hacienda community (hacendados and occasionally mayordomos) dominated the historical record. Most of the recovered records do not pertain to the daily life and working conditions of the peones, though we do see the workers in employment lists and censuses that include information such as their level of literacy, race, whether they spoke Nahuatl or Spanish, their marital status, age, education level, and health.[2] These lists, however, appear only during the second half of the nineteenth century. The earliest, and a rare, mention of workers is found in a late seventeenth-century bill of sale that includes among the hacienda's possessions "eight Indian workers and three who are absent."[3] In chapter 3, we will see exactly what the archival records can (and cannot) tell us about the lives of all of the people at the Hacienda Acocotla and in the surrounding region.

Chapter 4 begins in the middle of the muddy main street of one of those neighboring villages, La Soledad Morelos. Continuity between life at the hacienda and modern life in the village is clear. The village is home to the children and grandchildren of the hacienda's workers—some of the people we interviewed had even worked at the hacienda themselves as very young children. Today, many people in this small village live in traditional adobe houses surrounded by domestic house compounds, some of which are very similar to the architecture of Acocotla's *calpanería*, or worker's quarters. The subsequent pages summarize the data from a multiyear ethnographic and ethnoarchaeological study that Dr. Harold Juli began in 2003 (and that I continued). While this phase of research was still under way, Harold lost a battle with cancer in February of 2007. It was his wish that the project continue, and at his behest, I incorporate his collected data into this study. Though he was responsible for the collection of much of the ethnographic data, the analyses and interpretations of these data are mine alone. My discussion of these data is the subject of chapter 4, which presents an examination of domestic architecture and daily life in the descendant community.

The study as it is presented here serves two purposes. First, it establishes "normal" domestic and architectural patterns, allowing me to create a model of expected use of household space in the archaeological record. Second, the experiences that we had in the village of La Soledad Morelos drove us to explore the questions that are the subject of the rest of this book. We found ourselves wondering why, if life is so bleak today, do people not revolt, and, most important, we wondered about the connections between the past and the present. We wanted to know how the people we studied, people who befriended us and welcomed us into their homes and lives with generosity and warmth, ended up living the lives we found them living. We had all learned the master narrative presented in chapter 1 in school. There was a dissonance between that master narrative and the reality we found in the streets of the village that disturbed us. Chapter 4 details our experiences in the village, and we return to reflect on them in the book's conclusion, where we try to answer the questions raised by our research.

As in the preceding two chapters, the purpose of chapter 5 is to lay out the methods for obtaining our data. The chapter begins with a tour of the Hacienda Acocotla and explains how space was used before moving on to a description of two archaeological field seasons. The first, in June of 2005, was completed with the help of a dozen Mexican students from the Universidad de las Américas, Puebla. Our focus that season was on architectural recording, a survey of the field in which the hacienda workers would have conducted many of their daily activities, and some limited test excavations. A preliminary analysis of data collected during that season allowed us to plan our excavations for the winter of 2007. During our second season, we expanded our excavations to include five rooms in the calpanería and excavated an extensive midden in the field in front. The chapter ends by revisiting many of the "expected patterns" of household architecture that we had identified during our ethnoarchaeological work in La Soledad Morelos (in chapter 4). Somewhat surprisingly, we found that a number of our expectations did not hold true at Acocotla.

Chapters 3 through 5 all end with unanswered questions. If truth be told, this is how most field research ends. Scholars rarely have answers to even one of our questions on the last day in the archives, village, or field. Finding those answers takes months of analysis, synthesis, and study of comparative data. Chapters 6, 7, and 8 are the results of that process of long-term study and the story at the heart of this book. These chapters answer many of the questions left hanging at the end of the previous three chapters. Chapter 6 examines what an analysis of architecture can tell us about changing labor relations in nineteenth-century Mexico, painting the backdrop for the stage upon which the workers lived their lives. I integrate data drawn from archival records with data collected during the archaeological and ethnographic phases of the project to understand the experiences of the hacienda's workers and their relationships to managers and owners. Linking those changes to larger social processes and noting a startling mismatch to modern patterns of residence seen in the village of La Soledad Morelos, I suggest that the latter half of the nineteenth century was a period during which labor relations were being transformed at the family level, a transformation that may have contributed to social unrest during the early years of the twentieth century.

In chapters 7 and 8, I set the stage, populating the peones' world with the 87,142 artifacts that we recovered during our excavations. Chapter 7 focuses on the remains of foodways recovered from the calpanería. I look at what the remains of food and items like ceramic tablewares can tell us about the ways in which people organized their lives and the ways in which their lives were organized for them. Chapter 8 continues this discussion with an examination of what archaeologists call "small finds." I look at some of the more notable artifacts recovered during our excavations, and I consider what they have to tell us not only about the daily lives of the people who lived in the calpanería but also about how the workers constructed their identities. Together, these chapters show us the ways in which the hacendados and mayordomos attempted to manipulate and control the domestic lives of their workers, but they also show us some of the ways in which the workers resisted those attempts and give us a peek at normal, everyday life.

Finally, I spend some time in the conclusion thinking about why the questions raised in the earlier chapters matter. For many of us, the history discussed in this book is distant, foreign, and even exotic, but in fact the heritage of that history affects many of us on a daily basis. Once upon a time, people living in remote, indigenous communities in the Valley of Atlixco traveled a few miles from home to work at places like the Hacienda San Miguel Acocotla. Somehow, working conditions became so oppressive that these people decided their only recourse was armed rebellion. They won their fight and were awarded the land on which they had worked for generations. Quickly, that land became insufficient to maintain a basic standard of living. Today, the children and grandchildren of the people whose lives we excavated make the significantly more dangerous journey across the border to the United States, where they live and work in conditions not unlike those their recent ancestors experienced, though, unlike the families who lived in the calpanería, they must often leave their families behind. Making this journey often requires going deeply into debt, a debt that must be paid before the migrant can begin earning money to send home. Migrants who default on that debt often become victims of violence at the hands of the *coyote* who smuggled them across the border, just as their ancestors became victims of violence at the hands of hacienda owners and managers. Though the master narrative described in chapter 1 tells us that debt peonage has been abolished, in fact, this study suggests that debt peonage has instead been implemented on a transnational scale. The answers to the questions of why the indigenous laborers of central Mexico decided to rebel and why the remedies applied to that rebellion were insufficient are, perhaps, worth knowing.

One Hundred Years

From Independence to Revolution in Mexico

The general stifled a groan as he climbed stiffly off his horse. He would be forty in another year, too old for the strenuous life of a soldier at war, not that he was prepared to admit it to anybody but himself. General Fortino Ayaquica looked around as his men, following his lead, dismounted. Some of them were already glancing about with an appraising eye, looking for whatever each thought he needed most: food, valuables, women. He sharply ordered them to refrain from plundering, reminding them that that sort of behavior would not be acceptable today. He ignored the grumbling behind him as he turned back to look at the casco. *This meeting was important; they couldn't afford any distractions.*

Clearly, nobody had told the hacienda's peones *about today's conference. He had watched them flee for the safety of Acocotla's walls as he and his soldiers approached. They had abandoned their belongings, leaving everything unguarded in the field fronting the* calpanería. *They were worried more about their personal safety than that of their possessions. Given the way things had been going in the Valley of Atlixco lately, it was understandable.*

He looked around at the living space, guessing it was occupied by thirty-five or forty families. He stood clenching his jaw, fighting the anger he felt when he observed the conditions in which people were forced to live. General Fortino Ayaquica had spent his childhood in nearby Tochimilco, and it was haciendas such as this one he had been thinking of when he signed the amended Plan de Ayala three years earlier. He had chosen this meeting spot intentionally, convinced that Colonel Reyes couldn't possibly remain a Constitutionalist in such surroundings. Reyes would walk through this field, this so-called living space, passing between the rooms of the calpanería to enter the hacienda, and he would understand the position held by the Zapatistas. Fortino Ayaquica was convinced it was impossible to remain unmoved in the face of the poverty, hunger, and suffering seen in this field in front of the Hacienda San Miguel Acocotla.

The general turned as the approaching horses interrupted his thoughts.

At ten in the morning on April 17, 1917, the Zapatista General Fortino Ayaquica met with the Constitutionalist Colonel Eduardo Reyes at the Hacienda San Miguel Acocotla. According to an exchange of letters between the two, each man brought two officers, one assistant, and ten soldiers with him, although a letter sent by Fortino Ayaquica to his commander, the famous Emiliano Zapata, tells us that the Zapatistas had hidden over four hundred men in a nearby gully. Each met in hopes of convincing the other, through both discussion and manipulation, to switch sides; each believed that such a switch would bring peace to the Valley of Atlixco.[1] Both were unsuccessful in their mission, but the effort is understandable. By April of 1917, Mexico had endured six-and-a-half years of civil war known today as the Mexican Revolution. Soldiers in the employ of competing factions roamed the countryside, battling each other and laying waste to villages and farmland. People were exhausted, frightened, and hungry. Many perhaps wondered what had brought about the years of unrest.

The Hacienda in Colonial Mexico, 1519–1810

Fortino Ayaquica's choice of meeting place that April morning was likely deliberate. Haciendas were omnipresent across Mexico's postconquest landscape, and during the Mexican Revolution they would become a central part of Zapata's reform program, factors that have made haciendas the focus of extensive historical research.[2] They were most famously defined as businesses that were "operated by a dominant landowner and a dependent labor force, organized to supply a small-scale market by means of scarce capital accumulation but also to support the status aspirations of the owner."[3] More recently, historians have recognized that a hacienda is best understood through its relationships. Eric Van Young writes, "The great rural estate of the late colonial period was . . . more a set of interlocking relationships, or systems, than an entity with fixed and exclusive characteristics."[4]

Haciendas have proven difficult to define in part because of their variability through time and across the landscape. Studies of haciendas during
the last fifty years have been profoundly shaped by François Chevalier's
Land and Society in Colonial Mexico. The work of Chevalier was of fundamental importance because it explained the origins of the hacienda as
a feudal enterprise, an institution that was economically irrational, and
yet, as Chevalier showed, adaptive.[5] The hacienda, Chevalier explained,
was born out of an economic depression and simultaneous plummet in
the population that wracked Mexico in the seventeenth century.[6] Though
Chevalier's work continues to shape our understanding of the Mexican hacienda, historians have since found that the social and economic
situation was more complex than first thought. Few now agree that the
seventeenth-century economic depression Chevalier identified ever actually took place, while others see no evidence for a shortage of labor.[7] In
response, historians and anthropologists have developed models that describe the hacienda as a capitalist enterprise, closely linked to and dependent on the market economy, while also recognizing that the importance
of the hacienda was more than economic.[8] With the establishment of each
new hacienda came a social and physical reordering of an ancient landscape. The hacienda system brought European conquerors and the indigenous conquered into daily contact and provided a locus for the generation and institutionalization of new class, ethnic, and racial identities.
Some historians have characterized the hacienda as "the chief engine of
Indian acculturation," while others identify a pattern of conservativism
among indigenous communities associated with haciendas.[9]

Colonial haciendas were unlike their later nineteenth- and early
twentieth-century counterparts.[10] During the earlier period they were most
often small working farms, and in the latter they were much like the great
estates identified, defined, and analyzed by historians working on what are
now considered to be classic hacienda studies. Robert Patch writes, "From
recent research, the hacienda has emerged as an extremely diverse institution, the development of which was intimately linked to the complex
of geographic and socioeconomic conditions existing in each region."[11]
Some haciendas were enormous landholding fiefdoms, while others were
relatively small. The productivity of the land often determined the size of
the haciendas in a given region.[12] The arid northern highlands, good only
for grazing cattle, were home to haciendas with thousands of acres and
hundreds of workers. Fertile land that was especially good for cultivating
European crops like wheat hosted smaller haciendas with less acreage and
fewer workers.

The Mexican hacienda was of fundamental importance in structuring the postconquest agrarian world. Spaniards created the institution because of both status aspirations and economic necessity. After the arrival of European conquerors, inconceivable numbers of indigenous people died from disease and war. With native demographic collapse, pressures for creating a stable food source increased as sources of labor disappeared.[13] Food had to be grown, but the newly arrived conquistadors did not want to do the work themselves. The Spanish needed people to work in the fields, to grow grains such as wheat that were palatable to the Spanish tongue. Few could afford to buy African slaves in sufficient numbers to keep a hacienda running, and from the end of the sixteenth century on, the Crown was reducing the labor obligations of indigenous villages.[14]

The most frequently cited solution to this dilemma is debt peonage.[15] This was a system by which workers were freely extended credit in the "company store" (the hacienda's *tienda de raya*), credit that they were forced to draw on because their salaries were insufficient to cover their basic needs. The result of this unlimited offer of credit, at least within the traditional model of the system, was a debt impossible to repay. Debt tied the workers to the land and the hacienda, and they were unable to leave if working conditions were not to their liking. The costs, benefits, experiences, and reasons underlying the development of debt peonage have been much debated. Following this traditional model, some historians argue that this system was oppressive and, in the worst-case scenario, turned the indigenous workforce into virtual slaves with a mountain of debt impossible to repay.[16] Others argue that debts were often nowhere near as extensive as traditionally portrayed and might even be beneficial to the peones.[17] Knight argues, "Debts represented perks or incentives, designed to attract, retain, and reward workers. Far from indicating coercion, debts reflected the bargaining power of the worker and the (calculating) paternalism of the hacienda."[18] Knight further suggests that the aim of the hacienda was to acculturate the native laborers, not to "enslave" them.[19]

Of course, the conditions of life and labor varied not just from region to region but from hacienda to hacienda, as well as through time. The social and political relationships in the Mexican countryside were complex, and even the dichotomy of Spanish hacienda and Indian town is false. John Chance shows evidence from Tecali, Puebla, that native caciques (indigenous leaders) negotiated economic relationships with local, small-scale ranchers in a way that was shrewd and beneficial to themselves and their communities.[20] Chance argues that, contrary to what one might expect based on the arguments summarized above, native villages did not wither away with the introduction of haciendas but continued to exist and some-times even flourish. Conflict was not just between types of settlements, but, as we will see, during the latter part of the nineteenth century could be found among different types of workers within a single institution. Friedrich Katz argues that workers housed at haciendas were well treated and even content, while those brought in as day laborers were the least happy and, when the Mexican Revolution started in the early years of the twentieth century, would be the most likely to rebel.[21]

Though small-scale ranchers were largely absent from the Valley of At-lixco, Chance's point regarding the autonomy of indigenous communities is important to understanding rural life at the Hacienda Acocotla and in its associated communities. Indigenous communities responded to threats, real or perceived, aimed at their communities and traditional lifeways by neighboring haciendas. In 1754, the indigenous Atlixco Valley village of San Jerónimo Coyula had a survey produced as part of its lawsuit against neighboring hacendados who, they claimed, were encroaching on village lands.[22] This document is just one example of many. Indigenous villages were unwilling to play the part of passive pawns. As time passed, legal de-fense of communal lands became increasingly urgent as changing policies transformed land ownership and, by extension, labor.[23] During the colo-nial period, the Spanish Crown instituted paternalistic policies to provide a small measure of protection to the indigenous peoples and their land, such as establishing the doctrine of natural law, which made indigenous members of society legally equal to Spaniards.[24] Though many native communities were initially forced to move from their (often dispersed) preconquest homes to settlements (known as *reducciones* or *congregacio-nes*) that were more easily controlled by the Spanish bureaucracy, the Spanish Crown allowed these new communities lands for grazing live-stock and made land grants for cultivation to families and villages as a form of recompense.[25] Ultimately, these land grants added up to thousands of deeds that, in many cases, dictate land ownership patterns today.[26]

Land grants were easily made during the early period when populations were at their nadir, but over time population levels recovered and demand for land rose.[27] As part of the late eighteenth-century Bourbon Reforms, the Spanish Crown began chipping away at these communal landholdings, transferring properties identified as "barren" into nonindigenous hands in the name of economic development.[28] Women, who had been able to own land and had been protected by the Spanish Crown during the earlier pe-riod, became particularly vulnerable.[29] These moves during the late eigh-teenth century laid the groundwork for the rural unrest that played a sig-nificant part in Mexico's early nineteenth-century bid for independence.

An Extraordinary Century, 1810–1910

The master narrative portrays the War of Independence as a political battle led by Mexican-born Spaniards who wanted to escape the yoke of Spanish rule.[30] These Mexican-born Spaniards had long been dissatisfied with colonial policies that placed them on a lower political and economic rung of the social ladder than those who had been born in Europe.[31] When, as part of the European wars, Napoleon Bonaparte invaded Spain and placed his brother Joseph on the throne, Mexico's unhappy citizens had an excuse for making a bid for independence and transforming the colonial order—they refused to acknowledge the authority of the usurper.[32]

While politics and Mexico's desire to separate from Spain were central to the War of Independence, the revolt had a strong component of rural rebellion.[33] The famous "moment" of independence came early on September 16, 1810, when profligate Roman Catholic priest Miguel Hidalgo y Castillo summoned the local people, farmers mostly, to the square in the rural town of Dolores, Guanajuato, and urged them to take their land back. His famous speech, the *grito* (or cry), ended with the triumphant call, "¡Mexicanos, viva México!" ("Mexicans, long live Mexico!"). That cry was followed by more than ten years of war that ended with the realization of Hidalgo's dream—the establishment of the Mexican nation. The embryonic country gained its independence when Spain signed the Treaty of Córdoba in August of 1821.

With independence assured, Mexico's citizens may have expected that the new nation would settle into a period of peace. Unfortunately, this was not the case. Over the course of the next extraordinary century, the Mexican people would be subjected to more than forty changes in government (including foreign invasions from both the United States and Europe). When we stop to consider that Porfirio Díaz ruled for thirty of those one hundred years, the political turnover is staggering. The national turmoil was reflected at the local level in places like the Valley of Atlixco with regular and constant uprisings, waves of crime, and increases in domestic violence.[34]

The chaos on the national stage ended up profoundly affecting the living and working conditions of Mexico's rural, indigenous population. Though exploitative, the Spanish colonial government had done what it could to protect indigenous communities.[35] These protections vanished with the establishment of independence. In the Valley of Atlixco as elsewhere, the nineteenth century was characterized by a struggle between landowners who wanted to get more work out of their indigenous peones and indigenous communities who wanted to protect their members from overexploitation.[36] During the colonial period, members of the indigenous communities in the Valley of Atlixco had proven themselves legally savvy. They continued to use established legal strategies to protect themselves and their communities, but with decreasing success as the nineteenth century progressed.[37] Throughout the century, hacienda owners tried to redefine labor relations by increasing debt, implementing regulations to control worker movement, building prisons to lock the wives and mothers of the workers in, and, ultimately, constructing worker housing. The workers fought back, taking their bosses to court, reporting them to the authorities, or simply refusing to show up for work.[38]

In 1856, treasury secretary Miguel Lerdo de Tejada supported a law (known as the *Ley Lerdo* or Lerdo Law) that would review the use of lands held by the Roman Catholic Church and civil corporations with the aim of increasing national productivity through the confiscation of those lands.[39] Though Lerdo de Tejada's intent had not been to dismantle lands held communally by indigenous villages, his law ultimately served this purpose.[40] The trends established by the Ley Lerdo accelerated during the last quarter of the nineteenth century under President Díaz, who sought to identify *terrenos baldíos* (barren lands), expropriate these unused lands, and reassign them for more "industrial" uses.[41] Often, these "unused lands" were lands, granted under the colonial regime, that were held communally by indigenous villages for grazing livestock or for growing food, a loss to the communities that was compounded by Mexico's economic instability during the first three quarters of the nineteenth century. Rural, mostly indigenous communities responded to the economic instability and loss of their lands with violent, small-scale uprisings and rebellions. The ruling classes answered these rebellions by increasing their attempts to control the populace.[42]

The final quarter of the nineteenth century saw greater economic stability in some areas, along with rapid industrialization and modernization under the leadership of Díaz; however, these processes came at a cost for many agrarian institutions in central Mexico. Rather than acting to stabilize their economic bases, modernization meant that haciendas focusing on the production of food for regional markets faced increased national and international competition and falling prices.[43] Rather than decreasing tensions between landowners and laborers, programs promoting industrialization and modernization produced the opposite effect. Workers increasingly objected to the conditions under which they lived, and hacienda owners responded with efforts to increase control over their workers and stabilize their enterprises. In the Valley of Atlixco, this picture was further complicated by the presence of textile mills and their accompanying company towns that introduced both international concepts of industrial capitalism and worker violence and revolt that continued well into the twentieth century.[44] General Fortino Ayaquica, whom we met earlier, was an employee at just such a textile mill.[45]

By the last third of the nineteenth century, rural communities in central Mexico were under attack. Time and again, efforts to modernize Mexico instituted by Díaz and his government resulted in the accelerated erosion of traditional communally held lands in indigenous communities.[46] The erosion of community landholdings was not simply about the economics associated with landownership; it was also about the social aspects of the agrarian lifestyle and the introduction of industrial capitalist modes of labor control and organization. Though often couched in economic terms, the dismantling of communal village lands was about dismantling indigenous communities. Indian pueblos and their communal social organization were seen as a bar to "economic progress and the advancement of civilization" because they discouraged individuality.[47] To be indigenous was to be "left over"; it was an outmoded identity that belonged in the colonial past. For rural, indigenous farmers, the trends encouraged by Díaz represented a dismantling of the world as they understood it. They lost their village land, and their home lives were being transformed by outside forces—the traditions and expectations that people had grown up with no longer explained their daily experiences. Indigenous communities responded to these disruptions with violence.[48]

That violent response is one facet of the mayhem that would become the Mexican Revolution. People who had always been farmers wanted to continue to be farmers. They had been promised this right as part of the uprising leading to independence in the early years of the nineteenth century. One hundred years later, rural farmers were still struggling, and people like Zapata took up their cause. To address the needs, distrust, and rebellion of people like those discussed in this book, Mexican leaders found themselves acknowledging the importance of land ownership and the smallholder, agrarian way of life. For the rural poor, the ideal, as it was presented, was to own a bit of land, enough to feed your family and produce enough of a surplus to sell or trade for goods you could not produce yourself. It is an ideal that exists to this day.

The Mexican Revolution, 1910

The Mexican Revolution began on November 20, 1910, one hundred years, two months, four days, and twelve hours after the beginning of the

Mexican War of Independence. The origins of this second war, the Revolution, were also political, though the master narrative has emphasized the role of social, agrarian justice; the rural poor, increasingly under attack and disenfranchised, blamed the elite for their misery.[49] Shortly before the 1910 presidential elections (which had been advertised as free and democratic), Mexico's president of thirty years, Porfirio Díaz, jailed his opponent, Francisco Madero, and created an opportunity for the opposition to mobilize general dissatisfaction with Díaz's rule. Upon his release from jail, Madero fled to the United States, where he wrote a letter to the people of Mexico called the Plan de San Luis. In this statement, Madero argued that Mexico's recently concluded elections had been fraudulent and that he rather than Díaz was the legitimate president of the country. In the process, Madero articulated the frustrations of diverse factions throughout the country. To redress the wrongs he detailed, Madero called for an uprising against the federal authorities to begin at six in the evening on November 20, 1910. Though it did not initially seem to be the case, Madero's call to action was, perhaps, too successful. The November 20 uprising was an utter failure, but the rebels did not give up.[50] By early summer of 1911, Díaz had fled to France, where he would live until his death four years later.

Ultimately, three primary groups battled for control of Mexico—the Constitutionalists, who were primarily middle class, liberal/intellectual, and urban; the División del Norte, led by Pancho Villa but originally formed to support Madero; and the Zapatistas, under Emiliano Zapata, who fought for agrarian reform—though in many regions, local politics made the picture even more complex. During this time, Madero was confirmed as the democratically elected president of Mexico after a second round of elections in October 1911. The new president may have expected that his election, following on the heels of Díaz's exile, would mark the end of the Revolution, but he had lit a fuse that would burn for more than a decade. Madero's call to arms had allowed many of the nation's malcontents to find their voice. Nobody could agree on anything, including Madero's presidency. In February 1913, Madero was deposed and killed; his hard-won presidency lasted less than sixteen months.

Madero's brilliance was that his Plan de San Luis resonated with many of Mexico's dissatisfied factions; his fault was that he awakened those factions without quenching their thirst. Throughout Mexico, people objected to Madero's failure to address their particular agenda.[51] As far as this narrative is concerned, the most central of these figures was Zapata. Madero's promises of land reform had inspired Zapata. When Madero failed to pursue the reforms he had called for in the Plan de San Luis, Zapata issued his own call to arms, the Plan de Ayala, just days after Madero's inauguration in November 1911. His program was driven in large part by the desire to improve the conditions of rural agricultural workers living at and working for haciendas, individuals just like those we will meet in the following pages.[52] He wanted the federal government to take land from the wealthy, often absentee owners of central Mexico's haciendas and redistribute it to those who actually worked the land.[53] Zapata, born and raised just fifty kilometers from the Hacienda San Miguel Acocotla, had an intimate understanding of the daily living conditions of central Mexico's peones, though he himself had been born into a middle-class family of horse trainers.[54] His understanding of rural working conditions led him to issue the Plan de Ayala in 1911, and it was the reality of those working conditions that drove thousands to follow. Ultimately, the Mexican government was forced to acknowledge the demands of the Zapatistas with agrarian reforms, imperfectly and incompletely instituted, that dissolved the property ownership of the large landowners and redistributed farmland to people (individually and collectively in community parcels or *ejidos*) like those we will meet in chapter 4. Though the land received through these reforms became insufficient to meet minimum subsistence needs for the vast majority of families within just one generation, the men and women who farm the properties today remain fiercely proud and protective of the land they were awarded during the first half of the twentieth century.[55]

Fortino Ayaquica strode toward the front doors of Acocotla's casco with the posture of a trained soldier. He may have been nothing but a humble textile worker before the war started, but he had learned, quickly, to be a general. And he had learned that the way he carried himself, whether on the battlefield or in camp, was as important as anything in keeping control of his men.

As he approached the arched entranceway of the Hacienda San Miguel Acocotla, Fortino Ayaquica noticed an old woman standing in front of the doorway. She had not fled inside the walls like the rest, and she did not greet him with tears of fear. She stood proudly, head up, arms folded across her ample chest. She reminded him of his mother, and, for just a moment, he felt like the little boy he had once been, caught doing something he shouldn't by the formidable woman who raised him. He forgot his soldierly posture.

His remembered fear made him approach her with the caution and respect his mother had taught him to treat his elders with. "Señora, is anything the matter?"

Rafaela strode up to him and looked him directly in the eye. "Anything the matter?" She laughed bitterly. *"Who are you here representing? Other than your own desire for women and money, of course."*

Fortino Ayaquica felt his face flush hot with shame. Her accusations were not baseless; he had taken his share of the bounty of war. Dropping his eyes, he responded quietly, *"Emiliano Zapata, Señora."*

"Ah," she said, *"Then you are here to 'improve' our lives."* He looked up, hopeful that she had altered her opinion, and caught the flash of sarcasm in her eyes. *"Let me tell you,"* she continued, *"how you've improved our lives. My daughters can't leave their homes for fear that they'll be scooped up by one of your 'soldiers.' My sons hide when they hear hoof beats, afraid that they'll be shot or taken from their families to fight your battles. Without my daughters and my sons, my grandchildren would starve. I've lived at this hacienda since just before my youngest son was born. My daughter still lives here with me and her family. It has never been easy; we've often had to fight to survive. I saw as many of my children buried as I saw married. But, though life has often been tough, it has never been as tough as it has since this war started. And here you are, to 'improve' our lives once again."*

He closed his eyes, for just a moment. What she said was true, but he really had set out to improve lives. Opening his eyes again, he looked back at her, as squarely as she was looking at him. *"Yes, Señora, I know life has been difficult lately. But really, we are here today to talk about peace. Nobody will harm your family; nobody will take your belongings. My soldiers have their orders. And with God's blessing, we'll move one step closer to taking this land,"* he gestured with arms wide at the fields behind him, *"one step closer to taking this from the man you work for and giving it to you and your family—the rightful owners."*

Rafaela snorted in disgust and, ignoring the gathering soldiers, strode off to make the day's tortillas.

CHAPTER TWO

"A Place for Lizards and Archaeologists"

Historical Archaeology and the Hacienda San Miguel Acocotla

✻   ✻   ✻

Nearly one hundred years after General Fortino Ayaquica held his conference at the Hacienda Acocotla, I found myself in a jeep traveling along what may have been the same road on which he approached Acocotla that April morning. I leaned forward eagerly and scanned the landscape as I braced myself, one hand on the dashboard and one on the ceiling. Harold, whose attention was consumed with the difficult driving conditions, tore his eyes from the road long enough to tell me that the hacienda's casco was just ahead and that I'd see the tower, the tallest of the still-standing ruins, first. As the last word left his mouth, I noticed something over the tops of the leafless trees. "There it is." I said. Harold glanced up from the road quickly, "Yep. You spotted it."

As we drew nearer to the casco, I looked around eagerly. I was searching for a dissertation research project. I hadn't had any intention of choosing this one when I arrived in Puebla, but Harold was quickly winning me over. The project was fascinating, the students from the university were dedicated, and Harold's enthusiasm for his research and teaching was infectious.

Figure 2.1. Approaching the Hacienda San Miguel Acocotla.

Harold pulled up to the casco, and we climbed out. "Welcome to San Miguel Acocotla," he exclaimed as I looked around. It was a lovely early summer day. The sky had the clean, clear blue look that it gets in the Mexican highlands just after the rains start. Because we weren't far into the rainy season, the vegetation hadn't grown up and covered the ruins of Acocotla's buildings. I looked up in surprise at the arch that was Acocotla's front entrance. It was at least fifteen feet high. Before I could remark, Harold was tugging me off in another direction. "Come over here, Elizabeth."

He pulled me into a field to the left of Acocotla's main entrance and gestured at the remains of what seemed to be little stalls, not more than ten feet wide or deep. "What are these?" I asked.

"The workers quarters. This is where the peones lived, Elizabeth. This is where we are going to excavate."

I looked around, shocked. Even though I knew my historical facts well enough, they didn't prepare me. Reading about the workers' quarters is not the same as standing inside the remains of a room measuring less than one hundred square feet and imagining the little space filled by an entire family. The reality is a kick in the gut.

We chatted about what Harold thought could be accomplished with archaeological research before he dashed off to the next section of the casco. I was getting the full tour. I was glad—the place was magical. The ruins sit out in the fields, far from anything or anyone. During our time there, I heard neither traffic nor planes overhead, nothing but the buzzing of the bees housed in hives in one of the patios. There were bits of paint left on the walls and decorations molded in plaster; stairways led to a second floor long since vanished. The tumbled-down ruins just begged to be explored. Clambering over and around them made me feel like I was an eight-year-old with skinned knees and pigtails again. As we walked among the walls, sunbathing lizards startled and dashed for cover. With their movements, I thought, "A place for lizards and archaeologists!" It was how John Womack had described the Revolutionary-period haciendas of Morelos in his biography of Zapata, and as I looked at the crumbling walls around me, it felt like a perfect description.

Standing in the skeleton of Acocotla's chapel, the end of our tour, I turned to Harold and said, "Okay, you got me. This place is amazing. I'll work here with you if you'll have me." Harold looked back at me and grinned. Acocotla had its lizards, and now it had archaeologists, too.

*   *   *

The Hacienda San Miguel Acocotla

The Hacienda Acocotla is located in the Valley of Atlixco (in western Puebla). It sits on the lower slopes of the Popocatépetl volcano approximately 1,800 meters above sea level and just east of a line of hills that run south from the volcano's summit. The semiarid climate is famous throughout the region; it always seems to be the nicest of spring days. The rainy season lasts from late May through late September. When the Spanish began to settle the area in the mid-sixteenth century, they found the climate and conditions ideal for wheat production. Within fifty years, Atlixco became one of the primary production centers for the European-introduced grain.[1] Today, the valley continues to be used for agriculture.

Crops include maize (harvested in late August or September), jicama (the primary cash crop, harvested in October), and peanuts (harvested in November), as well as flowers and ornamental plants that are grown year-round for markets and greenhouses both in nearby cities and abroad.

The Valley of Atlixco has been occupied for millennia. Some of its Prehispanic sites have a continuous occupation dating to at least AD 550–650, and archaeologists have identified thirty-four sites dating to AD 900–1521.[2] At the time of the Spanish arrival, two Nahuatl-speaking communities, Calpan and Cuauhquechollan (modern-day Huaquechula), dominated the valley. Following the conquest, these two communities became encomiendas (sources of forced labor and tribute).[3] Each community was assigned to a single Spaniard, leaving the rest of the haciendas in the valley to obtain labor through other means.[4]

The Hacienda San Miguel Acocotla, which did not benefit from an encomienda, is located approximately ten kilometers southwest of the nearby city of Atlixco (fig. 2.2). Founded in 1577 by Lucas Pérez Maldo-

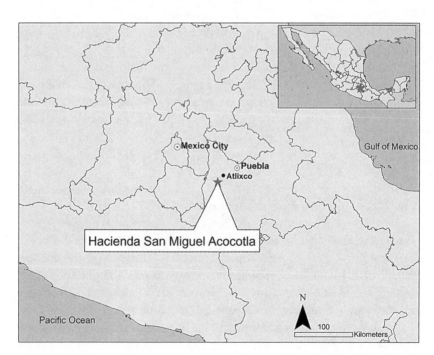

Figure 2.2. Map of central Mexico showing location of San Miguel Acocotla (ESRI Data and Maps 2007—Mexico [Map]. Redlands, CA: Environmental Systems Research Institute. Accessed using ArcView GIS, version 9.2).

nado, Acocotla operated for some 370 years until after the Mexican Revolution. During the twenty years following the Revolution, the federal government both expropriated land and enabled villagers who were former hacienda employees to purchase portions of the former hacienda through Mexico's agrarian reforms.

Acocotla is one of many haciendas littering the Valley of Atlixco, where haciendas were relatively small and had diverse economies dependent on the nearby markets of Puebla and Mexico City. Throughout its existence, Acocotla was valued in the midrange of its neighbors; it was neither the largest nor smallest, most valuable nor cheapest, most productive nor least.[5] Ownership changed frequently, and the owners were neither more famous nor more important than their neighbors. The workforce also changed regularly, as it did at haciendas throughout the region. The Hacienda San Miguel Acocotla was perfect for this historical archaeological study of nineteenth-century life and labor because, at least in the Valley of Atlixco, it was unexceptional.

Historical Archaeology in Mexico

Few historical archaeologists have avoided hearing that historical archaeology is nothing more than "the most expensive way in the world to learn something we already know."[6] At its best, however, historical archaeology does not simply find the material correlates expected from documentary research but instead uses documentary resources as just one of multiple lines of evidence. Historical archaeologists explore processes of social change during the last five hundred years, filling gaps in the historical record with archaeological data. Documentary resources are heavily weighted toward the victors, especially those with command of wealth, power, and land, victors who were almost always men. The daily experiences of most people, especially women, children, the poor, and ethnic minorities, are largely ignored. During the early years of the twentieth century, the central Mexican peasant revolt led by Emiliano Zapata was essential to the development and trajectory of the Mexican Revolution and the reforms that followed. People like those under study in this book, people largely invisible in the historical record, inspired Zapata and were inspired by him. To understand these grand historical processes, and to understand what has happened to the peoples of rural central Mexico since, we need to understand the lives of workers in the generations leading up to the 1910 uprising.[7] Historical archaeology provides an ideal vehicle for this sort of study, expanding our understanding of these processes in ways that are unavailable to historical research alone.

In Mexico, the discipline of historical archaeology has been around for less than a century. The earliest formal Mexican historical archaeological study dates to 1934, when Eduardo Noguera examined changes in ceramic technologies and production from the Prehispanic through the colonial period.[8] In the vein of Noguera's study, other typological analyses of historical period pottery followed.[9] In 1969, Thomas Charlton articulated the need for problem-based research in postconquest Mesoamerica in an article in which he presented a survey of Aztec settlement patterns in the postconquest period.[10] Excavation-based archaeological research grew following the passage of a 1972 law requiring archaeological rescue of sites affected by construction and other development. Patricia Fournier comments that most of the historical archaeological research during the 1960s and 1970s was either dedicated to historical restoration for tourism or conducted with the true aim of getting to the Prehispanic remains lying below the more recent materials.[11]

In recent years, problem-based historical archaeology has come into its own, with projects dedicated to understanding processes of social and economic transformation in the period following the Spanish conquest.[12] The archaeological study of haciendas has contributed substantially to the literature, making it something of a subfield within Mesoamerican historical archaeology.[13] The focus of hacienda studies has primarily been the recovery of information about the lives of indigenous peones, especially their physical living conditions and their relationship with the dominant power structure. For example, Rani Alexander has explored the relationship between haciendas and indigenous communities before, during, and since Yucatán's Caste War through archaeological settlement surveys combined with ethnohistoric and ethnographic research.[14] Allan Meyers has also explored hacienda life during Yucatán's nineteenth century through household archaeology, ethnohistory, and ethnography.[15] The research presented in the coming pages builds on this body of research, integrating historical, enthographic, ethnoarchaeological, and archaeological data to expand our understandings of the experience of life and labor at the Hacienda Acocotla.

Investigating Acocotla

During the project's initial phase, Dr. Harold Juli set out to find a hacienda that would allow us to understand the daily lives of hacienda workers.

He surveyed Puebla and Tlaxcala for a site that offered ruins ready for excavation (sufficiently ruined that they could be dug up without upsetting anyone and sufficiently well preserved that we could still identify their architectural features) but that would also offer opportunities for ethnographic and archival study. After looking at the remains of a dozen haciendas, Harold settled on the Hacienda San Miguel Acocotla as an excellent place to conduct research.[16] The abandoned property was a classic wheat hacienda with many of the architectural features seen at such haciendas throughout the region. Today, the main house, or casco, is in ruins, but the calpanería is easy to identify along the casco's south-facing wall (fig. 2.3). The calpanería comprises thirty-seven small adobe rooms and is adjacent to a field once used for a variety of domestic activities.

Acocotla's architectural remains were not the only thing that made it a promising research site; the village of La Soledad Morelos sits just two kilometers south on that rough road I had driven with Harold during my first visit. The village is home to people whose parents and grandparents had once worked at the hacienda as day and resident laborers. Some of the older people in the village had actually worked at the hacienda themselves when they were very young. Some had lived at the hacienda; others lived in the village, whose origins date back to at least the mid-nineteenth century.[17] Today, the village's inhabitants have community property rights to the hacienda's ruins. Harold had chosen Acocotla in part because he knew that the village would be a great place to conduct ethnographic, ethnoarchaeological, and oral historical research.

Figure 2.3. Calpanería room, Hacienda San Miguel Acocotla.

Following Harold's survey work, María del Carmen (MaryCarmen) Romano Soriano, then a student in the anthropology department at the Universidad de las Américas, Puebla, began archival research in Atlixco, Puebla, and Mexico City and ethnographic research in La Soledad. Her research led to a thesis dealing with the history of Acocotla.[18] In 2008 and 2009, Karime Castillo Cardenas completed an additional eighteen months of full-time research in the local, state, and national archives. Together, they produced hundreds of pages of transcribed documents that provide the foundation for the research in the pages to come. With the archival research under way, Harold began a multiyear ethnographic and ethnoarchaeological project in the descendant community. Ultimately, I would join the project as we expanded to the archaeological phase of the research. Together, we designed a program that was informed by and contributed to the substantial research on Mesoamerican household archaeology, ethnoarchaeology, and ethnography.[19]

Harold designed the ethnographic and ethnoarchaeological research in La Soledad Morelos to document the ways in which people inhabited and used domestic space, as well as to collect oral histories and memories of hacienda labor. With the help of students from the Universidad de las Américas in Cholula, Puebla, and Connecticut College in New London, we were able to collect more than one thousand transcribed pages of interview notes and questionnaire results, along with a complete survey of land use in the village and detailed architectural diagrams of twenty households. Archaeological remains alone make it difficult to know how people experienced things like domestic space, and sometimes even how that space was used is difficult to understand. Ethnoarchaeology illuminates some of these difficult to interpret experiences and helps archaeologists nuance their interpretations. For example, research in La Soledad Morelos showed us how important kitchen space was to members of the modern community; the lack of archaeologically identified kitchen spaces in the hacienda's calpanería led me to consider the ways in which family life may have been disrupted during the nineteenth century.

While conducting research in La Soledad Morelos, I often heard concerns from other scholars about the use of oral history. Many said "people lie" and suggested that, as a result, oral history was not useful in constructing the past. Oral history may be of limited use in recovering objective "facts," but if we are to connect the past to the present, people's perceptions of their history—what they believe to be true and what they have been told is true—is as important as any "fact."[20] The conditions under which we live are the results of innumerable historic events, historical "fact" or "truth," but the decisions we make, decisions that affect the historical truth of future generations, are based on both our contemporary conditions and what we believe about our past. To understand the lives of the people of La Soledad Morelos and the decisions they make, we needed to know more than the "master narrative" presented in chapter 1, more than we were able to dig up at the hacienda or in the archives; we needed to know what the villagers believed to be true. For this reason, we spent many hours conducting open-ended interviews, encouraging people to share their memories of life and labor at the Hacienda Acocotla.

While perception is important, so are "facts." Our archival research had provided a great deal of data about the owners and managers of the hacienda and more limited information about the hacienda's workers. Our archaeological research program was designed to complement what we had found in the archives and in La Soledad Morelos. While oral history and archival records tell us what people *say* they did, the archaeological remains show us what people actually did do. We completed extensive architectural recordings of the standing architecture at Acocotla, conducted a complete surface survey in the area where the hacienda's workers would have lived along with a few limited test excavations, and excavated a few targeted areas completely, including five rooms that would have housed some of the hacienda's peones. Our decisions of where to dig were made to maximize the recovery of data that would be parallel to data collected during the ethnoarchaeological phase of research in La Soledad Morelos.

Thanks to these multiple lines of data, we were able to develop an understanding of life at the Hacienda Acocotla over many hundreds of years. Documentary research provided one line of evidence that stretched from the hacienda's founding in 1577 through the last decade of the nineteenth century. Oral history and ethnographic research picked up where the archival record failed by bringing history up through the present day, and further, it nuanced the documentary record with stories of those who were frequently not included in traditional, historical sources. The archaeological record connected the extraordinary moments captured in the archives to everyday life. If we were to understand the history of this community before and after the Mexican Revolution, if we were to explore questions about why they revolted then and do not now, if we were to understand how their history has defined modern life, we needed to understand the conditions of daily life in the calpanería, and we needed to understand those conditions over the longest time scale possible.[21]

Theorizing Revolution

Though Mexico's rural workers had organized small-scale uprisings through-out the colonial and independence periods, the unprecedented effective-ness of Zapata's 1910 revolt has left many scholars wondering what, at that moment, made conditions right for the Agrarian revolts and reforms.[22] To understand the origins of the Mexican Revolution and the reforms that followed, we need to understand something about the origins of agrarian revolt. The literature dealing with peasant revolt is too extensive to sum-marize here, but we can extract a few concepts from the literature that are useful for understanding the stories in the coming chapters. The theories of social rebellion and radicalism developed by Eric Wolf, Anthony Giddens, Edward P. Thompson, and James Scott can help us understand what was going on at Acocotla and the surrounding valley when Fortino Aya-quica arrived there on that spring morning in 1917.

In *Peasant Wars of the Twentieth Century*, anthropologist Eric Wolf ex-amined the origins of peasant resistance worldwide.[23] Wolf compared peasant rebellions in Mexico, Russia, China, Vietnam, Algeria, and Cuba, finding a common thread among them: the introduction of capitalism. Wolf argued that the alienation brought about by capitalist systems is not limited to the alienation of labor as had been proposed by Marx but ex-tends to the alienation of complete agrarian social systems. This, he con-cluded, results in violent and radicalized uprisings as peasants find their long-established modes of production and conventional lifeways threat-ened. Wolf argues that in Mexico this alienation took the form of the loss of village-controlled communal lands during the nineteenth century and the accompanying destruction of village social systems as modern indus-trial capitalism was introduced from Europe and the United States by Por-firio Díaz.

While not exploring the origins of revolt, Anthony Giddens's 1973 study *The Class Structure of the Advanced Societies* shares some of the points of Wolf's argument. In his study of class structure and radicalism in France, Giddens finds that the conflict between feudal and/or postfeudal economic systems and capitalism results in a radicalization of the lower classes. He argues that socialism grows out of the "clash between capital-ism and post-feudalism."[24] Giddens is not the only theorist to argue for these dynamics. Five years before the publication of Giddens's study, Eng-lish historian Edward P. Thompson also found that the most militant re-sponses to the pressures of capitalism came from those whose production was least associated with the capitalist market.[25] Though Giddens is writing about France and Thompson about England, their analyses also apply to late-nineteenth-century Mexico. During this period, Mexico's long established "semifeudal agrarian" structures were being challenged by the modernizing forces of capitalism.

The idea of a "moral economy" is central to many of the arguments regarding the origins of social rebellion. Indeed, Thompson's thesis regarding rebellions among the English working classes invoked the idea.[26] Basically, a moral economy is an economy in which people's decisions are not based only on financial gain but also involve a desire or need to be "fair" and "good." Scholars like Thompson have argued that a moral economy is incompatible, sometimes catastrophically, with a capitalist economy. James Scott is perhaps the most famous scholar to apply the idea of a moral economy to agrarian insurrections. His book *The Moral Economy of the Peasant* offers one of the best-known theses on the subject of agrarian revolt and suggests the root of the conflict identified by Giddens and Thompson in more industrialized venues.[27] Scott's anthropological study of peasants and violent resistance movements in Southeast Asia shows a direct link between basic subsistence levels and rebellion. Scott posits that peasant farmers believe they have an inalienable, "moral" right to basic subsistence. Investigating the origins of rural insurrections, Scott finds that peasants in Southeast Asia will opt for financial scenarios that provide them with the most stability. When this stability fails and basic subsistence levels are threatened, peasants react violently. He argues that the origins of these patterns of rebellion may be found in the imposition of colonial rule by British and French forces and the accompanying commercialization of the economy.

These analyses share points that are important to our understanding of the experience of the peones working at the Hacienda San Miguel Acocotla, the rural uprisings associated with the Mexican Revolution, and the lives of Mexico's rural poor since. Agrarian insurrections may be linked to both the introduction of industrial capitalism and threats to the structures of daily life, whether the perceived attack is directed at subsistence levels or at social structures. Research at Acocotla suggests that the protection of homelife is of fundamental importance to people, akin to a "moral right." Mexico's nineteenth-century modernizing forces attempted to transform "Indians into Mexicans" in the name of progress.[28] In the coming pages, we will see how these processes played out in one community as the reorganization of labor and the nineteenth-century workers' quarters at the

cocotla dismantled family, domestic, and community struc-
ess that, ultimately, was violently rejected by the inhabitants
of Atlixco. Meanwhile, our work in the modern community
highlights two important factors in this discussion. First, once the constraints instituted by hacienda management were removed, people returned to structuring their homelives in the way they had been structured
for hundreds of years. Second, while the economic situation of the modern community appears to be no better, and is perhaps worse, than it was
under the hacienda system, people seem to be willing to accept poor economic conditions as long as they remain in control of their homelives.

The problem with the application of the theories discussed above is that
it has been difficult to recover details about the homelives of people like
those who lived and worked at the Hacienda Acocotla. These were not
people deemed important enough to appear in documentary records kept
in local, state, and national government offices and archives. Traditional
historical studies cannot tell us what daily life was like for indigenous
workers at central Mexican haciendas, and for many, this missing bit of
information is what we lack in understanding Zapata's rebellion.[29] With
the exception of a handful of haciendas held by a single family throughout
the colonial and independence periods, the majority of haciendas regularly changed hands. As a result, documentary research is often too spotty
to permit a long-term or detailed study, especially because documents
have frequently been lost or destroyed.[30] Further, documentary records
tell us very little about the day-to-day lives of the peones. To understand
the social processes at work at many haciendas during the last half of the
nineteenth century, processes that ultimately led to the Mexican Revolution, and to challenge the master narrative, we need a more complete
picture of agrarian life in central Mexico.

CHAPTER THREE

"Something We Already Know"

Too much of
this

*   *   *

The chair creaked as I leaned back. Karime looked up at the sound, grinning at the sight of me massaging the kinks out of my sore neck. We'd been in Atlixco's archives for only two hours, and I was already restless. She knew I preferred to be out in the field—interviewing people or getting hot and dusty digging—but this was part of my job, too. I smiled back as I closed my eyes, trying to clear from my head the images of the poorly preserved eighteenth-century letter I was transcribing. I often found that looking away from the document for a few moments allowed me to easily read what, a moment before, had been completely indecipherable. I doubted it would make much difference this time. The sheet in front of me had suffered a lot of water damage, but it was part of the story I was trying to tease out of the boxes surrounding me. I wasn't prepared to give up easily. As I opened my eyes and looked down, I realized that my trick wasn't going to work. The paper was just too damaged—for me, anyway. Looking back across the table at my assistant, I interrupted Karime and asked, "Can you make out anything more?" Thanks to the many hours she'd spent in the archives working on this project, her skills outpaced mine.

She stood and came to my side of the table, shaking her head at the condition of the paper. She checked my transcription against the original, finding where I had given up. After a few moments of squinting, she shook her head again, "No, I think this one is a lost cause." I nodded. It wasn't a particularly important document, just a note of yet another loan made to the perpetually money-troubled owner of the Hacienda Acocotla, Francisco Esteben de Malpica Ponce de León. Though we had plenty of documentation about this particular aspect of de Malpica Ponce de León's life, it was still frustrating to know I was missing a piece of his story.

I stood up, stretching again, and moved toward the table on the other side of the room where Natalia sat. The archivist had been unbelievably kind and helpful. She kept an eye out for pertinent documents while conducting her own research and laid them aside until we were next there. Thanks to her, our research was moving more quickly and smoothly than was normal. She smiled in sympathy as I returned the document she had gotten off the shelves for me only a few minutes earlier and stood to get the next document I had requested on my list that morning.

While I waited for her to return, I looked at the boxes surrounding me. Those boxes contained the stories of people who were beginning to inhabit my imagination. As I sat in the archives each day, my mind filled in details left out of the records and explored what the emotional experience of these characters might have been. These daydreams are the constant companion of historical research. I saw Lucas Pérez Maldonado, the hacienda's sixteenth-century founder, riding up to the indigenous village he was about to cheat out of land. How had the villagers and their cacique greeted him? How had he justified his behavior to himself as he rode home afterward? My brain fast-forwarded 150 years. Francisco Esteban de Malpica Ponce de León, who inherited the hacienda in the early years of the eighteenth century, was lying awake at night, worried about the money he had borrowed again that day. Why was he always so short of money? How did it affect his family? The stories of the hacendados were documented in detail, but others were not so well defined. De Malpica Ponce de León's daughter Catalina made three brief appearances in the historical record, once and most notably as part of a financial transaction between her father and the convent she was to join when she was sixteen. What had she felt the night before she professed her vows at Santa Catalina? Did she go willingly, with enthusiasm? Was she trying to escape a difficult relationship with her stepmother? Or was her trip to the convent nothing more than a business arrangement between her father and the convent to which he owed a great deal of money?

María Catarina, the indigenous widow whose husband left her with four young children and his debt to the hacienda owner when he died in the middle of the nineteenth century, showed up in the records when she found herself battling the hacienda manager for control of her six-year-old son's labor. What was she thinking during her first night alone after her *where are the citations for this?*

husband's funeral? How did she act when the mayordomo came to take her son away to pay his father's debt? Though each of these women left only fragmentary stories in the archives, together their voices, along with many more, told the story of the Hacienda San Miguel Acocotla.

Natalia returned with the next folio, chasing the ghosts back, for now, to the corners of my brain. I reached across the table to gently take the next piece of my puzzle, wondering who I was going to meet next.

✻   ✻   ✻

Lucas Pérez Maldonado founded the Hacienda San Miguel Acocotla in 1577. At the time, little more than half a century had passed since the arrival of Hernán Cortés and the fall of the Aztec Empire. Archaeological and ethnohistoric evidence for the human prehistory of the Atlixco region indicates a lengthy and tumultuous occupation.[1] The arrival of the Spanish was simply the latest iteration of war and conquest in a region that had been experiencing generations of violent turmoil. The Spanish conquest brought the dissolution of existing governments, social and religious reordering, and, ultimately, the deaths of millions due to war and the introduction of European diseases.[2] When Pérez Maldonado first arrived in the Valley of Atlixco (then called Atrisco), he found a few Spaniards and a scattered but entrenched indigenous population.

Pérez Maldonado rode into the village with a sneer on his lips. He was certain he would be able to make some profitable land purchases this afternoon. The Indians running around his horse seemed particularly ignorant, though the lonely friar in the nearby monastery of Huaquechula insisted that these savages had converted to Christianity. He looked around and tried to dismiss his doubts. The skins of pulque hanging from his saddle would ensure there would be no problems. Pérez Maldonado had learned when he first arrived in Mexico that the only thing he needed to cheat an Indian in a land purchase was a bit of their beloved liquor, however mild. He had had a great deal of luck out here in the Valley of Atrisco. The Indians had some sort of prohibition against intoxication, but they didn't seem to be able to refuse a guest or a gift. It took very little time, and even less pulque, to get them drunk enough to sign any paper he put before them.

He raised his gaze from the half-naked savages milling around his horse and the mud and filth in which they lived to look out at the beautiful, fertile valley beyond the village. In his mind's eye, the surrounding land was filled with his grazing cattle. He sighed, returning to the task at hand. First, he had to get the bills of sale signed. It was something of a race these days. So many Spaniards were showing up in the valley that already land was becoming scarce. He was determined to acquire as much as he possibly could. Pérez Maldonado suppressed a grimace. The worst part of this enterprise was having to drink the pulque. He would never develop a taste for it; best to get this business over with. He looked down at the Indian nearest his right stirrup and demanded to be taken to the cacique.

By all reports, Lucas Pérez Maldonado was not a nice man, eagerly taking advantage of the opportunities presented by the chaos the Spanish conquest produced in rural indigenous communities.[3] He was infamous for using copious amounts of liquor to lubricate negotiations, behavior that made him the subject of multiple lawsuits brought by indigenous communities complaining of the illegal manner in which their lands had been purchased.[4] It was through one such negotiation in 1577 that the land for the Hacienda Acocotla was acquired, one of many such purchases he made during the 1570s and 1580s.[5] By 1602, Pérez Maldonado and his wife owned more than 2,300 acres of land in the Valley of Atlixco.[6] Low population levels in the region, which had dropped from an estimated thirty-five-thousand families at the time of Spanish contact to a low of twenty-five hundred during the seventeenth century, facilitated his amassing of land.[7] Pérez Maldonado initially kept cattle on his Atlixco lands, but he quickly shifted his productive focus to wheat. Wheat would remain the hacienda's main cash crop for the rest of its history, though other crops, including maize, beans, chiles, jicama, and peanuts, supplemented the grain. Fruit trees and livestock, primarily cattle and goats, were also elements of the hacienda's economy, though these last were primarily for local consumption.

Pérez Maldonado's investment in the Valley of Atlixco proved to be an excellent one. In 1576, a severe plague (likely a hemorrhagic fever exacerbated by severe drought) swept through central Mexico.[8] The result (at least as far as the Spaniards were concerned) was a sudden lack of grain in the markets of Mexico City and a simultaneous glut of meat.[9] Between 1576 and 1578, wheat prices nearly doubled, leading the Spanish viceroyalty to offer numerous incentives to Spaniards willing to establish wheat haciendas.[10] The Valley of Atlixco had a climate that was perfect for the crop and was located an easy distance from both of the major consumption centers—Puebla and Mexico City. Soon, Pérez Maldonado had plenty of competition for land and irrigation water. By 1632, and thanks to the viceroy's incentives, ninety haciendas in the valley were producing fifteen thousand *fanegas* of wheat every year.[11] Acocotla was just one of those ninety haciendas in an increasingly crowded landscape.

The death of Lucas Pérez Maldonado brought about the division of his landholdings. In 1629, his heirs created two distinct properties—the Hacienda San Jerónimo Coyula (which took its name from one of the local villages) and the Hacienda San Miguel Acocotla. This division defined the borders of Acocotla's lands for the rest of its history. The Hacienda Acocotla stayed in the Pérez Maldonado family until 1632, when Diego López de Nava (son-in-law of Lucas Pérez Maldonado) sold Acocotla to the Convent of Santa Clara to pay the dowry of his two daughters who were about to take orders there. The business interests of Acocotla remained intertwined with the Convent of Santa Clara throughout the colonial period as the hacienda passed from owner to owner.[12] Following the 1632 sale to the Convent of Santa Clara, the property changed hands at least twenty-two more times until its final dissolution in 1946.

But what was this colonial hacienda like? Historical novels and *telenovelas* paint a romanticized picture of grand estates with imposing architecture and rooms full of fine furniture, expensive draperies, and beautiful men and women flirting in corridors and courtyards.[13] Those of us who think outside the walls of the finest rooms in the hacienda might imagine hordes of indigenous peones, ill-treated by the Spanish hacienda owner, doing the actual work while the Europeans sat in sumptuous luxury, waited on hand and foot by these exploited individuals. At the end of the day, the indigenous workers would stagger home, exhausted, to their tiny, inadequate housing provided by the hacendado.

If we were talking about the latter half of the nineteenth century, this picture would be correct; the sources for those novels and telenovelas that spark our imagination today are the lingering memories and physical remains of this period. But during the earlier colonial era, the Hacienda San Miguel Acocotla, the casco and its associated structures, would have been more like a working farm.[14] There would have been a few uninspiring buildings and a chapel for the hacienda's employees. A 1686 bill of sale furnishes a detailed picture of what Acocotla would have looked like only a century after it had been established.[15] The buildings were constructed out of adobe and roofed with a thatch of dried corn stalks. The casco was composed of a living room, four bedrooms, and a kitchen. Some of the rooms were described as having doors with keys, while others had no door at all; some may have been intended to house servants, though such details were not included. There were also two granaries, a henhouse, and an oven. Finally, the chapel was given the most attention. Though it, too, was constructed out of adobe, the chapel had a tiled roof with wooden roof beams. Its trappings included a satin altarpiece and all the accoutrements necessary to perform Mass. Of the buildings, the chapel represented the greatest financial investment, but emphasis in the bill of sale was placed on items necessary for conducting agricultural business rather than on architectural space or furniture. These items included fifty-five oxen, nine cows, a cart, yokes, rope, axes, and shovels. In the seventeenth century, the value of the Hacienda Acocotla could be found almost entirely in its functional purpose as a farm.

While the hacienda's mayordomo would have been constantly in residence, the city-dwelling hacendado would have visited only occasionally. Workers would have come daily from nearby villages that were either wholly independent or "sponsored" by the hacienda owner. In the first case, individuals who felt the need for a cash income beyond that available from the limited farming conducted on the village's communal lands might sign on to be day laborers at the hacienda. In the latter case, individuals would live in a village that was owned by the hacienda but was self-organized and governed, an arrangement seen in an eighteenth-century survey map produced by inhabitants of the indigenous town of San Jerónimo Coyula (fig. 3.1). The map shows a very clear delineation of space between the village's lands, the Hacienda Concepción de Coyula's casco and lands, and the village in which the hacienda's workers lived. Additionally, evidence suggests that a very few workers might actually have lived at the casco itself. In 1632, an assessment of Acocotla's value was made in preparation for its sale to the Convent of Santa Clara. "Ocho indios gañanes y tres que andan ausentes" ("eight Indian workers and three that are absent") were listed among the hacienda's assets between the plows and the water rights.[16] The 1686 bill of sale discussed above tells us of the existence of "jacales de vivienda de los gananes" ("huts for housing workers") but does not mention how big the area was, how many people were housed, or where it was located in relation to the rest of the structures.

The central Mexican countryside was more diverse than just Spanish-owned haciendas intermixed with Indian towns.[17] Urban areas like Atlixco dominated the commercial and cultural life of the region. Haciendas, which gobbled up large tracts of land, stood alone in the middle of their fields. Indigenous villages sat on the borders of the hacienda-owned lands, jealously guarding their communally held fields from encroachment. Somewhere between, *ranchos* contributed to the landscape in a complicated and ill-defined way. In theory, ranchos were smaller than haciendas and were often associated with sheep or cattle ranching but also would

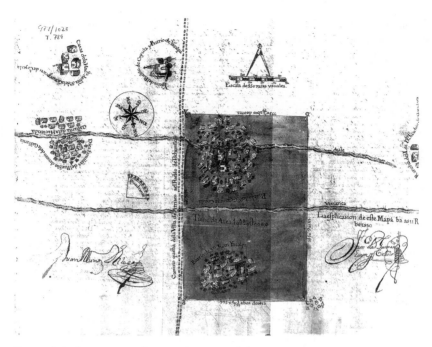

Figure 3.1. Survey map showing location of the town of San Jerónimo Coyula (center gray area), the buildings of the Hacienda Concepcíon de Coyula (upper left), and the hacienda workers' village (middle left) (AGN 1754, Tierras, vol. 789, exp. 1, f. 25).

have relied on agricultural activities. But who owned them? And where did they fit in the settlement patterns of rural central Mexico?

Some historians have argued that the difference between a rancho and a hacienda was the socioeconomic and racial status of its owner, which suggests both categories of property type would share similar physical and agricultural characteristics. Others have defined ranchos based on property size alone.[18] Property definitions seem to have been fluid in the Valley of Atlixco. The total number of settlements listed during the late eighteenth and early nineteenth centuries varied from twenty-six to fifty.[19] Settlements are listed in one document as a "hacienda" and in the next as a "rancho," while a "pueblo" regularly becomes a "rancho." Though today we struggle to fix labels to these different settlement types, it seems likely that this fluidity, at least in the Valley of Atlixco, makes any precise definition impossible. The economic and racial status of the owner or representative affected the legal definition of the property, but the definition was

relative and influenced most by the assessor. Of course, property definitions were not the only convoluted aspect of the Valley of Atlixco's landscape. Each settlement in the valley was inhabited by equally diverse
actors.

*Catalina stood with her eyes closed, breathing deeply and listening to the
sounds of a day in the country. Tomorrow, she would join the convent. Today, for one last day, she was free. It was a nice day for late November, and
she was grateful. As she inhaled the scents of the harvest, she pushed herself
to remain in control of her emotions. She had no desire to pursue a contem-
plative life, and indeed, she had not expected to have had to make such a
choice, but her mother had died when she was still young and her father had
remarried. That alone wouldn't normally have been enough to force her to
take orders, but her father, as usual, had money troubles. He had made arrangements with the Convent of Santa Clara. She would profess her vows.
The convent would lend her father three thousand pesos. He would pay half
of that back as her dowry; the rest would be kept to pay his not inconsider-
able debts. It would save the Hacienda San Miguel Acocotla. The sisters,
always savvy, had also extracted a promise that her father, de Malpica Ponce
de León, wouldn't borrow more money. She hoped he would hold true to that
at the very least.*

*Catalina opened her eyes. The sunlight almost blinded her, but gradu-
ally the forms of the Indians busy in the field before her came into focus. She
smiled as she remembered many happy moments indistinguishable from
this. The day before, her father had asked her how she would like to spend
her "last day." She silently added "of freedom," before smiling like the good
daughter she was and asking to be taken one last time to Acocotla's fields.
The only person more surprised than her father had been her stepmother.
"You want to do what?" her father had demanded as her stepmother's face
curdled with distaste. She asked again for nothing more than to accompany
him on one more trip when he went out to check the state of the jicama harvest. Her father had granted her request; how could he not?*

*She looked around, taking in the views, the fresh air. She took another
deep breath as she watched a hawk circle overhead. Blinking back tears, she
tried not to think about how much her mother had loved this place. Unlike
most "ladies," her mother never hesitated to leave the city behind in favor of
the hacienda's fields. As a child, Catalina came out to the fields with her
parents often. Her first playmates had been the Indian children who also
came with their parents for the harvest. The hacienda was not fine or grand
like some she had heard of—the buildings were really nothing more than*

mud huts—but the space was beautiful, the air clear. She had spent so many happy hours playing here while her parents reviewed the account books. She hoped that by taking orders at Santa Clara, she would save this place for her little brothers and sisters. Once again, her father's debts meant they might lose Acocotla, but there was freedom here like she'd never known in the city, a freedom she wanted them to share.

A Hacienda Owner and His Family

Catalina de Malpica Sosa y Guzman was the eldest child of Francisco Esteban de Malpica Ponce de León and his first wife, María Antonia de Sosa y Guzman. Born in 1698, Catalina was the second of nine children and one of seven to survive past infancy.[20] She was seven years old when her mother died and sixteen years old when she took her vows at the Convent of Santa Clara.[21] That is the extent of her story; nothing else is written about her. Documents found in the national, state, and local archives are weighted toward wealthy men of European descent. Indigenous and African individuals, as well as women and children of all ethnic backgrounds, do appear, but their inclusion in the historic record is most commonly as passive pawns in the world of those European men or, occasionally, in landmark moments in their lives. Catalina de Malpica Sosa y Guzman appears in a birth record, is mentioned in her father's will, and is the subject of one final document at the age of sixteen when she joins the Convent of Santa Clara in her hometown of Atlixco. This last note about her life comes from a financial agreement drawn up between her father and the convent.

Her father, Francisco Esteban de Malpica Ponce de León, lived a life that was strikingly better recorded. He was born August 2, 1667, to Francisco de Malpica Diosdado and Juana Ponce de León. Like his father, Francisco Esteban was native to Atlixco; his mother had been born in New Spain's capital city, Mexico. He had at least five siblings, but he seems to be the only child who survived to adulthood. De Malpica Ponce de León married María Antonia de Sosa y Guzman on April 5, 1693. He was twenty-five years old. During the thirteen years they were married, Francisco de Esteban and María Antonia had four children, three of whom survived their mother. In 1705, de Malpica Ponce de León's wife died, leaving him a widower with their three young daughters, Catalina, María Teresa, and María Magdelana. Shortly thereafter, de Malpica Ponce de León remarried. We don't know exactly when he and Bernardina Delgado y Soria wed, but by July of 1708 she had given him the first of five children, four of whom, two daughters, and two sons, would survive. De Malpica Ponce de León was not just a father and husband—he was a pillar of the community, named *alguacíl mayor* (sheriff or constable) to the local Office of the Inquisition and mayor of Atlixco. By 1719, Francisco Esteban de Malpica Ponce de León was dead.[22] He lived barely past the age of fifty, just long enough to celebrate the birth of his youngest son, Sebastian, on January 18, 1718.

While well documented, de Malpica Ponce de León's life was not extraordinary. Like many hacienda owners in central Mexico, he spent much of his life deeply in debt. The Hacienda Acocotla's primary product was wheat, a grain that was, at times, in great demand in New Spain and thus, at times, a profitable product. But because of the varying demand, prices fluctuated wildly. These fluctuations both affected the financial well-being of the hacienda's owner and provided a cause for frequent changes of hacienda ownership.[23] Historical records of de Malpica Ponce de León's life reflect this pattern and highlight the role of the Catholic Church in rural Mexican financial transactions.[24] The Church acted like a bank, a bank to which hacienda owners like de Malpica Ponce de León frequently found themselves owing money.

Though records of his debts are extensive, de Malpica Ponce de León was actually much more successful and financially stable than many others. The majority of Acocotla's owners seem to have been plagued with money troubles. Loans taken out by Acocotla's owners against the value of the property (and from the Church) were highest during the middle of the seventeenth century and throughout the nineteenth century when loans equaling between 30 and 100 percent of the total property value were regularly made.[25] Further, many of de Malpica Ponce de León's contemporaries turned to him for financial assistance, suggesting that he had money to loan. Evidently, this became a problem for de Malpica Ponce de León. In 1707, he made a promise that he would not lend people money. He explained that his habit of doing so was whittling away his fortune, and he made a commitment to pay a one-thousand-peso fine to Atlixco's church each time he violated this promise.[26] By these measures, de Malpica Ponce de León was a notably successful businessman—though one who was not without his problems.

Records of de Malpica Ponce de León's financial woes are representative of a pattern well established in the historical literature. They show us exactly what we expect to see in rural central Mexico during the early years of the eighteenth century. Other documents tell stories that are less expected and less well documented. The textual records of de Malpica Ponce de León's life hint at an aspect of colonial Mexican life rarely discussed—the presence of African slaves in rural central Mexico. Though we often think of the rural Mexican landscape as the setting for a dialectic struggle between Spaniard and Indian, in fact, the landscape was more diverse. Between 1705 and 1718, there are eleven records of the purchase and sale of slaves involving de Malpica Ponce de León.[27]

The story of African Mexicans is often ignored or glossed over, except in regions where they were able to maintain a substantial and distinct presence (namely, the east coast communities in Veracruz and the west coast "Costa Chica" communities of Guerrero and Oaxaca).[28] In the years following the Mexican Revolution, José Vasconcelos and others defined Mexicans as being part of the "cosmic race" or the "bronze race."[29] These efforts were directed at homogenizing a nation that had been torn apart by innumerable factions before and during the Revolution. Vasconcelos and his peers worked to make the nation they were creating "whiter" and thus, in their eyes, more progressive.[30] Their efforts were largely successful, and so today the role in nation building played by the slaves owned by de Malpica Ponce de León and his compatriots goes largely unacknowledged in the official narrative.

We do not know what role the slaves played in the Valley of Atlixco's economic activities, nor do we know if they worked at the Hacienda Acocotla itself. The slaves listed in de Malpica Ponce de León's purchases and sales may have been members of his urban household. Thus, a solid, quantifiable presence of Africans, blacks, and slaves living and working in the countryside continues to elude us. For now, the story at the Hacienda Acocotla must be limited to that of the quintessential struggle between European and Indian.

María Catarina sat in the darkened room. Her husband had been buried today. She had put her grief aside while she got her four children to bed, but now there was nothing to distract her. The neighbors had left behind a good supply of food; she couldn't even busy herself by getting started on tomorrow's tortillas. So she sat by the dying fire, thinking about her husband, worrying about how she was going to feed her children. She had only one son, and he was so little—only six years old. He would have to grow up quickly, she thought, shaking her head. He would have to find work and help feed her and her three little girls.

Lost in morose thoughts, María Catarina was startled when a figure appeared in her doorway. She jumped up, heart racing, until she realized it was just Luis Tlalpanco, the mayordomo at Acocotla. Her husband had worked for Tlalpanco at the hacienda until he got sick last week. Luis had been too busy at the hacienda to come for the funeral. "He must be making late condolences," she thought.

Tlalpanco walked into the room cautiously. His position at Acocotla meant he couldn't afford any perceptions of impropriety, and he was visiting the newly minted widow quite late and alone. He should have brought his wife, and he cursed silently at his lack of forethought. Still, there was business to be done. He offered the expected expressions of sympathy, squaring his shoulders for the conversation ahead. As the young woman accepted his condolences, he continued, "There are some matters that need to be dealt with, and quickly. Your husband left a debt of four pesos on the books at Acocotla. I need you to pay it now."

María Catarina looked back at him, appalled. Was this man crazy? Where did he think she would find four pesos? It was a sum equal to two week's wages. And she had just had the expense of burying her husband. She glanced out the door and into the compound. Through the darkening gloom, she could just barely make out the outlines of the building her four children slept in. She didn't know how she would feed them once the food brought by the neighbors for the funeral was gone, and this man wanted four pesos. He was insane!

She told him as much, and he shrugged his shoulders. It was her husband's debt, and she had inherited it. He told her coldly that the money must be paid. Trembling with sadness and exhaustion, she told him it was impossible. Tlalpanco turned on his heel and strode out of the room into the now dark compound outside.

María Catarina sighed with relief. He was leaving. In just a minute, she realized her mistake. He came back into the room with her six-year-old son in tow. Her son was rubbing the sleep from his eyes, blinking in confusion at being dragged out of his dreams so forcibly. "If you can't pay your husband's debt, your son will have to," Tlalpanco informed her. "It will take him a while to pay it at a child's salary, especially after I deduct the cost of his living expenses. But, then again, he doesn't look like he eats much. I will return him to you when his father's debt has been paid. Goodnight."

Tlalpanco strode out of the room, leaving María Catarina sitting on the floor next to the fire. She was overwhelmed with grief. What would she do now? How could she and her daughters survive without the only man of the household? She stared into the dying coals, too terrified of the future to re-light the fire or to go to sleep.

Managing the Hacienda

Acocotla's documentary history is dominated by its owners, but daily life would, in fact, have been subject to the whims of the hacienda's managers, or mayordomos. Contemporary accounts suggest that throughout the nineteenth century, hacienda owners lived in urban areas, spending only the occasional weekend at their rural properties for business or pleasure.[31] The hacienda's mayordomo would have been in charge of the day-to-day operations, and he would have most greatly affected the peones' working conditions and quality of life.

Acocotla's mayordomos most frequently appear in the historical record as the target of complaints filed by neighboring villages and workers. In 1826, the mayor of the nearby villages of San Pedro and San Pablo Cuaco wrote to the authorities in Atlixco to complain that the mayordomo of Acocotla had imprisoned the wives and mothers of the villages' workers in the hacienda prison. The mayor reported that the mayordomo was retaliating for a perceived failure on the part of the mayor to force his workers to meet their contractual obligations. The mayordomo was confident that such action would encourage the workers to come to work in the fields with greater reliability and punctuality. The mayor of San Pedro and San Pablo Cuaco understandably objected to the harsh methods employed by the mayordomo, while claiming that he could not be held responsible for the misbehavior and unreliability of his people. In the end, Atlixco's authorities supported the actions of Acocotla's mayordomo.[32]

This is, perhaps, an extreme example of abuse of power. More commonly, mayordomos were accused of overzealous collection of debts from the relatives of deceased peones. In 1826, the manager of the Hacienda San Agustín wrote to the authorities in Atlixco to request that the daughter of one of his deceased workers, Felipe Morales, return a metate, or grinding stone, purchased for her in the hacienda's store by her father prior to his death. The manager claimed that the metate represented an unpaid debt that Morales's daughter was refusing to honor.[33] Such tensions were not limited to the tumultuous decade following the establishment of Mexican independence. In 1864, señora María Catarina of the village of San Jerónimo Coyula indicted Luis Tlalpanco, the mayordomo of Acocotla, for taking her only son to pay her deceased husband's debt of four pesos. She argued that her six-year-old son was her family's only source of financial support and that the mayordomo's actions would leave her unfairly vulnerable.[34] Interestingly, the source of María Catarina's complaint was not Tlalpanco's illegal transference of the debt from her deceased husband to herself but that, in taking her son, Tlalpanco left her without a "man" to support the family.

Mayordomos occupied a position that was, by turns, precarious, contentious, and powerful. Antonio Calderón was Acocotla's mayordomo during and after the Mexican Revolution. His story illustrates the complexity of relationships among different classes of people living at a hacienda. Oral and documentary evidence tells us that during the years following the Mexican Revolution, Calderón refused to relinquish his control over Acocotla to the hacienda's prewar owner, Manuel González Pavón. Though González Pavón attempted to reclaim his lands through legal channels, he was, in fact, only able to return to the hacienda and sell off its lands following the murder of Antonio Calderón by one of the peones from a neighboring village. According to oral history, Antonio Calderón took advantage of the hacendado's absence to transform himself into an hacendado in everything but legal title, even moving his girlfriend into the hacendado's living quarters at Acocotla.

This same girl proved to be Calderón's downfall: she murdered him in 1936. I found this plot twist incomprehensible when it was first told to me by people in two of the descendant communities. What, I wondered, did this girlfriend have to gain by his murder? One imagines her financial position and status could not possibly have been enhanced following Calderón's death. Over time, I was able to piece together the entire story. The title of "girlfriend," it seemed, was a misnomer. When she had been a young girl, some suggested as young as twelve, Calderón had begun repeatedly raping her. Her life in the hacendado's living quarters at Acocotla was more torture than luxury. When she could no longer bear this life, she murdered him. It was a fortuitous turn of events for the hacendado.

These stories illustrate the extent of power wielded by hacienda managers throughout the nineteenth and early twentieth centuries. As the hacienda's labor bosses and bookkeepers, they were the target of anger and suspicion from above and below. Hacienda workers clearly resented the managers' control over their lives, while hacienda owners had to keep their managers under close control. Though the popular narrative often portrays the social world of the hacienda as a tug of war between Spanish hacendado and indigenous peones, in fact, the (often indigenous) mayordomo may have played the most important role in setting the tone and pace of daily life.

Working for the Hacienda

The hacienda's manager had two main sources of labor from which he could draw—resident and nonresident laborers. The former would have been housed on the hacienda property, while the latter would have lived in independent communities bordering the hacienda's lands. Though the experiences of these two groups of people are not identical, they are intertwined. Day and resident laborers (known as peones or *gañanes*) were a necessary part of any hacienda operation. At Acocotla, nineteenth- and early twentieth-century documents identify all the resident workers (with the exception of the hacienda manager) as indigenous.[35]

While Acocotla's records are largely silent on the subject of the hacienda's workforce until the second half of the nineteenth century, some earlier evidence for their presence exists. The earliest mention of workers dates to 1632. Eager to ensure that Indians never became slaves, the Crown prohibited the mention of Indian laborers in bills of sale in 1601 and again in 1609, but these edicts were frequently disobeyed.[36] Acocotla was no exception. As we saw earlier, a 1632 assessment made for the sale of the hacienda to the Convent of Santa Clara numbered a total of eleven indigenous workers among the hacienda's assets.[37]

Archaeological and architectural evidence speaks to the presence of workers during the nineteenth century. The first structure one encounters when approaching the south façade of the Hacienda Acocotla's ruined casco is a series of small rooms flanking the building's main entrance. These rooms make up the hacienda's calpanería, constructed during the 1860s to house the hacienda's resident laborers. The calpanería is an architectural form that appears at haciendas throughout central Mexico during the nineteenth century, and it is one that allowed hacienda owners to enmesh workers in a complex debt structure, minimizing worker mobility.[38]

By the second half of the nineteenth century, families living at and working for the Hacienda Acocotla had acquired considerable debt through the system of debt peonage. Debate surrounds the nature and extent of debt peonage; however, at Acocotla, it seems to have been a strategy of labor control that was regularly employed.[39] By 1910, on the eve of the Mexican Revolution, 90 percent of Acocotla's fifty resident workers owed the hacienda owner money, and debts ran as high as 110 Mexican pesos.[40]

Acocotla's owner paid his workers thirty-three centavos a day in 1910; a debt of 110 pesos represented more than 330 days of work, a sum seemingly impossible to pay. Though the law forbade the transfer of debts to family members upon the death of the debtor, historical records from the municipal archives in Atlixco indicate that this law was frequently ignored.

In the Valley of Atlixco, local authorities passed laws to help enforce the system of debt peonage and control the lower classes. Rural workers had to report their movements to the authorities and request permission to travel from one job to another, even if the change in employment meant a move of only a few miles. In August of 1855, Santiago Morales approached the authorities with a request to move his family two and a half miles from the Hacienda Coyula to the Hacienda Acocotla. He asked to go to Acocotla for the harvest season, and he promised to pay his debts to the owner of Coyula before making the move.[41] Thanks to labor shortages, an hacendado was often willing to pay a peon's existing debts to enable that individual and his family to leave another hacienda and work for him, and it may be that Acocotla's mayordomo was purchasing Santiago Morelos's labor in just this way.[42] A few years after the Morelos's move, regulations, billed as policies to "protect the well-being of workers," were implemented. The regulations stated that if a worker could prove that his employer had abused or mistreated him, he would be allowed to end his employment. He could only take advantage of these protections, however, if he could pay any debts owed to the hacienda and report a new employment situation to the authorities in his home village. If the worker could not meet these obligations, he was required to continue in his employment, regardless of mistreatment or abuse.

Debt was one way the local government and hacienda owners tried to control worker mobility, but more direct, heavy-handed measures were taken as well. We have already heard the story of the wives and mothers imprisoned by Acocotla's mayordomo, and it seems as if this was not an uncommon strategy during the first half of the nineteenth century. Archival records mention prisons only a few times. Hacienda owners were writing to the local authorities to request permission for the construction of prisons during the 1830s.[43] During the same decade, one petulant mayordomo wrote to the mayor of the village of San Jerónimo Coyula requesting the return of indebted workers who had run away from his hacienda. He complained that he had to rely on the village authorities because he did not have a prison in which to lock the workers.[44] Though these are the only appearances of prisons in the archival records in the Valley of Atlixco, the practice was widespread enough that thirty years later Emperor Maximilian sent orders to Atlixco's governor instructing him to stop hacienda owners from imprisoning their indigenous workers.[45]

These documents are evidence of a real problem. In spite of the debts, regulations, and even prisons, workers had a reasonable degree of mobility. Beginning in 1837, lists of workers living at the Hacienda Acocotla were kept on a semiregular basis, and eighteen of these censuses from the years 1837 through 1893 can still be found in Atlixco's municipal archives.[46] In contrast to traditional views of debt peonage that portrayed peones as virtual slaves tied to the land, these lists show that Acocotla's workers had a high degree of mobility.[47] During the fifty-year period covered, Acocotla's lists identify 240 adult males.[48] More than 75 percent of these men appear on only one census (meaning they spent as little as six months at the hacienda), and the number of men who appear on multiple censuses drops off rapidly over time. Though one man appears on every single census over a thirty-five-year time span, 80 percent of workers had left by the second year, and more than 90 percent of the workers had left by the seventh year. Further, with the exception of one family, male children left the Hacienda Acocotla for employment elsewhere once they were grown, regardless of whether or not their parents continued to live and work at Acocotla.

Life in the Village

Not all hacienda workers resided on hacienda lands. Many came as day or seasonal laborers from nearby villages. Understanding what life was like in those villages helps explain what workers gained by accepting employment at Acocotla. The hacienda's workers came from the communities of Tejupa, La Trinidad Topango, San Jerónimo Coyula, and La Soledad Morelos. The village of La Soledad Morelos is located approximately two kilometers south of the Hacienda Acocotla. Prior to the Mexican Revolution, the village was known as Rancho la Mojonera, evidently because it was located at the boundaries of the lands belonging to the nearby haciendas surrounding the settlement (a *mojonera* is a boundary marker).[49] The first mention of the rancho in the documentary record comes in 1853 in the form of a census of mostly indigenous individuals paying a poll tax; sixty-one men between the ages of sixteen and eighty-five were listed. In 1872, La Mojonera makes another appearance in a complaint made to the authorities regarding an attack of one of the members of the village by bandits.[50] The settlement next appears in a census published in 1903, which describes La Mojonera as a "ranchería" and identifies a total population of 612 individuals (including 293 men and 319 women).[51]

The history of the Rancho la Mojonera is uncertain due to the absence of documentary evidence prior to 1853 and the paucity thereafter. The village may have been an indigenous settlement that existed prior to the establishment of the nearby haciendas. Alternatively, it may specifically have been established by the surrounding haciendas as a place to house workers, a pattern that has been identified on haciendas in Yucatán.[52] For our purposes, it is enough to understand that La Mojonera was an established community during the second half of the nineteenth and early years of the twentieth centuries that provided day laborers to the Hacienda Acocotla (and probably others nearby). Today, descendants of the hacienda's workers continue to live in the village.

Unfortunately, archival records are rarely more complete than fragmentary archaeological remains. To understand what life was like in the villages associated with the hacienda, we have to draw on archival records from neighboring villages, many of which also had a working relationship with Acocotla. While La Mojonera is virtually invisible in the historical record, the history of the indigenous village of San Jerónimo Coyula is much better documented and helps us understand what life was like in Mojonera. San Jerónimo Coyula was likely an established settlement when the Spanish first arrived in the region. Documents held in the village's town hall suggest that the settlement is of great antiquity. Among these, a hand-drawn map from 1639 shows the village in relation to other Prehispanic settlements. The village itself is shown as a Catholic Church surrounded by traditional Nahua "house" or "lineage" symbols (*calli*). Today, inhabitants of San Jerónimo Coyula continue to speak Nahuatl and self-identify as indigenous, though the language is used less often by the village's younger inhabitants.

Records such as that shown in figure 3.1 suggest that the inhabitants of San Jerónimo Coyula fought to maintain control over their village lands and other resources during the centuries following the Spanish conquest. The 1754 map was part of a legal case in which the people of San Jerónimo Coyula were complaining that the neighboring hacienda owner was infringing on their communal lands.[53] Documents dating to the late eighteenth or early nineteenth centuries and currently held in private hands speak of the community's rights stretching back to "the time of Cortés." Today, the community remains insular and hostile to outsiders. The current mayor speaks with great pride about his community's antiquity and resistance to attempts at domination made by iterations of would-be conquerors during the last five hundred years.

Water rights provide an example of the perpetual struggles in which the villagers found themselves entangled. Battles over control of the valley's limited irrigation water were of great importance throughout the colonial period, and it is an issue that continues to be contentious to this day. As recently as forty years ago, one of Coyula's citizens was assassinated for his role in constructing a reservoir that reduced the amount of irrigation water available to villages downstream. His murder and the controversy leading up to it are representative of a pattern with deep, historic roots. Throughout the colonial period, indigenous people in the Atlixco Valley avidly defended their water rights, an ecological necessity in a desert farming community.[54] Defense of their communal land and water rights is an expected response of the people of San Jerónimo Coyula, but things did not always go smoothly. The social landscape complicated the fight.

In 1784, members of the village of San Jerónimo Coyula chose to drop a lawsuit against hacienda owners in the region that would have been decided in favor of the villagers. According to the lawsuit, the Castillos, owners of the haciendas Coyula and Acocotla during the early years of the seventeenth century, had made an agreement with the village's leaders regarding the fair and equitable (paid) use of water rights. One hundred and fifty years later, Coyula's leaders were complaining that the contemporary hacienda owners were failing to live up to the ancient agreement. Ultimately, the people of Coyula dropped their claim for fear of retribution from the hacienda owners, who were also their employers. Their lawyer explained to the court that the people of San Jerónimo Coyula lived in fear, misery, and poverty. He told the court that the villagers did not have the spirit to resist their employers, who held them in a state of terror, and so, for these reasons, they were dropping their legal claims.[55]

These legal documents hint at the attitudes held by Coyula's inhabitants toward the interlopers, but they tell us little of the daily conditions of life in the village. In fact, reconstructing daily life in San Jerónimo Coyula is difficult from historic records alone. Momentary glimpses afforded us by stories such as that of María Catarina, discussed earlier, give us an idea of life in the village. Some vital and government records help fill in some of the gaps. Between 1839 and 1855, twenty censuses were taken of the village of San Jerónimo Coyula. A few of these were simple notes summarizing the population losses and gains to factors such as birth, death, and moving and list between 375 and 462 individuals living in the village in 1841 and 1842.[56] More complete censuses, taken in 1842, 1843, and 1855, suggest that the village actually held approximately eight hundred inhabitants.[57] The more complete censuses tell us about family size, which averaged around 4.2 individuals per family, and that between 185 and 200 families in total lived in the village during this period. Electoral rolls were also taken, listing all adult males who voted in local and regional elections.[58] These lists identify anywhere from 90 to 260 men between the ages of sixteen and seventy-five and catalog their literacy levels. Literacy accounts varied quite a bit. Anywhere from 3 percent to 10 percent of the voting men were listed as literate. Finally, a single tax roll lists 211 men, twelve of whom are described as disabled and unable to pay taxes. These twelve men's disabilities are evenly divided between blindness and lameness.

Death records, among the most poignant of data sets, tell us a great deal about living conditions. Figure 3.2, which shows the number of deaths per

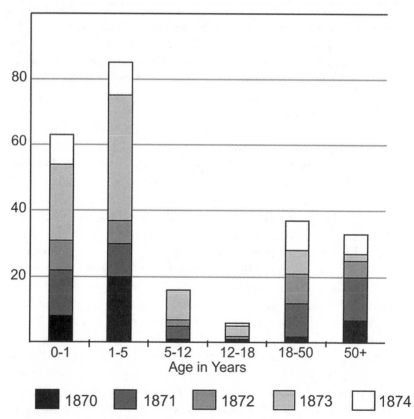

Figure 3.2. Number of deaths by age group (1870–1874) in San Jerónimo Coyula.

age group between 1870 and 1874, emphasizes the high rates of child and infant mortality.[59] Children died regularly of fevers, dysentery, epileptic seizures, and whooping cough, whereas adults seem to have most often succumbed to either injuries or complications brought on by injuries, as well as chest pains. Only two women are listed as having died in childbirth. Epidemics seem to have struck with regularity. Figure 3.2 captures one such epidemic of smallpox that passed through the village in 1873. During its height in the late spring and early summer, three or four children died each day. Records recount instances of as many as three siblings dying in the space of only four or five days. Taken together, archival records of life and death in San Jerónimo Coyula suggest that life was difficult. People were poor, struggling to survive. In spite of this, village members worked hard to maintain their ethnic and community identity, an endeavor in which they were largely successful.

⁜   ⁜   ⁜

I leaned back and glared at the computer screen in front of me. I tried rereading the chapter about the history of the Hacienda San Miguel Acocotla I had just finished writing, but I was still unhappy with the results. Shaking my head, I worried about the fact that the women and children in my story all seemed to appear as victims. Was this really their life, or was I imposing my preconceptions on their story? I looked at the towering pile of archival transcriptions sitting on the table next to my desk, mentally flipping through their pages, thinking about the ways in which women and children were presented, included, and discussed. At first glance, the documents did seem to portray women, children, and ethnic minorities as passive victims in a male, European-controlled world. A more careful examination of the documentary evidence, however, suggested that while these individuals were often victimized, they were far from submissive. For example, María Catarina found herself battling for custody of her son after her husband's death. Though her loss of custody to the hacienda manager was a form of victimization, she didn't accept the attack. Instead, she enlisted the help of the (male) mayor in fighting for her son's return. But how well did moments like this capture the experience of María Catarina's life?

"What would remain of me after I was gone, and what would it say to people?" I mused. Smiling ruefully, I admitted to myself that a college professor and archaeologist was unlikely to inspire much careful record keeping on the part of the archivist. Official files and records would of course remain, but they were the sort everybody had, and they would be intermixed with more personal hints—record of my birth, my transcontinental move from Canada to the United States when I was nine, perhaps the annual childhood border crossing on a pilgrimage to visit my father who stayed on the west coast of Canada, newspaper clippings for high school awards won, a record of graduation from first one and then another university, a driver's license obtained unusually late in life, an oddly eclectic work history, some dry professional articles about research in a field I had fallen, unintentionally, into, the record of my death. . . . I imagined nothing would remain of digital files such as e-mails and instant messaging logs for anyone living as mundane a life as mine. I shuddered at the sudden image of a poor historian attempting to reconstruct my personality based on the reams of teaching evaluations stored by the university and fervently hoped she would read them with a critical and honest eye. But how much would any of this paperwork really say about who I had been?

I looked around my office at the colorful bits and pieces of me scattered across bookshelves and windowsills. How much of this, how much of what I really thought of as ME, would make it onto paper? My feet rested on the hand-woven Zapotec rug purchased in a street market in Oaxaca. I smiled at the feeling of it under my feet as I remembered handing money to the eleven-year-old girl who had woven it. It was her first rug, and her first sale. Every time I looked at it, I felt the warmth of the sun on the back of my head and the feeling of watching her father's face as he watched the daughter he had both raised and taught make her first sale. My glance floated over to the silly Lucite pyramid from Teotihuacán. I chuckled a bit as I remembered purchasing it at the base of the Pyramid of the Sun with the young man, then sixteen, whom I had nannied when he was just an infant. We had bought it as a joke, and the joke, continuing to this day, had been well worth the $1.10 I had spent on the little pyramid. My glance slipped to the next item on my windowsill—a beautiful vase from Michoacán. My graduate school roommate had given it to me as a Christmas present when we spent four days of luxury at a Mexican beach resort one Christmas holiday. She and I were both in the field working that year and were both unable, for the first time in our lives, to make it back to the States for holidays with our families. The vase was a reminder of a holiday that was simultaneously wonderful and awful. My gaze wandered to the overflowing bookshelves that lined my office. To the outsider, they were simply the office decoration adopted by most academics. To me, they represented escape from a childhood that had been too poor to allow for the ownership of very many volumes. They were my security blanket, a buffer between my present and my past. These bits and pieces scattered across my office defined me more completely than anything else could, certainly more than limited paper remains. Taken alone, they were just inanimate objects, but when combined with the historical record of my life, they offered more to the historical puzzle.

I closed my eyes, listening to the old-style Cuban jazz floating from my speakers. I imagined what it would sound like if only the highest and lowest notes were left in the song, the rest replaced by silence. For the skilled and familiar listener, the tune or, at the very least, the genre of music might still be identifiable. The remaining notes might hint at the tenor of the song, but the true joy and tragedy of the music would be lost. The historical record of my life would be like those high and low notes—hinting at the truth but glossing over most of the emotional complexities. The lives of the women, children, indigenous, and African inhabitants of the Valley of Atlixco were no different in their historical impact than mine will be someday. The historical research presented here allows us to hear the high and low notes, but if we want to hear the entire melody, we need to expand our sources of information. By drawing on the available oral historical, ethnoarchaeological, and archaeological resources, I hoped I would be able to add a few more notes to the tune I was trying to reconstruct.

I stood up to refile all the paper on my desk and reshelve the books. Everything already had its place in my office, and so I finished the task quickly. When my desk was clear, I began to pull the next data set from my files, boxes, and shelves, hoping that this set of information would add that depth to the story.

✻   ✻   ✻

CHAPTER FOUR

The Legacy of Revolution

*   *   *

I picked my way through the muddy, partially flooded main street, greeting young men as they rode by on their horses. They had assisted with my excavations at the hacienda, and they smiled, friendly and seeming happy to see me. My students trailed behind me, looking shocked at the conditions in which the villagers lived. This was the town's main street? I could see the question in their eyes as they looked around, whispering. I expected the exchange students from the United States to feel out of their element, but the astonishment evident on the faces of the Mexican students I found, in turn, astonishing. The poverty in La Soledad Morelos is out of the ordinary to many, but Mexico is full of such villages. Why the surprise and discomfort?

I considered the question as I hugged an electrical pole, trying to skirt a large puddle without flooding my boots. Starting a long day in the field with cold, wet feet is unpleasant—best to keep them dry until the sun was a bit higher and the air a bit warmer. I slipped away from the pole and my cause was lost. I sighed and shrugged. It was our first day in the field. I knew the month held many days of cold, wet feet. It was hard to complain as I looked down the main street, named Independencia, toward the elementary school. The sight made me ashamed of my irritation.

We would be collecting oral historical, ethnographic, and ethnoarchaeological data in La Soledad Morelos for the next four weeks. I turned to my assistant, MaryCarmen, and consulted her about where to start. She told me it was her compadre Juan Antonio's birthday. Lunch at his house would be a good way to introduce the students to members of the village, and thanks to MaryCarmen's relationship with the family, we would all be warmly welcomed. But first, we would take the students to meet the elementary school principal, teachers, and children. Word that we were in town would spread quickly after the visit.

*   *   *

Looking around, my students saw a tiny, poor village, but had any of the 612 individuals who lived in La Soledad Morelos in 1903 walked into the village with us, they would have found it surprisingly, perhaps overwhelmingly, large. The population has more than doubled in the last one hundred years; the village has expanded dramatically in just three generations. One elderly man told us that during the Mexican Revolution the village had only seven adobe houses. The rest of the houses were made primarily out of *chinamite* (dried cornstalks) and palm leaves. Few people, he told us, had lived in the village, and all worked on the nearby haciendas. The population swelled during the second quarter of the twentieth century when the post-Revolutionary agrarian reforms caused the dissolution of those same haciendas. Peones who had been living at the haciendas moved to villages, including La Soledad, as the hacienda buildings fell into ruins and the lands were expropriated.

According to the 2005 National Census, La Soledad Morelos has a population of 1,916 people and 364 individual homes or house compounds.[1] While conducting a survey during the first two research seasons in the summers of 2003 and 2004, we identified 444 lots including 381 house compounds, noting two under construction and twelve clearly abandoned, which suggested the census is accurate. The village's main street, Independencia, runs for just under a kilometer from the northeast to the southwest. There are no paved streets in La Soledad (fig. 4.1), and with the exception of delivery trucks and police patrols, very few vehicles are seen. The majority of the village's inhabitants rely on horses for their primary transport, and a nice saddle is seen as a mark of status. It is also common to see young men on bicycles. For longer trips, a bus runs on weekdays to the nearby city Atlixco between the hours of 8 a.m. and 4 p.m. Individuals with a bit more money (largely thanks to family members working in the United States) may own pickup trucks, though these tend to be saved for special occasions.

Most municipal buildings line the village's main street. A small, government-funded medical clinic sits at the entrance to the village

Figure 4.1. The main street (Independencia) of La Soledad Morelos, June 2004. (Photo by Isaac Guzmán.)

Figure 4.2a. Medical clinic, La Soledad Morelos. (Photo by Isaac Guzmán.)

(fig. 4.2a). It is a single, concrete-block room surrounded by a chain link fence topped by barbed wire. A nurse comes from the nearby city for a few hours every Tuesday, and women line up with their children waiting for a consultation. This is the only access to Western medicine that the majority of the villagers have; 99 percent of the 1,916 people living in La Soledad have no access to either private or public, government-funded medical care, though national health initiatives supplement this from time to time (fig. 4.2b).[2] There are no doctors in the village. A single pharmacy sells nothing stronger than aspirin (villagers reported needing to go all the way to Atlixco to buy "modern medicines" like cough syrup). Those who have an emergency and can afford to pay a doctor take a forty-five-minute bus ride, when the bus is running, to Atlixco. Those who cannot afford a doctor or who cannot wait until public transportation is available visit the local *huesero* (a bonesetter, masseuse, and healer).

A *telesecundaria* is located next to the clinic. Young people who have the inclination to study beyond the sixth grade and who can be spared from the responsibilities of family and work may attend this school. The building is composed of a few rooms equipped with television sets. A satellite dish sits on the roof, receiving lessons broadcast daily from Mexico City. The television sets are the teachers, though one teacher is employed

Figure 4.2b. Public health announcement for a national vaccination program. (Photo by Isaac Guzmán.)

to supervise. During the summer of 2005, there were approximately thirty-five children pursuing an education beyond the sixth grade. The rest of the village children had gone to work in the fields with their families.

The primary school is located a few blocks farther down Independencia. In 2004, the school had 487 students, fifteen teachers, and a principal. The teachers and principal commute from Atlixco. The school has four computers, an Internet connection, and digital projectors provided by the government in lieu of textbooks. Teachers in the primary grades make do largely with paper and pencils. Teachers in the upper grades each have one of the four computers in their classroom and construct lesson plans based on what is available on the Internet. No other computer access is available in La Soledad Morelos. The 2005 census lists 521 children of primary-school age, so it seems fair to estimate that between thirty and fifty children were not attending school. While school is free, the required uniforms are not, nor are shoes optional. A number of families cannot afford to send their children to school, and so they send them to the fields instead.

I interviewed one young man, about seven years old, over a shared sandwich in the fields one day. He was sent out to mind the livestock everyday, and he took to hanging around our excavation site, asking questions, offering help, and sharing our lunches (though, very proud, he would only share our food if we insisted it was too much for us and would be thrown away). I asked him if he had ever been to school. He shook his head, looked at the ground, and said, "I want to learn to read, more than anything. But my mother says I have to watch the goats." For adults fifteen and older, the average number of years of schooling is 3.98, and approximately three out of every ten adults are illiterate.[3]

The Catholic church (fig. 4.3) is adjacent to the primary school. Unlike most villages in Mexico, La Soledad has no town square, no gathering place. The church's plaza serves as a gathering spot as best it can. The church has no resident priest. Instead, a traveling cleric comes to say Mass on Sundays in the early afternoon. Villagers who need him outside of this regular visit, for christenings, marriages, or funerals, for example, must find the money to hire a priest to come to town.

While the majority of La Soledad's residents are Catholic, evangelical Christians are beginning to find their way into the village. There are no evangelical churches in La Soledad yet. Services are held informally in members' homes, and attendance has been gradually increasing. Women especially are converting. Conversion to an evangelical religion affords

Figure 4.3. Catholic church, La Soledad Morelos. (Photo by Isaac Guzmán.)

these women a measure of control and self-determination and can even provide protection from alcoholism and spousal abuse.[4] Though conversion affords protection and increased stability at the family level, it can be destabilizing at the community level.[5] In June 2005, the rainy season was four weeks late. As the weeks stretched on and the crops were in danger of failing, our Catholic informants told us repeatedly that the rains had not come because God was angry that there were evangelicals in La Soledad Morelos. They were planning to attack the evangelicals, kill a few, and chase the rest out of town when, luckily, the rains started.

Other municipal buildings located along the main street include a kindergarten, the Oficina de la Unión Campesina (the offices of the farm workers' union), and the Presidencia (the mayor's office); the Partido Revolucionario Institucional (PRI—the Party of the Institutionalized Revolution, Mexico's dominant political party) controlled the latter two offices. Additional municipal spaces included a soccer field, a jail, and a whorehouse. We were surprised to discover the jail and whorehouse. Though authorities from both the nearby city of Atlixco and the town of Huaquechula pass through La Soledad on patrols, the town has no standing police force. La Soledad's jail is an artifact of community policing, used "unofficially" to control those who need controlling. The whorehouse is indicative of the lack of available social services. Widows and women whose husbands have disappeared during their northern migrations staff it; the women have no other ways of making ends meet.

The town is divided into four barrios, or neighborhoods. Each barrio has its own mayordomo and round of fiesta responsibilities. With this division come distinctive and separate social identities and allegiances. People who live south of Independencia claim that the people living in the northern half of town are "dangerous," "unfriendly," and "crazy." The people living north of Independencia were largely unavailable for comment. Six months before we began research in La Soledad Morelos, a couple claiming to be from Mexico City arrived in the village to buy people's daughters (twelve years old and younger) to "take to be secretaries in Mexico City." While a number of families in the area of town north of Independencia were in the process of finalizing arrangements, federal authorities arrived to arrest the couple in question. Evidently, the couple had actually come to the village to buy young girls to take to Tijuana and other border towns to work as prostitutes. As a result, the people in the two barrios north of the main street were extremely suspicious of outsiders, and these closed communities became even more closed. We were able to interview only three families living in this part of the town. The rest of the interviews conducted during all our field seasons were taken from families living in the two southern barrios.

The barrios are also home to rival gangs, a product, people in the village say, of young men returning from the United States with corrupted morals (fig. 4.4). The gangs seem to mimic traditional barrio organization and are constrained by the barrio's borders. Anthropologists have noted the ways in which children, when left without adult authority figures, create their own system of authority and rules.[6] The gangs in La Soledad seem to serve this purpose. Though the 2005 National Census listed only three men as migrants to the United States, in reality migration is much more widespread.[7] The structure of the gangs, mimicking the traditional barrio structure, may be in place to bolster conventional systems faltering because substantial numbers of middle-age men — father figures — have left for *El Norte*.

In spite of considerable outmigration, the village continues to have an economy based on agriculture, with supplemental income from remittances sent by family members working in the United States. From August to December, villagers are busy with the harvest: first corn, then jicama,

Figure 4.4. Goats and gang grafitti. (Photo by Isaac Guzmán.)

and finally peanuts. Jicama brings in the most money and, with the exception of remittances sent from the United States, is the primary source of cash for the people of La Soledad. The harvest ends just in time for the Christmas festivities beginning on December 12 with the celebration in honor of the Virgin of Guadalupe. Celebrations continue through January 6, with emphasis on La Soledad's feast day—December 25. The people of La Soledad Morelos are quick to explain that their December 25 fiesta has nothing to do with Christmas; it is a celebration of the day of a Virgin housed in the chapel of a neighboring hacienda. The fact that this celebration takes place on December 25 is nothing more than a coincidence, but they are very proud that their feast day coincides with Christmas.

From January through May, little agricultural work is available. Those who can scrape together five thousand US dollars to pay a coyote head across the border for a few months of work, mostly at restaurants, in the United States. Many return with the rains in late May or early June to begin the planting season. Migration is not just common but a fact of life. During the course of the project, we studied twenty households intensively. Of these twenty, eighteen households had fathers or elder sons working illegally in the United States. As a result, three out of every four children in the studied households are growing up without a father. Families who have made this sacrifice, however, are in a position of economic strength with which their neighbors cannot compete.

*   *   *

As I paused for breath, one of the students called out, "Professor Newman, what is the point of this? I mean, I thought the Acocotla project was about archaeology and history." I had ducked these questions in the classroom, suggesting they think about it on the drive out to the village. For these students, archaeology meant the distant, Prehispanic past, a past to which modern connections are often tenuous. I stopped and turned, waiting for the stragglers to catch up to the rest of the group. Gathering the students around me, I asked if anyone might venture a response. Some of the braver students did, and I was pleased to see that many were close to an answer. The connections between past and present had been anything but obvious in the classroom, but here in the street, they became clearer. After listening to the students puzzle through their responses a bit, I gave them the answer as I saw it.

*   *   *

Why Ethnography in a Book About Archaeology?

Life in contemporary La Soledad Morelos is just the beginning, or perhaps the end, of the story. The conditions of daily life described in the preceding and following few pages are the heritage of four hundred years of life and labor at the Hacienda San Miguel Acocotla, as well as the result of post-Revolutionary reforms introduced by the twentieth-century Mexican government. The research we were embarking on in La Soledad Morelos that morning was part of a body of work that is using ethnographic research among former hacienda workers and their descendants to reconstruct the lives of Latin America's rural poor and nuance the master narrative.[8] In La Soledad Morelos, many of the village's 1,916 inhabitants had parents and grandparents who lived at or worked for the hacienda. A few of the hacienda's workers are alive today, still able to share their memories of life at Acocotla during the Mexican Revolution. Today, this continuity between life at the hacienda and life in La Soledad Morelos is clear. Research in this descendant community colors the interpretations of the archaeology at the Hacienda San Miguel Acocotla and informs our understanding of nineteenth-century rural life.

Why do the people of La Soledad Morelos live like they do today? More important, why are they content with the economic situation in which they find themselves? Fewer than one hundred years ago, agrarian peasants in central Mexico rose up in violent rebellion, protesting the conditions under which they were forced to live. Some of the individuals we interviewed in La Soledad Morelos participated in the Mexican Revolution, and others grew up listening to their parent's stories of insurgency. Was employment with a nearby hacienda so awful? Was it so much worse than the conditions under which the contemporary community lives? The last was hard to fathom as I stood ankle deep in the mud in the middle of the main street surrounded by shocked students on a cool June morning.

The master narrative of the Mexican Revolution tells us that cruel and exploitive hacienda owners drove rural peasants to rise in revolt during the early years of the twentieth century. These problems were resolved by the post-Revolutionary agrarian reforms, the story continues, and so today the formerly exploited peon cheerfully farms his own plot of land, supporting his family with the corn he and his community grow, secure in the knowledge that, no matter what, he has enough land to feed his wife and children. Both my university students and the people of La Soledad Morelos had been taught these facts in elementary school, but time spent in La Soledad Morelos makes one reexamine the assumptions inherent in

this story. Though individuals living at and working for the nearby haciendas certainly had difficult lives, what, exactly, made those lives too difficult
to bear? What pushed people to the drastic recourse of violent rebellion?
The economic situation today is bleak, as evidenced by the preceding description, and yet people seem prepared to peacefully build families and
lives under these conditions. Why don't they rebel when their parents and
grandparents did so without hesitation? The official story seems overly
simplistic.

*   *   *

I looked around at the students. They were nodding, processing the information and opinions I had just offered. I turned and continued to make
my way down the main street. We soon reached the gates of the school,
and the young students playing in the yard ran to meet us. They recognized those of us who had come to their village during past summers.
They chatted with us through the gate, filling us in on the changes that
had taken place in their families since we had last visited while we waited
for one of the children to return with the school's caretaker. He arrived
quickly, smiling his greetings as he unlocked the gate and let us into
the schoolyard. We made our way to the principal's office, a windowless
cement-block room, and entered. Abram greeted us warmly. Mary-
Carmen and I sat across his desk, and he filled us in on the latest village
news.

After getting caught up and exchanging a few more pleasantries, we
moved on to the real purpose of our visit. Every year, two students from the
United States would spend part of their time during our field season teaching English to the students in the upper grades of the elementary school.
From the outside, it was a superficial service to offer, but in reality, in a
village where the vast majority of the men would seek illegal employment
in the United States, a few words of English were highly prized. I introduced the two students who would be spending a few hours each day at
the school, and we left them with Abram to meet their students and the
teachers with whom they would work.

The remaining students and I waved goodbye to the children in the
schoolyard as we made our way to the next stop on our "tour." Juan Antonio's house would be busy by now with preparations for tonight's fiesta.
The women of the family, along with friends and neighbors, would be,
literally, elbow deep in tortilla preparation, and the stews would be simmering in the giant *cazuelas* kept for parties. Our primary research objective this month was to study domestic compounds and the ways in which

space is used. Though we had previously collected detailed data about the town and settlement patterns, we wanted to examine the ways in which individual, traditional compounds were constructed and inhabited in hopes that it would allow us to contextualize and interpret excavation data at the Hacienda San Miguel Acocotla. I encouraged them to meet as many people as possible this afternoon and explain our project. The party not only would be an ideal chance to make initial observations but also would provide introductions to many people in the village. As we walked toward Juan Antonio's home, I reviewed what we knew about architecture and land use in the village.

*   *   *

Land Use and Domestic Architecture in La Soledad Morelos

During the 2003–2005 field seasons, we collected data on domestic architecture and use of space in the village, surveying land use and architecture for all 444 lots in town. We identified and mapped three categories of domestic architecture: traditional, mixed, and modern. We also identified lots used for agriculture within the town, public/municipal buildings, and abandoned/empty lots. House lots totaled 381, including twelve abandoned and two under construction. This total represents 86 percent of the land use in La Soledad Morelos (discounting outlying agricultural fields). Of these, modern house compounds were the most common. Two hundred and thirty-seven lots contained modern architecture. While collecting data on house types, we quickly learned that "modern"-style houses were a strong indicator that the inhabitants had close family members in the United States sending remittances.[9] The fact that more than half of the houses exhibited modern influence hints at how widespread migration is, in spite of the census data indicating the contrary. One hundred and seven houses were categorized as mixed, and traditional house compounds were the rarest, with only thirty-seven identified. We also identified thirty-six structures as either municipal or public use buildings, seventeen lots as agricultural, and ten empty, unused lots. Municipal and public buildings included the clinic, schools, and church. Agricultural lots were planted with a variety of crops but most commonly were used for either corn or *nopales* (a type of cactus).

A number of factors were used in creating the typology of domestic architecture in La Soledad Morelos, including materials used in construction, form and layout of houses, and form and layout of house compounds.[10] These categories were then used to assign each house lot to the category of "traditional," "mixed," or "modern." Traditional house compounds were identified first by materials used in construction. They were constructed primarily out of adobe and roofed with red pantiles, though occasionally other materials such as brick were present. The compounds were composed of disarticulated rooms, each standing alone with a single door leading into a patio area, a design and layout seen throughout the highlands of Mexico.[11] Traditional house compounds could also contain what we termed "indigenous" architectural elements, such as *temascales* (sweat baths; fig. 4.5) or *hornos* (adobe ovens used for baking bread on Day of the Dead), but the presence of these items was not deemed necessary. In fact, these architectural elements were rare. Within each compound, four distinct layouts with a total of eight possible variations were identified.

Mixed houses were identifiable by the inclusion of modern building materials (cement blocks, tile, and corrugated tin roofs), and they occasionally had interconnecting rooms but often exhibited traditional elements

Figure 4.5. Temascal in traditional house compound, La Soledad Morelos. (Photo by Isaac Guzmán.)

as well. Most commonly, mixed house lots were lots that contained both traditional and modern architecture. Finally, modern house lots contained structures made out of modern materials. These houses were the only structures in La Soledad to have an upper floor and internally connected rooms. In both traditional and mixed house compounds, outside activity areas were often as important, sometimes more important, as the interior spaces of rooms, but in the modern category, outside activity areas were of significantly lesser importance. While some mixed compounds are included in the following discussion, emphasis is placed on traditional compounds, as these appear to have been most analogous to the Hacienda Acocotla's calpanería.

*   *   *

As MaryCarmen knocked on the door at the entrance of José Antonio's home, I explained to the students that this was one of the traditional house compounds. I told them to take careful mental notes of the compound's attributes. We would discuss these on our way back to the cars at the end of the workday. I also reminded them to make as many personal introductions to different members of the village as possible. Our goal was to study twenty separate compounds (5 percent of the total households in the village) over the course of the next month, and for this, we would need invitations. As they nodded their understanding, José Antonio's wife, Marta, opened the door and greeted MaryCarmen effusively.

Her warm greeting was extended to me and my twelve students. We walked into the compound and were almost knocked over by the smell of spicy *moles* steaming from enormous cazuelas in the smoke kitchen. Near the simmering pots, a group of women worked under a tarp stretched out to shade the area adjacent to the overflowing kitchen. The women were preparing the mountains of tortillas that would be consumed during the festivities. We had come at a good time. MaryCarmen's relationship with the family would mean she could join the cooking women and bring a couple of the female students. After a few moments of introductions, MaryCarmen and the students sank their hands into the tortilla dough, laughing, and talking with the women.

The rest of us, men, foreigners, and me (foreigner, teacher, and, at times, boss) were relegated to a place of honor at a shady table with the men. At first, unsure in the presence of foreigners and visitors, the men's conversation quieted. Soon, though, they relaxed. Some had worked in the field with me, and, to them, I had taken on a sort of genderless status.

I wasn't married with children like all the women my age they knew. Instead, I worked in the fields next to them every day, giving them orders and, at the end of the week, paying them. I no longer counted as a woman in their eyes, and indeed, had I tried to join MaryCarmen in the kitchen, neither our hosts nor their guests would have been any more comfortable had the man of the house gone into the kitchen space and begun to make a tortilla himself. As everyone relaxed, the conversation at our table quickly became as spicy as the simmering mole. I suspected the conversation flying over and around the tortilla preparation was no tamer given the tone of laughter floating over from the women's side of the yard.

Soon, the band arrived and began to set up for the afternoon's festivities—festivities that would continue into the early morning. The music went a long way toward breaking down the gendered division of space, though still no men ventured anywhere near the kitchen. More neighbors drifted in, and the party began to pick up speed. My students and I wandered through the growing crowd, meeting and greeting new faces and old acquaintances while eating our share of the delicious turkey in mole verde. After a few hours, I signaled my students. It was time to collect the two Americans at the elementary school and head back to campus. As we walked back to our trucks, we compared notes. The students had done a good job of observing the layout of the compound we had visited, and their observations would be refined over the coming month. We should be able to describe the compounds in accurate detail by the time the field season ended in July. I felt a sense of satisfaction. It had been a productive day in the field, something that boded well for the month to come.

*   *   *

Over the course of the coming month, the students successfully met our goal of studying and mapping twenty compounds. They interviewed at least one member of each household regarding the use of domestic space, architecture and architectural materials, domestic activities, and daily life. When available, men and women of multiple generations were included in interviews about the same domestic space. We also collected oral histories focused primarily on subjects including the surrounding haciendas, the history of La Soledad Morelos, and life before, during, and after the Mexican Revolution. Ultimately, when the interview notes were compiled, we had more than one thousand typed pages of information. This mountain of data meant that we could record modern life accurately, but it also meant that we would be able to enhance our interpretations of our archaeological finds with information that is simply not recoverable from excavations alone. By developing an understanding of the way people used their modern domestic space, as well as the way they felt about that space, we could understand something about the way their grandparents and great grandparents experienced life in the calpanería during the nineteenth century.

On average, domestic compounds in La Soledad Morelos measure 559 square meters but range from 256 to 1,575; the measurements include indoor and outdoor activity areas. With one exception (which had no fence), the studied compounds are bounded on four sides by adobe or cement block walls within which rooms are arranged in one of eight possible layouts.[12] Rooms are single-storied and constructed out of adobe and pantiles or cement block and corrugated tin roofing (fig. 4.6). Only one compound had rooms with windows, and very few of the rooms had doors in the doorways. The number of rooms and/or activity areas in each compound ranged from two to nine, but between five and eight areas was most common (fig. 4.7). Most compounds had a single sleeping/living structure for each nuclear family, though occasionally either multiple sleeping/living structures were identified for a single family or one structure housed multiple families. Each compound contained a separate kitchen area for each nuclear family.[13] All compounds contained space for a variety of

Figure 4.6. Traditional architecture, La Soledad Morelos.

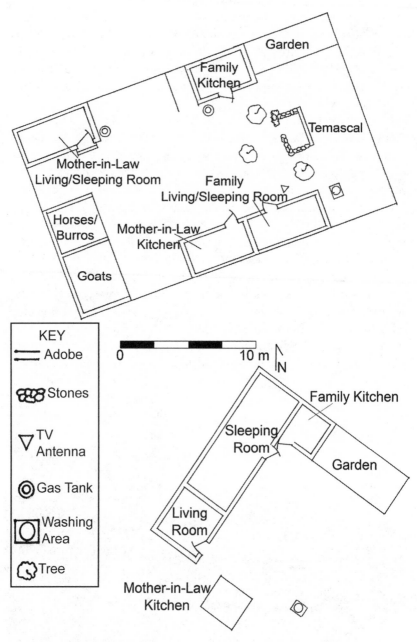

KEY
Adobe
Stones
TV Antenna
Gas Tank
Washing Area
Tree

Garden

Family Kitchen

Temascal

Mother-in-Law Living/Sleeping Room

Family Living/Sleeping Room

Horses/ Burros

Mother-in-Law Kitchen

Goats

0   10 m   N

Family Kitchen

Sleeping Room

Garden

Living Room

Mother-in-Law Kitchen

Figure 4.7. Domestic compounds, La Soledad Morelos. (Drawings by Lew Stevens.)

animals, such as pigs, goats, and turkeys. Many compounds also contained dedicated space for burros, horses, sheep, and chickens.

On average, housing compounds contained 4.5 people, though the populations ranged from one to eight. Most commonly, six to eight people inhabited the same compound. Of the twenty households surveyed, only two had men between the ages of fifteen and sixty in residence. All but these two households mentioned having at least one man, husband or son, absent and working in either Mexico City or, more commonly, the United States. While the majority of younger men went to the United States at ages as young as twelve for only a few months each year, many of the village's older men had left permanently. It was common to find compounds inhabited by three generations of women—grandmother, daughter, and granddaughter. Seventy-three percent of children in the sample were growing up without a father present, though more than half of these were living with a grandfather.

All households had running water and electricity, though we were told the water was not potable. The water, our informants explained, has *bichos* (bugs), and so they only drank soft drinks bought from the store. Running water was generally limited to one or two taps located outdoors and was used for washing up dishes, watering plants and animals, and bathing. None of the houses had a connection to municipal drains or sewers, nor did they have indoor plumbing. Latrines, when they existed, were pits dug in the ground and sheltered by an impermanent structure or a reused building.

Electricity was used primarily to power small television sets. Though a number of families owned refrigerators, these were never plugged in and were used instead like coolers to keep food from getting warm. Modern gas stoves were common but were used mainly when it rained. Most women preferred cooking over an open fire in semi-open, detached kitchen areas, and most men preferred food cooked in this manner. Only one of the houses in our sample (and only one of three in the entire village) had a private telephone. Most of the village used a "public" phone located in one of the small stores in the center of town. The proprietors of this store received phone calls and called a village member to the phone by making an announcement over the town's loudspeaker. Though many now have prepaid cell phones, people rarely have money to add airtime to the phones, making them status symbols rather than vehicles of communication.

Small neighborhood stores, ubiquitous throughout Mexico, were common in La Soledad Morelos, and one of the sampled compounds contained a store. The stores sell a variety of goods. The best business is in candy, chips, and soft drinks, but they also sell basic necessities such as milk, toilet paper, and canned chiles. In the one studied case, the store was the only room in the compound built out of modern materials. The owner used the structure as both store and sleeping space, putting blankets on the floor at night and sleeping there rather than in the designated *dormitorio*.

✳   ✳   ✳

We sat around the table at *Carnitas el Mexicano* for our celebratory end of field season lunch. I leaned back, satisfied and happy for many reasons. The restaurant had a reputation for delicious, tender *carnitas*, and I had eaten my share. We had just finished a field season, problem-free, in which we'd met all the goals I'd set out for the students and for myself. Best of all, I was surrounded by twelve happy students who were as enthusiastic about the project as the day they had started. Though not every day had gone so smoothly or ended so cheerfully, the students seemed happy with the work they had done, interested in the experiences they had had, and excited about future work. It was time to sum up what we had learned.

"So, what do we know about life in La Soledad Morelos, and how is it going to help during excavations at the Hacienda Acocotla?" I asked, looking around the table.

It was an instant mood killer. The students thought they were done with school for the summer, admittedly one source of their aforementioned enthusiasm. They sighed, pushed aside their plates, and hauled their field notebooks out as I ordered another round of sodas for everyone. I waited a few moments, giving them a moment to flip through their notes, before prodding them, "Well, what surprised you about how people lived? What observations did you make that challenged your presuppositions?" More silence, and then one of the bolder students put up her hand.

"Well, when we first went into the village, I was really shocked by how small and dark the houses were. But after spending a month with people in the house compounds, I came to realize that the structures are really only for shelter when necessary. Almost all of the day-to-day living happens outside in the compound."

"Good!" I exclaimed, jumping up and narrowly missing our waiter, "Our first 'rule'—daily life happens outside. What implications might this have for archaeology at the hacienda?"

Another student, rolling his eyes, said, "Well, obviously, if you want to know what people were actually doing, you'd need to look outside the rooms of the calpanería, not inside them."

"Excellent." I nodded, "Maybe that seems self-evident now, but would you have assumed that outside was the place to look for such things when we began a month ago?"

He shook his head, sitting back to consider this.

"So what do people do outside?" I continued, "And when people do go inside, what are they doing inside? What are the activity patterns in a household? What other 'rules' can we define? What should we expect to see at the hacienda when we excavate?"

The students started scanning their field notes with interest, curious about finding answers to the questions I'd posed. All the careful drawings and notes we'd made of people's homes would allow us to build a model of expected patterns of architecture and use of space in Acocotla's calpanería. Our model would inform my excavation strategy, and ultimately my understanding of the remains, as I tried to both prove and disprove what we'd found to be true in the contemporary community.

✳   ✳   ✳

Inhabiting Space Now and Then

As that first student astutely noted, outdoor space is more important than interior space in La Soledad Morelos's house compounds. Exterior space is frequently as important as interior space in agrarian communities, and La Soledad Morelos is no exception to this well-established pattern.[14] The students and I had all noted that being invited inside structures was rare (though people were happy to grant us access into even the most private structures once they understood that we were studying their homes), and we frequently encountered people at work outside in the compounds. Partially, the light available in the open-air spaces of the compounds was necessary to many daily tasks such as cleaning seeds and textile work; however, the constraints of work were not the only factor in use of space. Weather permitting, people ate meals, entertained guests, relaxed, and worked in the semiprivate spaces of the enclosed but open-air compounds. Because this space was used so frequently, the patio was often swept clean daily, an activity that might impact the discovery of activity areas in the archaeological record.[15]

In La Soledad Morelos, the size and form of the compounds had more to do with wealth than with the number of inhabitants. The twenty compounds studied by the students during our field season contained, on average, 174 square meters of space per inhabitant, which included an average of 8.9 square meters of interior, roofed space per person. These numbers fall within the expected range set by many archaeologists who argue that eight to ten square meters per person is the average required to house a nuclear family.[16] Our work in La Soledad Morelos highlights the fact that though the averages hold true to the expected numbers calculated by others, in reality the numbers vary. Exterior compound space ranged from 50 to 432 square meters per person, while interior, roofed space ranged from 8.1 to 36.9 square meters per person. Thus, our study suggested that while a reasonable guess might be made as to population for a large number of structures based on the averages of space, single compounds or households could not be studied in the same way.

The life history of a single compound also contributed to the amount of available space. One of the compounds was inhabited by a solitary woman who had 36.96 square meters of space to herself. This woman described her situation by saying, "Ahora estoy solita como perro sin dueño" ("Now I am alone like a dog with no master"), but she had not always lived alone. In fact, at one time, the space had also housed her husband and children; only five of her children had survived past the age of three. Though she gave birth to a total of fourteen children, nine died between the ages of one and three and a tenth at the age of ten. Her surviving family would have lived in a maximum of 5.3 square meters per person.

As we worked our way through the field notes, we noted that the outdoor space, while not as tightly bound or easily defined as a formal room, was imbued with social meaning and was heavily gendered. The "smoke kitchen," an especially notable manifestation of this dynamic, was the exclusive territory of women and children (fig. 4.8). Men rarely entered this space, gathering instead outside in the compound in shady areas. Strangers, male or female, were rarely invited into the kitchen space and instead were made comfortable under a tree in the open air. Kitchens, however, were the one space marked architecturally that would show activity areas in the archaeological record. Today, La Soledad's kitchens are a space not only for cooking and preparing food but also a place where women and children gather to gossip, sew, and play while keeping an eye on simmering food. They provide warmth from an open fire in cold weather and shade from the sun during the warmer times of day. When a woman visits her neighbor, she heads for the kitchen and settles in to share a cool drink and trade the latest town news. In La Soledad, as in many places, kitchens are the nucleus of domestic life; sharing a hearth defines a nuclear household's membership.[17] Though the amount of space in a compound was

Figure 4.8. Smoke kitchen, La Soledad Morelos. (Drawing by Lew Stevens.)

not necessarily representative of the number of people living there, the presence of kitchens was, without exception, indicative of the number of nuclear families living in the space. In every case we studied, each compound had a separate kitchen for each nuclear family living in that compound (see fig. 4.7). The reasons behind this are cultural. In Mesoamerica, women spend much of their time preparing tortillas, as they have for hundreds of years. The work is physically intensive and time-consuming. In La Soledad, each woman heading a nuclear family has her own architecturally defined space to perform this task (regardless of whether or not she is actually preparing those tortillas).

The meaning of the Mesoamerican kitchen space stretches back beyond memory. The hearth and its associated responsibilities (primarily food production) have been central to Nahua conceptions of femininity for hundreds of years.[18] The Aztecs described the good woman as follows: "She would have food and drink available. She would have food for others to eat; she would revive and refresh the spirits and bodies of those who lived in misery on earth."[19] At birth, an Aztec girl's umbilical cord would be buried next to the hearth and below a metate, an act that tied her to the home and her duties as food producer.[20] Following the conquest, the kitchen space may have been what James Lockhart identifies as the *cihuacalli* or "woman house." The cihuacalli was an architectural space identified in sixteenth and seventeenth century documents (though largely in text, with one exception appearing in pictorial form) that seemed to hold different inheritance rules from the rest of the compound.[21] Lockhart notes that the "woman house" does not pass with the rest of the compound to the male inheritors in Nahua wills but instead remains with the widow or daughter of the family. He is uncertain if this space is a kitchen, though that is exactly what the Spanish call it, or if it is a room used for other activities, such as weaving, or a space where women gather.[22] Studies of preconquest, Postclassic households in the region suggest that architectural patterns, at least for the first 150 years after conquest, remained the same and that this pattern of women having a dedicated architectural space for "their work" was something that predated the arrival of the Spanish.[23] In La Soledad Morelos, the kitchen space serves this purpose.

But what of the architecture and construction of the house compounds? What dictated how, why, and with what materials people in La Soledad Morelos constructed their homes? Though building materials were often dictated by availability, perceptions about how a house should be built also played a part. During interviews in each of the compounds, students asked, "What is the best building material?" One woman told us that cement block was best, but every other informant responded, without hesitation, "Adobe." We asked each informant why they answered as they did, and those who identified adobe as the best building material explained that it was far more durable than cement block, it leaked less, and it was easier to repair.

In separate interviews, we asked informants what building materials they would choose if they were constructing a house. Without exception, every single person responded, "Cement block." This answer surprised us, given that the same respondents had earlier told us that adobe was the better material. We asked them to explain the reasoning behind their decision. While the details of the answers varied, all informants shared a consensus that adobe was old-fashioned. Cement block, though less durable, they explained, was modern. Not one person wanted to connect themselves to the past, and all were most interested in materials that signaled modernization and progress.[24]

The form of architecture is more easily explained. The architecture we identified as traditional in La Soledad Morelos (and that which was defined by the inhabitants themselves as "old-fashioned") arguably has its roots in traditional Nahua constructions.[25] These architectural forms may date to the beginning of the colonial period, and perhaps even earlier.

Lockhart identifies compounds similar to those in La Soledad Morelos—single, disarticulated rooms, built of adobe, lacking windows, grouped around an open-air compound—as distinctly Nahua, though he admits that this style is not dissimilar to the Spanish conception of domestic space (with the notable exception that the Spanish constructed houses with interconnecting rooms).[26] In fact, a glance at domestic architecture in rural, agrarian communities around the world suggests that small, disarticulated, single-doored, windowless rooms placed along the perimeter of an open compound may not be an unusual architectural form; it is certainly common in Mesoamerica.[27]

The Nahua way of conceptualizing a particular domestic space and emotional responses to it were unique both to the culture as a whole and to each individual living in or visiting the household; however, the architecture remains silent on those subjects. When viewed cross-culturally, the ruins, standing or excavated, speak to an inexpensive and accessible design ethic. Certainly, Mesoamerican architects had been designing incredible, complex structures for millennia when the Spanish conquistadors arrived in Tenochtitlan, but those elaborate and status-laden structures, then as now, were not available to the masses. Disarticulated rooms with single doorways and no windows are easy and inexpensive to build, and the ease and cost of design must be factored in to any discussion of architectural forms.[28] Though we define certain types of architecture in La Soledad Morelos as traditional, the dichotomy between traditional and modern may be based less on history and culture and more on access to economic resources.[29]

True to this design ethic, people with income from the United States have modern-style homes, constructed with multiple stories, windows, doors, and little outdoor space. Though small and simple by US standards, these houses appear staggeringly opulent in La Soledad Morelos. The community does not seem to be shy about public displays of what wealth they have.[30] In Maya communities in Belize, researchers have linked the willingness to invest income in housing (and thus to mark differences in status and wealth to the entire community) to a proliferation of wage labor, an engagement with a wider, non-community-based market, and the accompanying disruption in the balance of financial power between men and women of the same household.[31] In La Soledad, the heads of households and holders of the purse strings are often women because the majority of men are working and living elsewhere, but women too are investing in increasingly elaborate and "modern" houses, often built out of the most "modern" materials available.

Flipping through field notes on that July day, my students noted that the activities that took place within the rooms often had no correlation with the room's designated purpose. Most of us sleep in our bedrooms, cook in the kitchen, and watch television in the living room. In La Soledad Morelos, people were frequently found sleeping in the store, storing things in the living room, and living in the patio.[32] Examples of the difference between room designation and use abound. As mentioned, one studied compound contained a small store. Our informants in this particular compound explained that, at night, they bring mats into the store and sleep on the floor. The "living/sleeping" room is used mainly for storage. This pattern in the use of space would leave virtually no markers in the archaeological record. In addition, items in certain spaces that one might assume are indicative of room use may not be. For example, the majority of the compounds surveyed had both gas stoves and refrigerators. One might assume that these items would be kept in the kitchen, but in fact they were generally kept in the living/sleeping room. The modern gas stove is used only when it is raining. The area designated as a kitchen, and most frequently used as such, contains an open hearth, often a mano and metate for grinding corn (though two of the compounds also had what was designated as a "mill," which was a separate room dedicated for grinding corn by hand), pots and pans, and so on, as well as miscellaneous other stored items, including, most commonly, animal feed and seeds for next season's planting. While reviewing our notes, we realized that assumptions about room use would need to be made with care when we excavated the workers quarters at the Hacienda San Miguel Acocotla.

Finally, abandonment processes were also complex because, in fact, in La Soledad Morelos, as in many communities in Mesoamerica, buildings were rarely abandoned after a single occupation.[33] Just as room use changed from moment to moment depending on need and desire during a day in the life of the household, so too did the patterns of use of a building over its entire existence. When a room is no longer fit (or necessary) for human habitation, it becomes a place to store things. When storage is no longer necessary or feasible, the room becomes a place to shelter animals. We also came across many cases of reuse, both of buildings and of entire compounds. One man had inherited his parents' housing compound, adjacent to his own, upon their deaths. He converted all of the rooms in their compound into storage for animal feed, seeds, and firewood and said he had been using it as such for more than twenty years. More expensive architectural elements, such as a rare door, were scavenged and installed in his own compound, while the "bare bones" of the parental structure remained standing. He did the minimum amount of repair work necessary to keep the buildings in sufficient shape to protect his stored materials from the elements.

We found that buildings were abandoned during their "human-use stage" only in extreme cases. During the research period, the students mapped an abandoned house compound that appeared to have been left intact. Living/sleeping rooms in La Soledad are generally characterized by the presence of the household altar, with religious statues, candles, incense, and so on, typically placed near the doorway. The main abandoned structure still had evidence of this altar, something that would have been moved to a new living space had the inhabitants reused the structure for purposes other than habitation. The presence of the altar suggested the room had ended its life as it began it. We interviewed neighbors of the compound, asking why it had been abandoned as it had. Each family told us, with minor variations, a similar story. One informant said, "The family is dead because the lady, the mother, put a tablet used to preserve grain in everybody's soup to kill them and to kill herself as well. She did this because nobody in the pueblo (La Soledad) wanted the family here and because of this her husband and children had no work."

Some suggested that the underlying motivation was that the family did not have enough money to feed themselves and the mother could not bear to watch her children starve. Others seemed to indicate that the mother was simply obliging the rest of the village by ridding them of this unwanted family. The reason this family was so hated by the rest of the village is unknown, but after the deaths, nobody wanted anything to do with the buildings or land. The family had been buried on the property, and the compound was left untouched.

※ ※ ※

Class was officially dismissed for the field season. I stood back and looked at the blackboard, enjoying the quiet for the first time in a month. After lunch, the students and I had returned to the classroom on the university campus to finalize our summary of the field season. Based on the conversation we had had over our carnitas and additional consultation of our field notes, we had developed seven rules that would impact the ways in which I excavated the hacienda and help me interpret what I found:

1. Outdoor space is more important than interior space. If I were going to look for activity areas, those areas would most likely be found outside, not inside. That said, the ways in which the compounds were structured, with a wall surrounding the patio, provided a level

of privacy that was absent at the calpanería. Would this affect what I found? And how would the contemporary habit of sweeping the patio clean impact the archaeological record?

2. Amount of space per person varies widely. If I wanted to know how many people were living in the calpanería, I'd need to examine the historical records. The amount of living space at the hacienda would have little to do with the number of people inhabiting it.

3. Kitchen space is important. If I could locate the kitchen spaces, I would be able to estimate the number of families present. Further, these would be the best architecturally marked areas to study activity patterns, as well as the lives of women and children. They would be hard to find, though, given the ephemeral nature of the modern architecture. Archaeologically, they would probably be marked by nothing more than a few post molds and a hearth, and, if we were lucky, we might find the remains of one or two walls.

4. Choice in building materials depends on more than "common sense." If I wanted to understand the architectural choices made at the hacienda, I would need to acknowledge that not all decisions were driven by pure practicality. Our informants had told us time and again that they would choose modern building materials over those they believed to be more durable. Further, the people of La Soledad Morelos show no shyness when it comes to architectural displays of wealth. The ethic of egalitarianism was absent in the village, and likely had been at the hacienda as well. Perhaps most obvious, the inhabitants of the calpanería would have had little opportunity to make decisions about these things, but the status represented by the "nicer" architecture at the hacienda may have helped attract workers from the village.

5. Architectural form would, however, be simple and practical. During excavations at the hacienda, we should find small rooms with single doorways opening onto a patio area. Windows would be rare, as would doors. Rooms would most likely have been used for a variety of purposes over the course of their lives, devolving from human-occupied space to storage and/or space for animals.

6. Room function would be difficult to discern. Artifacts found in the calpanería's rooms would likely not speak clearly to a formal, designated purpose thanks to both the variability in room use and abandonment processes seen in the contemporary community. Artifacts would represent a jumble of habitation, room use, storage, and postabandonment processes.

7. Rooms would not have been abandoned directly following habitation. Except in extreme cases, rooms would continue to be used after they were no longer inhabited by people, and the artifact assemblages would reflect that. A recoverable signature for rooms reaching the end of their life would potentially be the absence of more expensive building materials, including roof and door elements.

I nodded to myself, satisfied. This information was an excellent starting point for the excavations I would conduct at Acocotla's calpanería.

In spite of my satisfaction, I was unsettled. Yes, I had my data. I could go out and dig and maybe better interpret what I was finding archaeologically. But this research reminded me that there is more to the story than the official historical record offers. Today, grandparents are raising children without the help of parents; women are left alone to raise teenage boys without the help of a father and are battling the attraction that gangs hold for these young men. Children are dying unnecessarily thanks to a lack of basic health care. The elderly who aren't lucky enough to be raising their grandchildren are left alone, "like a dog with no master," as their adult children head out of Mexico in search of greater economic opportunity. More than anything else, I couldn't forget the story of La Soledad's murder/suicide—a woman had poisoned her entire family, and herself, because she couldn't bear to watch her children starve. How did a community become so fragmented that this was her only choice? Why are Zapata's reforms not our current reality? If nothing else, surely her husband ought to have a plot of land just big enough to grow corn and feed his family?

Today, Latin America's neoliberal reforms are dismantling the social safety net put in place following revolutions like Zapata's. The woman and her family who ate one last meal together, and countless others like those living and dying in La Soledad Morelos, are falling through the cracks created by the push toward privatization and the move away from state-sponsored programs to support the poor. Somehow, my study in La Soledad Morelos was no longer just about the past. That master narrative I'd been taught, the one that transformed exploited hacienda workers into independent (happy) farmers thanks to Revolutionary reforms, suddenly rang hollow. To understand the village I found myself in, I needed to understand the history of La Soledad and its inhabitants—not the history I was fed in the official "soup." It was time to start digging.

*   *   *

CHAPTER FIVE

San Miguel Acocotla

The Archaeology of a Central Mexican Hacienda

＊　　＊　　＊

I smiled to myself as the truck crested the edge of the *barranca*, and I caught my first glimpse of the Hacienda San Miguel Acocotla. I was eager to see how the site's crumbling walls had fared in the year since I'd last visited, but I put the pickup truck in park and clambered out to talk to my students who were perched in the back on top of our excavation equipment. I pointed to the structure across the fields, reminding the students about the tower that had been built during the Revolution. I told them to look to the north as we came closer. They'd see the hacienda's chapel there and, across the road, what remained of the threshing floor fronting the hacienda's east wall.

I climbed back into the truck, putting it into four-wheel drive, which was necessary to make it through the last bit of "road" during the rainy season. MaryCarmen would be waiting with don José, and I couldn't afford to take any more time.

Don José lived at the hacienda as a child just before the implementation of the post-Revolutionary reforms. He would be taking us on a tour of the casco, explaining what each space had been used for when he and his family worked there during the first decades of the twentieth century. It was the fourth such interview I had participated in but the first for this group of students. The students were equipped with clipboards, pencils, paper, and numbered maps (fig. 5.1). Using the preassigned numbers, they would take detailed notes of the old man's reminiscences. At the end

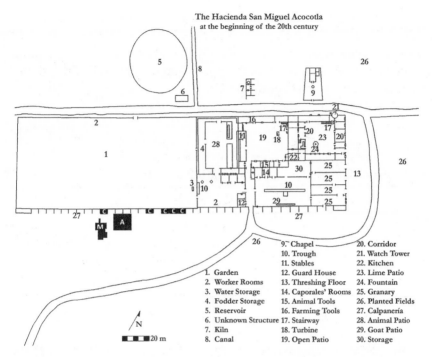

Figure 5.1. The Hacienda Acocotla at the beginning of the twentieth century.

of the workday, we would compare notes, putting together a comprehensive picture of how the hacienda's buildings had functioned.

I glanced in my rearview mirror as we approached the hacienda's chapel, noting that my students were pointing to it and taking notes. I had discussed the results of our archival research in class earlier. Based on the documentary record, the chapel served the entire hacienda community from at least the early seventeenth century onward, but the architectural style's close match to the rest of the hacienda suggested that it had been remodeled during the mid-nineteenth century with the casco.[1] We turned to the left, passing the casco's east façade and the remains of the threshing floor. Following the road, we turned toward the right, passing the last of the wheat storage sheds and nine of the calpanería's rooms, arriving finally at the casco's south-facing main entrance.

MaryCarmen was sitting with don José and his daughter in the archway leading into the hacienda's casco. Don José, dressed in his finest for the outing, was sitting in his wheelchair, ready to take center stage. I parked the pickup nearby, climbing out of the driver's seat as the students leapt out of its bed. The students were looking curiously at the ruins around them. It was their first visit, and they would be spending the next month digging here. MaryCarmen made the introductions while don José's daughter stood up and prepared to push him over the grass through the casco. We were ready to begin our tour.

✻   ✻   ✻

A Tour of the Hacienda San Miguel Acocotla

During the latter years of the nineteenth century, thirty-seven small rooms flanked the imposing entrance we found ourselves in front of that morning (fig. 5.1, no. 27; fig. 5.2).[2] The remains of these rooms, Acocotla's cal-panería, are still visible along the south-facing wall. They would be the focus of our investigations during the coming month. The architecture today appears to be limited to adobe complemented by a few stones and bricks, but the nineteenth-century façade of the hacienda would have

Figure 5.2. Calpanería, Hacienda San Miguel Acocotla.

been finished in white plaster, and the rooms of the calpanería would have been roofed in red pantile. Both the pantiles and bricks were likely produced in the hacienda's brick kiln located to the north of the casco (fig. 5.1, no. 7). The hacienda's resident workers and their families inhabited the calpanería during the second half of the nineteenth century. As many as 121 men, women, and children lived in these 3.5-meter-by-3.5-meter rooms, though the population fluctuated.[3] Don José thought about one hundred people had lived there when he was a child. Don José, agreeing with others I had interviewed, told us that the field fronting the calpanería was used for day-to-day activities such as sewing or tool repair. A communal smoke kitchen constructed out of chinamite was located somewhere in the field. He said all the residents of the calpanería shared the kitchen and surrounding field to prepare and consume meals, though a woman who had been hired to come from nearby La Soledad Morelos staffed the kitchen.

We stood silently in the field for a moment. In my mind, a few dozen people populated the field, and the ruined calpanería stood as it once had—a gleaming row of tiny rooms. I blinked, and the vision was gone. I broke the silence and suggested we move back toward the casco's main entrance. Don José told us that the empty archway was once barred with an imposing wooden door. Passing through the doorway, we found the remains of a two-room guard house (no. 12) on the left-hand side of the passageway, and before us, the hallway branched in three directions. Don José told us that the tienda de raya was once located inside the guardhouse. There, the hacienda's peones would have been able to purchase basic necessities and luxury goods, from metates to bottles of liquor, on credit from the hacienda manager.

He led us past the guardhouse and to the left into a large patio area. Don José explained that rooms bounding the edges of this patio stored farm implements and other tools necessary to hacienda life and work. He told us that his mother had said that a few rooms along the south wall (no. 2) may have also housed some of the hacienda's more trusted workers, though these rooms are not in evidence today. A small doorway on the western side of this patio led us into a large, enclosed garden (no. 1) that had been constructed during the Mexican Revolution to provide a protected food source for Acocotla's residents.[4] We returned to the patio and moved toward the ornate arch that dominates the north side of the patio. This arch led us to the animal patio, an area that housed cows and horses (no. 28) and provided storage for animal fodder.

We retraced our steps through the arch and patio to the central corridor and guardhouse where we had entered the casco. This time, we followed the right-hand path into the Patio de los Chivos (Patio of the Goats, no. 29). This area housed the *caporales*, the most trusted of the hacienda's peones. The caporales were responsible for the hacienda's animals, and don José indicated that they had a proprietary interest in the goats. Though the caporales and the goats shared this living space, we presumed that occupation of the rooms on the northern wall (no. 14) of the patio was limited to the humans. Don José spoke of the caporales with a great deal of respect, suggesting that the position was a mark of status, and the position may have been envied by those who failed to attain the rank. If nothing else, residence inside the walls during the Mexican Revolution would have provided a measure of protection.

We left the Patio de los Chivos and returned one more time to the central hallway. We took the final path north through another arched entryway to the Patio Abierto (the Open Patio, no. 19), which provided storage for tools, as well as more stable space for horses and cows. This area was normally accessible only to the manager, the caporales in their business with the herds, and the peones who were employed to cook and clean in the hacendado's living quarters; however, everybody entered this area every Saturday to collect their week's wages from the mayordomo. This space also housed the mayordomo's office (no. 22), above which was the hacendado's kitchen (above no. 22). Both were located in the southeast corner of the patio adjacent to the arch leading to the final area of the hacienda.

We walked past the remains of the manager's office and through a set of double arches into the Patio del Limón (Patio of the Lime, 23; fig. 5.3). This patio would have been the hacendado's living quarters on the rare occasions he and his family were in residence. Other than the hacienda owner, his family, and guests, the only people allowed into this space would have been the manager and the few peones paid to cook and clean for the family. The Patio of the Lime got its name from the lime trees that once surrounded an ornate fountain still in evidence in the center of the patio (no. 24). The area has been looted (thanks to a rumor that the last hacendado hid his gold in this patio before fleeing the area during the Revolution), and the rooms surrounding the patio are pockmarked with exploratory excavations. In spite of the destruction, numerous decorative elements are still visible, including ornamental arches and pillars, designs painted in red on white plaster, and a glass mosaic that frames a window. Though the architectural elements remain impressive, the furnishings used to dress up the space may have been less so. Descriptions of hacien-

Figure 5.3. Entrance to the Patio del Limón.

das dating to the first half of the nineteenth century tell of empty, echoing rooms with barely a chair to sit upon. One woman in residence at a hacienda outside of Mexico City explained that she gave up trying to keep the house furnished as every piece was thrown out of the windows during two successive revolts.[5]

* * *

We made our way back to the main entrance of the hacienda. It was rough going for don José's daughter; the ground wasn't exactly wheelchair friendly. We chatted as she negotiated the weeds and broken cobbles, and she filled us in on the village news. When we reached MaryCarmen's jeep, I helped don José into the front seat while his daughter folded the wheelchair up and put it in the trunk. I thanked the old man for his help, and he generously thanked me for the opportunity to share his memories. The students and I waved him and his daughter off as MaryCarmen started on the rough track to the village. As they disappeared from sight, I turned and faced the students.

"So, now you all have a good idea of how the casco was used a century ago, and you have an idea of where the calpanería belonged in the community hierarchy. Let's have a seat under the tree over there and talk about what we're going to work on this week."

We walked as a group over to the one tree that offered shade in the open field and settled on the ground to talk.

"First, we'll make detailed maps of a few of the calpanería rooms. Given the amount of destruction the casco has experienced during the last year, this is particularly important." I explained how the students were going to make the architectural drawings, reminding them to make careful notes. For many, archaeological fieldwork has an air of romance. In reality, days in the field involve, more than anything, paperwork.

I divided the students into groups of two and assigned each pair two rooms to map and describe. As they began, I spent a moment making sure my own notes were complete for the morning. When I'd noted everything I needed to remember, I got up and joined my students.

* * *

Mapping the Calpanería

We concentrated our research on the rooms on the west side of the hacienda's entrance (there are nine remaining rooms east of the entrance), in large part because these twenty-eight rooms were associated with the field in which, we had been told, the peones conducted their daily activities. We mapped and described the architecture of ten of the rooms (fig. 5.4). All the rooms are constructed out of adobe, which was either puddled or

Figure 5.4. Mapping the calpanería.

made into bricks and placed in rows.[6] Earthenware bricks would have been produced in Acocotla's own kiln and were used in construction throughout the hacienda alongside the more common adobe. In general, the walls are in a poor state of repair, though fragments of plaster cling to the adobe in a few places. Figure 5.5 shows the façade of one of the rooms

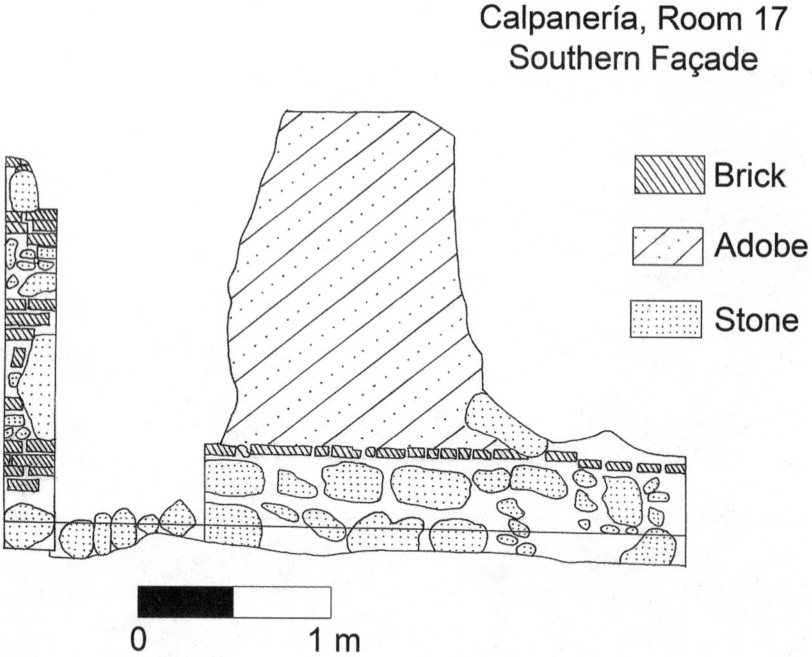

Calpanería, Room 17
Southern Façade

Brick
Adobe
Stone

0   1 m

Figure 5.5. Room 17, façade.

with its door placed in the southwest corner. The floors of the rooms were scattered with adobe bricks and brick fragments, stone, earthenware bricks, some broken roof tiles, and bits of concrete.

*   *   *

It took the students a full week to finish mapping the rooms, something which surprised them more than me. Mapping the architecture was a slow but vital task. The damage to the casco's structure was noticeable from one year to the next. In part this was due to exposure to the elements, but not all damage came from the weather. A few people in the descendant community want to turn the ruins into a community-run museum. The vast majority, however, are waiting for the casco to collapse completely so its land can be reclaimed for farmland. In the increasingly populated and hungry village, even this small tract is coveted, so the villagers were "helping" the structure's collapse along a bit. Any record we were able to make of the structures before they disappeared forever was important.

With the mapping finished, we began a transect survey of the field fronting the calpanería. The survey would allow us to identify possible activity areas in the field and would inform our decisions about where we were to dig next. It was the Monday morning of our second week. I sat the students down under the tree to explain what we would be doing now that the mapping was complete. Together, we decided to use the façade of the calpanería as our baseline for setting the starting point of the transects. We would mark the beginning line of each transect every ten meters along the façade, and the transects would run perpendicular to the calpanería for the entire length of the field. I handed out large tape measures, spray paint, oversized sheets of graph paper, drawing boards, and pencils. Together, we measured and marked the transects, ending up with thirteen. I assigned the pairs of students two transects each as I explained what they would be doing.

※　　　※　　　※

Surveying the Calpanería

We were able to see that there were ceramic and glass artifacts scattered across the cleared field. The artifacts hinted at the lives lived in the field, lives that don José and others had recounted in their memories. We designed the transect survey to collect the artifacts and identify possible activity areas as a guide for our excavations. We were especially interested in finding a kitchen (or kitchens—an architectural space central to domestic life in the descendant community), or perhaps a structure that predated the nineteenth-century remains of the calpanería. The field we were surveying had been plowed, but luckily, we could count on artifacts remaining close to where they had fallen one hundred years earlier. While a plow disturbs the vertical provenience (or how deep in the soil an artifact is), studies have shown that it has little effect on the horizontal provenience (where the artifact is in relation to other objects on the surface).[7] Because of this, I was confident that the artifacts visible on the surface would allow us to pinpoint activity areas below the surface. Perhaps artifacts necessary to the preparation of food would point us toward a kitchen.

We positioned transects from east to west across the field, numbering them one to thirteen. The length of these transects varied according to the irregular boundaries of the triangularly shaped field and ranged from twenty to ninety meters. After drawing detailed maps of the concentrations identified along each transect, the students collected the artifacts and bagged them by transect and concentration number. As they completed a diagram of each transect, I created a master map that showed the aggregate information and helped us decide where to place our test excavation units.

That week, the students collected more than 11,600 artifacts. Most of the materials proved to be architectural remains, locally produced ceramics, and bottle glass, all dating primarily to the nineteenth and twentieth centuries. The dates made sense in light of the oral historical accounts we had collected. We found the greatest density of artifacts (or number of artifacts per meter) in the center of the field along transects 7, 8, and 9. Transects 2 and 4 also had significant densities of artifacts per meter, though this seemed mainly to be from the collapse of the calpanería, as almost all were the remains of some sort of architectural component.

*   *   *

We were halfway through the field season, and the students were ready to start digging. I had spent the weekend reviewing the maps and artifacts and had a good idea where I wanted to place our test units, or *pozos*. Each one would be one meter by one meter, and each would allow us to explore multiple questions. I explained to the students, again under the tree on another hot Monday morning, that we would be looking for answers to the following questions:

1. What did the stratigraphy (or soil layers) look like? Nobody had dug at this site before, and we had no idea how many layers of human occupation we would encounter or how deep we would have to dig in each unit.
2. By extension, how long was the occupation at the site? Had people lived here only in the nineteenth century, or had there been people here before then?
3. Was the plow disturbance as minimal as we expected? And if so, would we be able to identify activity areas that we were interested in studying?

The questions might seem mundane to some, but they were questions that had to be answered before our excavations could become more "in depth" in later seasons. I pulled out the map, and the students gathered around. I had marked the locations of our test units on top of the surface survey map I'd created during the prior week. As I assigned each pair of students one test unit, I explained why they would be digging there.

"Isobel and Ernesto, you two will have pozo 1. I placed it there because, when you were doing the transects, you found a lot of architectural remains." Given the close proximity to the calpanería, this made sense, but it would be interesting to see if there was anything underneath all that given the density of the artifacts. Perhaps there were additional structures below ground.

They nodded and asked if they should grab their equipment and start. I told them to wait. I wanted everyone to hear the reasoning for digging each area of the field.

While conducting the surface survey, the students had identified a number of broken manos—an artifact necessary for tortilla production. When mapped, we realized that these manos had been found in a large, circular pattern, so I placed one unit adjacent to but outside the circle, and a second unit in the center of the circle. I really wanted to find the kitchen, and I suspected these were our best clue to its location.

I pointed to Ynez and Federico, continuing, "You are going to take pozo 2. There isn't much in the way of artifacts there, but it is just on the edge of the circle of manos. I'd like to see if we can find a kitchen."

They nodded their understanding as I moved on. "Sofia and Estéban, you are going to take pozo 3. This is our best bet at locating the kitchen. It is dead center in a circle of manos and in the midst of a lot of ceramics that seem to be related to cooking and serving food."

Moving on, I looked at Graciela and Roberto. "You guys are going to take pozo 4 here," I said pointing to the map. "There is not really anything here on the surface, but I need to know if the surface adequately reflects what is underneath. If you find something, we'll know we can't trust the results of the surface survey. If you don't find anything, we'll know that the survey might just be reliable after all. Especially if," I continued, pointing to Sofia and Estéban, "they find a kitchen."

Finally, I turned to Rebeca and Eduardo. "Okay, you get pozo 5. I am curious to see if there is any Prehispanic occupation here. During the transect survey, you found a spindle whorl that was at least six hundred years old. I'd like to see if that is indicative of anything that old under the surface. Sound good?" They nodded.

"Any questions?" Everybody shook their heads. "Then let's get started."

✳   ✳   ✳

Testing the Field

Following the completion of the transect survey, we opened five one-meter-by-one-meter test units in the field fronting the calpanería, naming these units P.1 through P.5 from east to west. We excavated in ten-centimeter levels constrained by natural strata until we found sterile soil, locally called *tepetate*. In most units, tepetate was encountered anywhere from sixty centimeters to almost one meter below the modern ground surface. For the region, these were very shallow deposits.

Happily, the surface survey really did seem to produce what we had hoped in a number of the cases. In pozo 1, the students found lots of building materials but very little else. The artifacts identified on the surface did indeed seem to relate to the collapse of the adjacent calpanería room. Pozo 2 turned up a light scattering of trash, mostly ceramics, in the first forty centimeters and then, below that, nothing. It was the shallowest unit we excavated. As I had hoped, pozo 3 turned up evidence of the smoke kitchen.

A few days into the excavations, Sofia called me over excitedly. She and Estéban had cleaned up the unit and found a perfectly intact rim of a bowl in the soil. As we dug further, we discovered that we had an intact *olla* (or cooking pot) filled with carbonized plant remains sitting in the center of a hearth. Lying nearby was a large portion of a metate. We identified what appeared to be a line of stones at the southwestern edge of the unit. We expanded excavations in this area (which became pozos 6 and 8) to see if the line of stones extended and might represent the base of a small, impermanent structure (fig. 5.6). The line of stones did, in fact, extend into both additional units. As discussed earlier, oral historical accounts indicated that a single kitchen made of impermanent architectural materials had occupied the field fronting the calpanería. Thanks to our research in the domestic compounds in La Soledad Morelos, we were able to match the remains we saw in front of us to the architecture of a modern kitchen.

Happy with this success, I was curious to see if the other units also held what we had hoped they would. Pozo 4 had been placed to test if a result of "nothing" in the surface survey indicated "nothing" below the surface as well. As Graciela and Roberto dug into the unit, we found (much to their delight) that it did, indeed, contain absolutely nothing. Just north in pozo 5, Rebeca and Eduardo were having a much more interesting time of it. We had placed this unit because of the discovery of half of a rather beautiful Prehispanic spindle whorl during the surface survey, and we wondered

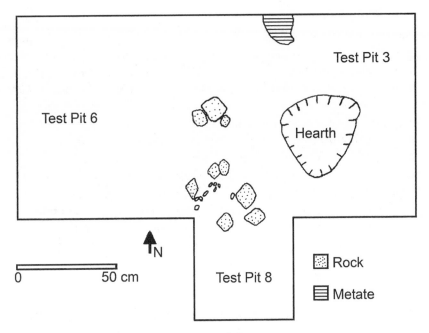

Figure 5.6. Smoke kitchen (pozos 3, 6, and 8).

if it indicated a Prehispanic occupation. Would the earth below ground hold more Prehispanic remains? It didn't contain any more ancient remains, but it was full of a wide variety of artifacts, from common, locally made cooking pots to a beautiful, hand-carved bone cross. This unit was placed in the midst of a dense midden (or trash heap). I was as delighted with this discovery as I was with the location of the kitchen. A midden is an archaeologist's favorite place to be thanks to the unusually high numbers of artifacts of all sorts that they contain.

Because it seemed likely that we would want to expand excavations in the midden during our next field season, we decided to test its extent. After all, it is not uncommon to find a simple pit that was dug and filled with trash. It wouldn't be a good use of our resources to waste some of our precious excavation proposal and funds on a small pit. We placed two small fifty-centimeter-by-fifty-centimeter units on either side of the main unit, two meters from the eastern and western edges of pozo 5. I hoped that one of these two units would show evidence that the midden continued. I was stunned when they both did. We knew, then, that the midden was at least one meter deep and six meters wide east to west. It was destined for extensive excavation in our next field season.

As we finished the test units, I had some of the students begin excavations inside one of the calpanería rooms (room 21). To maintain limited control over the horizontal position of artifacts, we divided the room into four quadrants and began excavations in the northwest and southeast sections. The materials recovered from these excavations looked much like those recovered during the surface survey and included unglazed ceramics, glass, lithics, and some iron nails. Shortly before our field season ended, we found a thick layer of ceramic roof tiles (or pantiles) between ten and fifteen centimeters below the surface. The tiles appeared to be the remains of a collapsed roof. We did not have time to explore further but hoped based on this find that we would be able to locate a sealed and intact floor surface. The dense deposit of ceramic tiles would have preserved anything on the floor. The find was a promising indication that excavations in the calpanería rooms would be productive.

✳   ✳   ✳

We had gotten quite a bit done during our four-week field season. I looked around the lab at the bags of artifacts piled everywhere. I had no idea how many artifacts we had collected—wouldn't until the analysis was finished. As a general rule of thumb, a month of excavation meant six months in the lab completing the analysis. As I stood there, I felt like six months was optimistic; there were a lot of artifacts. This year, a former student from the university with a specialization in historic ceramics would complete the analysis. I had to return to the States, and by Mexican law, the artifacts couldn't travel. Marta Adriana would send me her report by March so that I could plan the next field season.

The months had flown by. Sitting at my desk on a chilly, gray day, I reviewed Marta Adriana's artifact report. While I read, I sketched on top of copies of last season's field maps, adding indications of the spatial distribution of artifacts. The sketches were rough, but they helped me decide where I was going to propose excavating this coming field season. The test unit placed in the midden had been very productive. The materials dated largely to the second half of the nineteenth century, which coincided with what we knew was at least part of the occupational period of the calpanería. We would start with large-scale excavations there. I reached over to the master map and added an excavation unit. I had no idea how big the midden was, so I decided to plan for an area big enough to give me some of the edges of it. Using pozo 5 as the center point, I marked an excavation unit that ran two meters north to south and seven meters east to west.

I glanced north of the midden to the small rooms of the calpanería. The collapsed roof tiles we had found during the last days of digging the previous June indicated that we would find intact and protected living surfaces. The artifacts above the collapsed roof didn't offer much information and many were quite modern, but given the way artifacts would have collected on top of the roof after it collapsed, this wasn't surprising. I expected we would find materials contemporary with the midden and some, perhaps, that dated earlier. Digging a few of the rooms would prove informative. I decided we'd pick four or five of them randomly in the field, and I made a note on my steno pad.

I looked at the map, sighing. "One more area . . . " I thought. "The kitchen?" I shook my head. I was pretty sure we'd found what we needed to find during the test excavations. It seemed fairly certain that the area around pozo 3 was a kitchen, and the other units hadn't turned up evidence of another kitchen. A large, horizontal unit would allow me to get a good look at the living surface in the calpanería's field. I decided we would open a large ten-meter-by-ten-meter excavation unit. I reached over to my master map, making one final mark that I labeled "Unit A." I turned to my computer to start working on the permit request that would be submitted to the Mexican government.

Once again, I found myself driving up to the entrance of the Hacienda San Miguel Acocotla. There were no students with me this year. I would supervise the excavations, and Su Lin, an archaeologist from Mexico's National School of Anthropology and History, would help. We'd hired a dozen young men from La Soledad Morelos to assist us. They were about to receive a crash course in archaeological methods under our supervision. In Mexico, students and professionals alike are tasked with the job of taking field notes and supervising an army of laborers. These laborers are often hired from nearby communities, and none has a formal education in archaeology. Most leave the site at the end of the day to tend the crops in their fields at home. That said, many of these laborers have more field hours than a lot of PhDs back in the United States. A man who worked well on a project would be picked up again and again and might come to the newly minted archaeologist with thirty years of excavation experience. Such was not my luck. Very little archaeological work has been done in the region in which Acocotla sits, and experienced workers would not be easy to come by. I had simply asked don Andrés, the owner of the field we would be excavating, to send me a dozen able-bodied men. I expected we would walk onto the field and find twelve of don Andres's relatives waiting for us.

Contrary to my expectations, I was surprised to find only about a dozen dogs, in varying states of health, glaring at us. I looked at Su Lin, puzzled, and she shrugged her shoulders helplessly. "Buenos días?" I called out hopefully. A dozen men emerged from behind the wall of the calpanería, six more dogs trailing behind. They introduced themselves, and I asked about the dogs. They all looked at one very young man, Alejandro, who was about fifteen years old. Alejandro had an affinity for dogs. He brought all of his with him to the field, and would every day for the rest of the two months we were slated to dig. I looked around the field sighing silently to myself, wondering if any of the dogs would prove to be skilled excavators.

I walked back to the truck with the men and showed them the equipment. Together we unloaded it, and I explained what they were going to do with it. They were clearly humoring the crazy gringa who, evidently, had money to burn on pointless exercises, but they politely listened before carrying the screens, shovels, buckets, bags, and miscellaneous other equipment out to the field. Su Lin and I chose a few areas to start with, marking them out and mapping them while the men waited with skeptical looks. Then we showed the men what they would need to do to get started. While they broke through the first layer of sod in what we were calling unit A (the large, horizontal ten-meter-by-ten-meter excavation unit) and in room 21 of the calpanería, I walked Su Lin through the paperwork we were going to need to complete every day.

❊   ❊   ❊

Digging the Calpanaría

Su Lin began with unit A, where we divided the ten-meter-by-ten-meter excavation area into quadrants and began excavating in the northwest and southeast. Everything was excavated in arbitrary ten-centimeter levels constrained by natural strata, just as it had the previous season. Below the plow zone, the southeast quadrant contained nothing of interest, and we reached tepetate at only thirty centimeters below our datum. In this region, clean soil is sometimes used as fill to support new constructions. To ensure that this was not the case, we excavated two randomly placed test pits to a depth of 120 centimeters below datum. When neither test pit produced artifacts or a change in stratigraphy, we closed the area and concentrated on the northwest quadrant, confident that we had, indeed, found the total depth of cultural deposits in the southeast.

The northwest quadrant produced materials similar to those found in the southeast; however, at a depth of seventy centimeters below the datum, we found what appeared to be a feature in the southwest corner of the quadrant. It consisted of a pile of rocks, approximately ninety centimeters in diameter, a few fragments of brick, a large fragment of a *comal* (perhaps a third of the vessel), a mano, and a few animal bones. There was no burning in the area to indicate that the feature had been a hearth, nor was the pile associated with any other remains to indicate that it had been part of some sort of structure. After mapping and photographing the feature, we collected the artifacts and continued to excavate the entire unit. The purpose of feature 1 remains a mystery; it may simply have been a concentration of trash and collapsed wall from the nearby calpanería. We continued to excavate the quadrant in ten-centimeter levels to the sterile soil reached at a depth of eighty-five centimeters. Again, to ensure that we had reached sterile soil, we excavated a test pit to 120 centimeters below datum; and again, when we found no artifacts or change in stratigraphy, we chose to close unit A without exploring the other two quadrants.

While Su Lin was supervising the excavations in unit A, I began excavations in room 21 of the calpanería. Our excavations in this area proved extremely fruitful, so we ultimately chose to excavate five of the rooms of the calpanería during our eight-week field season. We intentionally chose to excavate five rooms in varying states of preservation, including rooms 11, 18, 20, 21, and 22 (room 11 was the most preserved, and room 22 was the least). Again, we excavated each room in quadrants to maintain horizontal control over recovered artifacts and in ten-centimeter arbitrary levels within natural stratigraphic layers to maintain vertical control. With the exception of a few anomalies, each of the rooms presented remarkably similar features and stratigraphy. The following description offers a composite sketch of all five excavated rooms, though some interesting divergences from the norm are also discussed.

Figure 5.7 shows the plan of a completely excavated unit. Near the southwest corner of each room, we found a large stone marking the threshold. As mentioned earlier, each room measured approximately 3.5 by 3.5 meters. With the exception of room 22 (where there was no evidence of a roof), we found an intact, collapsed roof of red pantiles in every room (fig. 5.8). The depth of the roof ranged from ten centimeters to as much as

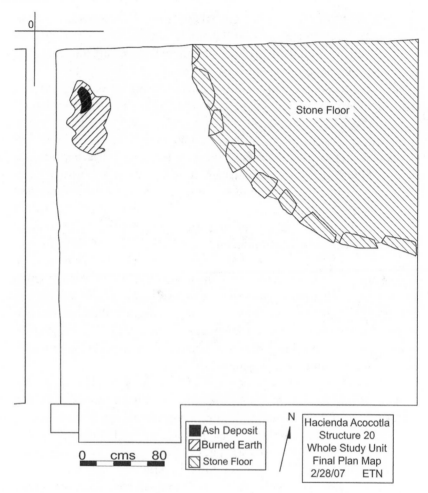

Figure 5.7. Room 20, plan map.

forty-five centimeters, depending on the amount of collapsed wall and other materials that had accumulated on top of the roof; however, all were at approximately the same level in relation to the field in front of the rooms and the architectural threshold identified during excavations. This suggested that, with the exception of room 22, the rooms in the calpanería had all been abandoned and then collapsed at approximately the same time.

In rooms 20, 21, and 22, we encountered a compacted earth floor immediately below the roof (when a roof was present). In each of these

Figure 5.8. Room 21, roof collapse and prepared floor surface.

rooms, we found a hearth in the same spot in the northwest corner (see, e.g., figs. 5.7 and 5.9). The hearths were simple. In each case, a shallow hole had been dug in the floor in which a fire had been lit. The only variation to this pattern was found in room 21. There, we also found a small, deep hole filled with ash (fig. 5.9) and, in the middle of the hearth, the

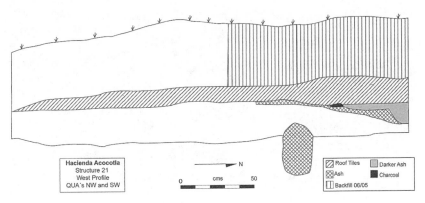

Hacienda Acocotla
Structure 21
West Profile
QUA's NW and SW

N

0   cms   50

Roof Tiles   Darker Ash
Ash   Charcoal
Backfill 06/05

Figure 5.9. Room 21, west wall profile.

broken neck of a ceramic jar that would have served as a support for a cooking pot. Though we had already identified a dedicated kitchen area in front of the calpanería, it seemed that the fires inside the rooms would have been used for some cooking as well.

We continued excavating below the floor of rooms 20, 21, and 22 and found a dense fill of mixed artifacts. Approximately ninety centimeters below datum, we found a second compacted floor surface. There was no hearth or other features at this level, though numerous artifacts, including glazed and unglazed redwares, majolica, lithics, glass, and metals, were resting on the floor. At this level, in the southeast quadrant of room 21, we found a chert core, flake, and scraper made of the same material. The accompanying artifacts date to the mid-nineteenth century, so it seems that stone working continued until quite late in Acocotla's history. Below this second floor, we reached sterile soil. After ensuring that there were no further occupations below a clean architectural fill, we closed excavations in each of these units.

Figure 5.10a. Room 20, stone floor.

Room 20 presented an architectural anomaly that remains as yet unidentified. While excavating the northeast quadrant, we discovered a rough cobble floor sitting directly on top of the roof fall (fig. 5.10). The floor was bounded along a circular edge to the west and south by faced stones. The north and east faces of the floor met the adobe walls of room

Figure 5.10b. Room 20, stone floor on top of roof collapse.

20 and were approximately 180 centimeters on each side. This floor appears to have been built shortly after the roof of the room collapsed, though we cannot say for what purpose.

Rooms 11 and 18 offered a slightly different construction history. In these two rooms, we encountered a badly preserved plaster floor directly below the roof fall (fig. 5.11). We continued excavations below the floor and quickly reached sterile soil. Evidently, these two rooms had only a single occupation. Below the level of the plaster floor, the profiles of the excavation units showed no evidence of any construction. The adobe walls described in the first part of this section had been built directly onto natural deposits. Based on this evidence, I believe there was an expansion and reconstruction of an earlier calpanería. As already discussed, documentary sources mention the construction of a calpanería during the second half of the nineteenth century. Likely, rooms 11 and 18 were part of this construction phase. Rooms 20, 21, and 22 had an earlier occupation and were part of a remodeling of the entire area fronting the hacienda. At that time, they would have had their floors raised to the level of the other rooms that were being constructed.

While I was working in the calpanería, Su Lin began to explore the midden we had identified during the summer of 2005. With the intention

Figure 5.11. Room 18, plaster floor.

of excavating a complete profile of the midden, we placed a large excavation unit (two meters along the north/south axis and seven meters to the east/west) centered on the original one-meter-by-one-meter test unit excavated in 2005. This entire area was excavated to a depth of ninety centimeters below datum, where we reached sterile soil. Two one centavo coins were found in the midden, one in the upper levels dating to 1906 and another sixty centimeters below datum dating to 1864, giving us a date of the second half of the nineteenth century and beginning of the twentieth century for the deposit. These coins also seemed to suggest that the midden had accumulated gradually over time, rather than being deposited all at once.

Upon completing excavations of this unit (which we called non-structure [NST] 100), it became clear that we had found only a single edge of the midden on the eastern side of the excavations. To explore the extent of the deposit, Su Lin and I decided to extend trenches in one-meter-by-fifty-centimeter sections from the north, west, and south walls. Figure 5.12 shows the extent of the final excavations, with each individual excavation unit numbered sequentially, as well as the relationship of the excavations to the standing hacienda architecture. We identified the edge of the midden approximately two meters to the north and one meter to the west of our original excavations (NST 101 and 102), and I hoped we would quickly define all four edges of the midden. Doing so would free Su Lin and the men she was working with to open excavations in a new area of the field.

As I stood in the field thinking about where I would like to excavate next, I heard one of the men call Su Lin over. "Elizabeth?" she called a few moments later. I turned and walked toward her. There, at the bottom of the end of the last trench, one of the workers had located what appeared to be cobbles on top of plaster. To make sure that we weren't dealing with a structure of some sort, we extended the trench. At the bottom of the next trench, we found the edge of a single brick laid into the ground. We knew then that the deposit represented more than just some discarded building materials and decided to open more of the midden. Ultimately, we determined that we had found a carefully laid, square brick floor measuring 3.5 meters on each side, a measurement strikingly similar to the size of the calpanería rooms (fig. 5.13). The floor, as well as the collapsed cobbles and plaster, appeared to be set directly onto tepetate. We managed to uncover the last bit of the patio just two days before we were due to finish our field season, and we needed the remaining time to backfill our units. Unexpectedly, the excavations of the midden had taken most of our eight weeks, and

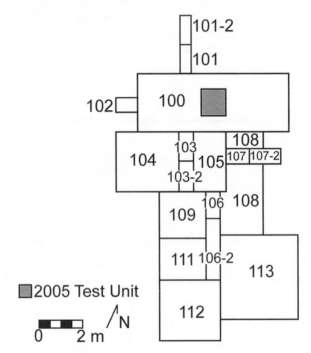

Figure 5.12. Midden excavations, winter 2007.

we had collected nearly fifty thousand artifacts—more than half of all that we would collect.

*   *   *

I flipped the lights back on, and the students blinked their eyes at the sudden brightness. I had finished my fieldwork ten months earlier and had been analyzing artifacts ever since. To relieve the solitary monotony of

Figure 5.13. Midden unit, brick patio.

artifact analysis, I volunteered to teach a seminar in historical archaeology at the local university. A few of the students in the course had worked with us during the first season at the hacienda and wanted to know how the research had turned out, so I decided to end the semester with a lecture about my work at Acocotla. I had just finished a slide presentation giving them an overview of the work we'd done in the field and was hauling a box of a few of the more interesting artifacts we'd found out from under the table.

I set the box on the table and began unpacking and passing the artifacts around. After reminding students the importance of keeping each artifact with its tag, I continued, "So what did we learn doing archaeology at the Hacienda San Miguel Acocotla?"

As the students thought a moment, I began explaining what I had learned from the excavations, reviewing the expectations I had set during the ethnoarchaeological work in the village of La Soledad Morelos that some of them had participated in.

1. Outdoor space is more important than interior space. I reminded them that we had been told that people had conducted most of their daily activities outdoors in the field fronting the calpanería, as the descendants of the calpanería's inhabitants do today. During excava-

tions, we found that these activity areas were very hard to identify, in spite of the substantial quantity of artifacts found on the surface. Perhaps people had used outdoor space but swept the area clean, as they do in the modern community. Given its public nature, the thirty or so families living together may have preferred to conduct activities in the privacy of their homes.

2. Amount of space per person varies. There was certainly no indication of the size of population at the hacienda's calpanería. Most of us would consider the small rooms too small for an entire family, and yet they had certainly been ordered this way. Archaeological evidence showed that each room had been set up as a single household, and ethnographic research agreed with this arrangement. A calculation of the past population size based on roofed space expectations set in La Soledad Morelos today (50.9 people) would not be drastically far off the average population taken from archival records (61 people), but in reality, the population ranged anywhere from 10 to 121 people during the second half of the nineteenth century. The only way we had any idea of how many people lived in the calpanería was through an examination of the historical documents.

3. Kitchen space is important. The one activity area we were successful in identifying during our excavations had been the smoke kitchen found the first season in pozo 3. The kitchen's distance from the calpanería and its unique nature as a feature type suggested that the oral history telling us that a single woman had come from the nearby village of La Soledad Morelos to cook for all the inhabitants of the calpanería was the most likely scenario. This, I was fairly certain, would prove significant because it was a substantial departure from the way modern households were organized. The dynamics of food preparation, labor relations, and family structure as represented by that one kitchen were subjects I would explore further.

4. Choice of building materials depends on more than "common sense." These rooms look small and poor today, but maybe once upon a time they had been attractive to villagers whose houses were nowhere near as grand. Perhaps workers were willing to put up with the conditions of life and labor at the hacienda because they were afforded the opportunity to live in homes associated with the prestigious casco.

5. Architectural form would, however, be simple and practical. The calpanería's architectural style was, in many ways, an excellent match

to what we'd found in the traditional and mixed compounds in La Soledad Morelos. The style was very similar, and the calpanería had been as unadorned as the compound exteriors are today.

6. Room use would be difficult to discern. Thus far, this did indeed seem to be the case. I'd spent a great deal of time with the artifacts, though I wasn't finished yet, and very little about them or the archaeology told us how rooms had been used.

7. Rooms would not have been abandoned directly following habitation. This seemed to be a likely explanation for the difficulty in identifying room use, but there was one problem with this interpretation. The intact hearths found in each room argued that the rooms had, in fact, been lived in right up until the roof collapsed. Perhaps this was the catastrophic event that ended the calpanería's useful life.

I let the students finish taking their notes before asking, "Any more questions about the dig before I let you go for the evening?"

Hands shot up, "What did you finally decide was going on with that structure under the midden?"

"Yeah," said another, "And what was up with that little stone platform on top of the roof? That was weird."

I nodded in agreement before admitting that I had no idea what the structures were.

"What do you mean you don't know?" they exclaimed as a group.

"Well," I said, "Finding something you cannot immediately explain or identify is not unusual, especially when you are working at a site like Acocotla where little exists to compare it with. When you dig a Prehispanic site here in Cholula, or in the Maya area, or at a big site like Teotihuacán, you have a pretty good idea about what you think you'll find, and a great idea about how to interpret the contexts thanks to the hundreds of archaeologists who've dug before you. Our interpretations at the Hacienda San Miguel Acocotla are informed by other excavations and artifact analyses, but with the very limited precedent of similar digs, interpreting everything we discover can be tricky. Allan Meyers's excavations at the Hacienda Tabi and Rani Alexander's work at Yaxacabá, both in distant Yucatán, do help us understand what we find at Acocotla; however, with no similar digs in same region as Acocotla is located, sometimes, interpreting everything we discover is difficult or even impossible."

"So what was the point of the excavations? What do you really know about life in the calpanería?" one of the students challenged.

I said, "That is why excavations are only one part of the puzzle. I've gathered data from historical documents, I've studied the modern community and collected oral histories, I've done the excavations and a careful architectural study of the hacienda's casco, and I've analyzed artifacts and faunal remains. Taken alone, none of these things tell us very much, but now it is time to integrate the data sets. Come back for next week's lecture, and I'll answer your questions."

*   *   *

CHAPTER SIX

Crossmending

The Archaeology of Architecture and Home Life

Rafaela pulled herself reluctantly awake. The sun would be up soon, and she had things to do. The fire had burned down to coals, but the room was still full of smoke from the night before. She slipped out from between her husband and children and neatened herself as best she could in the small, dark room. She smoothed her plaited hair, retied the ribbons at the ends, and smiled as she touched the small gold earrings in her ears. She was the only woman in the calpanería with anything as fine. Her husband's mother had given them to her as a wedding present, and she wore them proudly every day. She straightened her skirts, slipping her spindle into the pocket, ready for idle moments.

She bent over her youngest child, who was sleeping closest to the fire. She brushed the hair from Petra's forehead, frowning as she felt how warm the two year old was still. She had lost five children already and didn't intend to lose a sixth. The hacendado had sent his doctor to look at Petra. The man had given her some medicine, but the child wasn't any better. She would have to find the money to take the girl to a curandero, or at the very least buy a charm of protection. For all she knew, the hacendado himself had sent the curse. Rumors in the calpanería claimed that he had made a pact with the devil.

Rafaela went to the fire and stirred up the coals, adding a bit of tinder to get it burning again. She lifted the heavy olla off the fire where it had been simmering full of corn all night. The warm ceramic felt good in her cold hands. Carefully, she carried it outside to the kitchen. Feliciana was already at work, grinding corn for the midday meal. Rafaela felt a pang of guilt. Her mother had raised her to be a good wife and mother, to care and cook for her family, but her family needed the money she earned working next to her husband in the fields every day. She carried the olla across the field and set it over the already burning fire, ready whenever Feliciana wanted it. The two women exchanged a few words, comparing notes on children and commenting on the fact that the rains still had not arrived.

Rafaela turned and walked back toward the calpanería. The row of small, white rooms looked so tidy. She knew she was lucky to live there, even if it meant her entire family had to work on the hacienda's lands. She touched the small cross at her neck, thanking the Virgin for not having sent a husband like Feliciana's. The poor woman was married to a man who did nothing but drink, and Feliciana worked to support her family. Though Feliciana didn't spend much time talking about family affairs, Rafaela knew that the woman got up shortly after midnight to grind corn and make tortillas for her family. As soon as the tortillas were done, she left her home in La Mojonera and, in the dark, walked all the way to the hacienda by herself. Feliciana spent the day cooking the midday and evening meals for the inhabitants of the calpanería before returning home to face a drunken, violent husband.

Rafaela ducked through the doorway, reentering her family's living quarters and prepared to wake her husband and children. It was nearing dawn. If they weren't in the fields ready to work when the sun came up, they would lose the day's wages. It was a penalty they could ill afford. She sighed softly, preparing to break the peace of the morning, and reached to wake her youngest child.

The preceding is nothing more than a palimpsest pieced together with data gleaned from the ethnohistorical, ethnographic, and archaeological research discussed in the last three chapters. We don't know what Rafaela thought as she got out of bed the morning in question, but we do know she existed. Rafaela's name is recorded in Acocotla's accounts as part of an inventory of sorts.[1] We know that she lived in the calpanería with a husband who was fifteen years older than she. We know that in May of 1893, she had six living children ranging in age from two to eighteen years. The document, a list of workers living at the Hacienda Acocotla, tells us that Rafaela was a Catholic and an Indian. It tells us that she was illiterate and that she spoke only Nahuatl (listed as *Mexicano* in the nineteenth-century census). The record states that she had been vaccinated and that she had no visible physical defects. It tells us only what the hacendado chose to report to the government based on what that government thought mattered. It is the sum of information available to us about Rafaela and the fifty-five other indigenous workers identified in the same document.

Some might suggest that Rafaela's story is unimportant. She was just a small cog in the machinery that kept the Hacienda Acocotla running, and the hacienda was just a medium-size venture in a densely cultivated valley. Rafaela's role on the national, state, and perhaps even local stage was nonexistent, but her story is that of thousands of women living at haciendas throughout central Mexico. These stories played a central role in the trajectory of the Mexican Revolution and the reforms that followed. Her experience, and the experiences of her husband, children, ancestors, and descendants, illuminates the lives of the poor and rural peoples of Mexico during the profoundly transformative years of the late nineteenth and early twentieth centuries.

While it is impossible to reconstruct Rafaela's life specifically, we can attempt to assemble a more complete picture of daily and domestic life in Acocotla's calpanería. By combining ethnographic, oral historical, and archaeological research using data collected at the hacienda and among the descendant population, we can give Rafaela a voice she otherwise would not have. The details of Rafaela's morning are all based in fact, though we do not know which details belong to her and which belong to others like her. Thanks to the 1893 document, her name and family relations may be taken as a certainty, but we cannot be confident of the accuracy of details such as the exact age of family members. We know that she and her family lived in the calpanería.

Archaeological research provides the material backdrop to our story. From the outside, the calpanería would have looked trim, a line of small, white-plastered rooms with red roof tiles and regularly spaced doorways. We know that Rafaela and her family likely occupied a single room. The room would have been small and windowless. A fire, built directly on the dirt or plaster floor in the northwest corner, would have drawn air from the open doorway. This fire would have warmed the space and allowed for food preparation. The smoke kitchen, a small structure that would have sheltered women from the elements as they prepared meals, would have been located across the field. There is no other architectural evidence for use of the field for regular activities. It would not, however, have been a bucolic environment, with the large, open midden full of both broken household items and rotting trash fronting the western half of the calpanería.

We know that some women used spindle whorls to produce cotton thread. Most of the women wore inexpensive copper earrings accented with glass beads, but at least one wore fancier gold earrings. Comparative data and archaeological evidence suggest that the hacendado provided medical care to his workers. Lack of faith in the doctor's medicines may perhaps be found in the presence of charms intended to protect children from illness and the evil eye. Christianity, in some form, is attested to by the crosses that would have been part of a rosary or worn as jewelry.

Oral history supplements the data and provides emotional detail to the narrative. Feliciana's story is true, though her name was not Feliciana. During interviews in the descendant community, one woman in her nineties told us about her mother's life and experiences working at Acocotla. Feliciana's story is taken word for word from this interview. Emerging from this story is the subtle but important information that the hacienda owner or manager hired women to come from nearby La Mojonera to cook rather than rely on the women living in the calpanería to prepare meals for their own families.

The 1893 list of the calpanería's inhabitants identifies only adult males as employees. Oral history expands our understanding of the demographics of the hacienda's workforce and explains the need for imported cooks. While collecting stories of life at the hacienda from people who had lived in the calpanería as young children and people whose parents had lived at Acocotla, we came across repeated accounts of women and children being put to work in the fields. Both men and women told stories of going to work at the hacienda at ages as young as six, and many of them remembered going to work with their mothers. Children worked the same hours as adults (at least twelve-hour days six days a week), though they were paid a fraction of the wages. Nobody reported having the opportunity to go to school, and everybody admitted they were illiterate. One woman, born shortly before the start of the Mexican Revolution in 1910, told us "our education was the bullet."

Work at the hacienda seems to have been especially difficult for young women. Two of the women indirectly indicated that they had been raped by the mayordomo at ages as young as twelve years old. These are extreme examples of the difficulties faced by women on central Mexican haciendas. Rafaela's story illustrates a more subtle tension that the women of Acocotla's calpanería faced. They lived in a world that expected them to be wives and mothers, to clean and cook, to reproduce and care for their young, responsibilities that were carefully and clearly defined by society, regardless of social class.[2] The failure of the hacendado and his manager to identify women and children as paid labor on their censuses is indicative of the social unacceptability of the roles that these women were playing.

The preceding demonstrates the ways in which a historical archaeologist interweaves data from diverse sources to understand the lives of those largely left out of the historical record. Chapter 5 concluded with students wondering what all the data we had collected at Acocotla meant. The next three chapters answer their questions and help us understand the daily lives, past and present, of the people in Acocotla's calpanería and the village of La Soledad Morelos. The "true" stories of the fifty-six men, women, and children recorded in the 1893 census are largely lost to history, but the memories of the way they lived, the material remains of those lives, and the ways in which their descendants live now echo that truth. These echoes offer the opportunity to understand a bit about life at the Hacienda Acocotla.

Power and Social Control: The Redesign of Acocotla's Casco

Thus far, we have explored the ways in which the ethnographic study of architecture and domestic space in the modern descendant community might contribute to our understanding of the architectural remains at the Hacienda San Miguel Acocotla, and we then actually dug up the remains of homes in Acocotla's calpanería. This chapter integrates the data to build an understanding of the social dynamics embedded in, broadly, Acocotla's casco and, more specifically, the calpanería and its domestic space. While many have rightly cautioned against reading too much into architectural remains recovered during archaeological excavations, historical archaeologists, art historians, and folklorists have used architectural analyses to great effect in helping us understand past social dynamics.[3]

The dynamics behind the design and construction of the Hacienda Acocotla are complex. Examination of the domestic space of the individuals living in the calpanería is not simply the study of the individual households. Today, most people live with an architectural separation between home and work. During the nineteenth century, a time that saw rapid industrialization throughout the Americas, such a separation was much less common. As part of the processes of industrialization, corporations constructed housing for their workers, a management strategy that allowed them, at least in theory, to control most aspects of their employees' lives.[4] Though not a factory, the Hacienda San Miguel Acocotla is no exception to this pattern. When looking at Acocotla's calpanería and the associated casco, we are not examining a "normal" pattern of domestic use and abandonment. Rafaela and her neighbors did not own their homes; they did not have leases. The people who made decisions about the design and organization of Rafaela's home were people who would never live in the space. Perhaps even more important, the people who made those decisions were Rafaela's employers, people who were more concerned with Rafaela's productivity as a worker than her comfort at home.[5] Though unusual, this arrangement is far from unique. So what, or who, dictated the plan of Rafaela's home, and why was it constructed and organized as it was?

A rat scuttled across her foot, and doña Ana swallowed a scream. So much for her dream of a genteel country house in which to entertain her city friends. What had she gotten herself into? The place was decrepit; nobody had lived here for years. Her friends had country homes outside of Mexico City, and her husband's move to Puebla de los Angeles provided her with the opportunity to find a country house of her own and return the years of invitations her friends had extended. All those weekends of pastoral luxury they had provided would be nothing compared with her hospitality. The Valley of Atlixco not only was famed for its beauty but also was an inexpensive place to buy property. The broker had assured her he'd found the perfect place, and she had believed him. It would be exotic enough to entice her friends. She'd be the first to own property in the remote valley, but still it was well known enough that people would come.

The broker was, of course, wrong. Acocotla was simply not up to the standards she required. She didn't know if she should laugh or cry. What would people think? She grimaced as she looked out the window. At least the little chapel was pretty, and the view of the volcano Popocatépetl rising behind it was unmatched. The chapel needed some updating, but it was better looking than anything else she owned. And its cemetery was picturesque. Her ancestors weren't buried there, but somehow the graves gave the place an air of history, conferring a hint of the pedigree she desperately wanted. She turned back to look through the arches and into the main patio, trying to focus on her new home's positive attributes. It almost worked, and then a chicken scuttled past. She shook her head. Chickens in the patio. . . . Did she really need to see anything else?

She returned to the patio where Juan waited. The broker bowed obsequiously. "Would doña Ana like to see the kitchen?" he asked? "The KITCHEN?" she thought, "Did she look like a woman who EVER set foot in the kitchen?" These country people were impossible. She frowned at him and turned back to the patio in freezing silence. It was horrible, full of crumbling adobe. And of course there were the chickens. But the purchase had been made sight unseen. Her husband had warned against it. She had insisted. She used her inheritance to pay for the property without consulting him. Thank goodness she hadn't spent it all. She would use the rest for the work that needed to be done, and she would do it before she had to bring her husband here. Doña Ana turned back to the broker and, wondering why she should trust him but recognizing her own desperation, asked if he could recommend a decent architect . . .

Thirty years before Rafaela moved into a room in the calpanería, doña Ana Cristina Treviño de Ruelas purchased the Hacienda San Miguel Acocotla, which was, at the time, in foreclosure.[6] An assessment made in 1859 offers a detailed description of the hacienda and its casco as doña Ana would have found it.[7] The casco would have been significantly smaller than it is now, measuring only about fifty meters by fifty meters square. This measurement approximates the size of the Patio del Limón today, and it is likely that this area comprised the entire casco in 1859. The structure had two stories, spaces for living and working, a kitchen, a granary, stables, a threshing floor, a carpenter's shop, and a chapel with a burial ground. The buildings were all constructed out of adobe, and most were in ruins. The surveyor tells us "the building is deteriorated because several walls have been burrowed by rats."

Though we don't know who was responsible for the redesign of Acocotla's casco, archaeological evidence recovered during our excavations in the calpanería indicate that the remodeling would have taken place during doña Ana's tenure. If nothing else, one imagines she would have wanted to evict the rats. Doña Ana's redesign of the casco not only was a "sign of the times" (Mexico's period of rapid modernization during the second half of the nineteenth century) but perhaps also an attempt to bring order to a world in chaos. The architectural reconfiguration that we see at Acocotla is of fundamental importance to understanding the experiences of the people, of all social classes, who inhabited the casco.

In the Valley of Atlixco, the century between the War of Independence and the Revolution was dangerous and unstable. Elites struggled to maintain control over the economy and government. The poor felt their long-held control over basic subsistence and village independence slip from an increasingly tenuous grasp as a result of the political and economic struggles on the national stage.[8] In 1814, owners of haciendas in the Valley of Atlixco wrote to the government to request forbearance in their fiscal responsibilities, citing attacks by insurgents, the payments they were required to make in support of the army, and lack of labor due to frequent epidemics resulting in the death of the Indians responsible for the haciendas' harvest.[9] Conditions in the region did not improve. By 1859, when the hacienda was assessed in the document described above, archival evidence shows that tensions ran high in the valley. Many of Acocotla's nineteenth-century records deal with the responsibility of the hacendado to send men and horses to local authorities to assist in policing the area. Other documents speak frequently of murders and assassinations by and of the local populace. Fluctuations in the number of resident workers housed in the calpanería speak to either economic instability or the difficulty of maintaining a consistent worker population.[10] Doña Ana would have had to contend with all of these problems if she were to invite her friends to her palatial country home.

Doña Ana leaned over the rough table erected by her architect. She examined the plans carefully, frowning in concentration and nodding thoughtfully. The broker had given her an excellent recommendation for an architect. Though the man was more used to designing the newer textile mills that were popping up throughout central Mexico, he seemed to understand her requirements—safety, beauty, efficiency, productivity. He'd assured her that he could design a structure that would welcome her friends, protect her business interests, and lull her workers into some form of loyalty.

She squinted at the plans that don Javier had laid out for her, but the truth was she had no idea what she was looking at. She looked up just in time to see him emerge from the hut he had constructed to provide shelter while he supervised the laborers. She noticed he was holding two glasses of wine. "Thank goodness," she thought. She was so parched, she wasn't sure she'd be able to speak. She'd have to remember not to invite her friends to come in March. Her husband had warned her that it was the height of the dry season, but she'd had no idea how bad the dust would be.

"Perhaps you could just walk me through the plans one more time so I can be certain I understand," she suggested.

He smiled smoothly, "Of course."

Together, they leaned over the table. She would feel safe, he assured her. He went on to describe the inner patio where her residences would be. Her friends would travel through the working areas of the hacienda to reach them. Radical, maybe, in exposing the working areas so prominently, but he suggested that her friends would be impressed by her business acumen and even more impressed by the luxury of the private residences in contrast. As an added benefit, the complexity of the structure would keep everyone, from peon to honored guest, in his place.

Social theorists exploring programs of discipline, power, and social control have suggested that the design of architectural space can create an environment that naturalizes a stratified social hierarchy.[11] Basically, this means that the way a building is designed, constructed, staffed, and used can dictate the way you and your friends, neighbors, and coworkers behave. Think of a large bank in a busy city. Anybody and everybody can walk up to the ATM on the sidewalk. You may withdraw a large sum of money, looking nervously over your shoulder as you do, furtively tucking the cash into your wallet, wondering who on the street behind you is watching your every move while you groan internally over another $2.50 fee paid to a bank you don't have an account with.

Perhaps, after months of nervously withdrawing your hard-earned cash on the street corner most convenient to you, you decide to form a slightly more developed relationship with the bank. You can now walk in and conduct your business with a teller in whispered tones. The exchange is still far from private, but given that you had to walk by a security guard to get into the bank, and given that you are communicating with a real, living human being, you may feel a bit more protected. Presumably, the people in the bank have been screened as you have, and maybe you don't worry about hiding your wallet quite as much. If you are willing to entrust the bank with a bit more money than the average person, say, in the form of a substantial CD, you may be ushered into a cubicle and offered a chair. You can conduct your business in relative comfort and privacy. Your access to the physical spaces of the bank, and your prestige in the eyes of both bank staff and other patrons, increases in direct relation to the amount of money you have entrusted them with. Not just anybody can waltz into the office of the branch manager. When someone does, those left waiting in line for a teller are subtly reminded that they are standing, economically and socially, where they belong.

A bank is an easy and familiar example, but it is not the only example. Many would argue that delineated space controls our behavior and even self-worth in endless ways both now and in the past. Archaeologists working on historical sites in the New World have identified architectural designs from the late eighteenth and nineteenth centuries that are intended to create and control a subservient population. During this period, the development of both public and private spaces was intended to exhibit, maintain, and perpetuate discipline, an intention that was derived from Baroque theories of power that "attempted to establish stratified social hierarchies by creating environments that proclaimed a natural law dependent on divinely ordained, natural hierarchies."[12] Patterns of power have been identified by historical archaeologists studying architecture and landscape design in a wide range of settings in both the Old and New Worlds, such as urban areas and government buildings; factories and their associated residences; plantations in former English, Dutch, and Spanish colonies; and even domestic architecture and landscapes.[13]

When we look at the redesign of Acocotla's casco, we are examining architectural answers to questions the designers, or their customers, may have posed. Today, as we approach the casco's main entrance, we find ourselves looking at the calpanería. When doña Ana purchased Acocotla, the calpanería did not frame the main entrance and dominate the façade as it does now, but by the time she sold the hacienda, the shift had been made. Why this particular reconfiguration? The organization of worker housing we see at Acocotla stands in stark contrast to contemporary structures in the surrounding region. The calpanería at most local haciendas had interconnecting rooms and walled patios and was rarely placed in so public a place as the hacienda entrance.[14] In the Valley of Atlixco, no other calpanería is so configured.[15] Doña Ana was not simply doing what "everybody was doing" when she or her architect redesigned the casco.

Though unusual, in a world where the rich were faced with the necessity of figuring out how to control the poor and their labor, the design of Acocotla's calpanería makes sense. Intent to control the worker population may have encouraged someone like doña Ana or her architect to develop a subtle, unstated architectural dynamic. By creating a domestic area for the workers that was very public and "on display," the hacendada may in fact have been forcing (or at least intending to force) the peones to engage in what social scientists call "self-reflexive monitoring" of their behavior.[16] In much the same way that drivers on a busy but familiar road slow down as they approach a place where there is often (but not always) a speed trap, the inhabitants of the calpanería may have had to behave as if someone were watching because their boss *might* emerge from the hacienda or pass by on the road in front unannounced at any moment. Some scholars have likened this sort of architectural design to Jeremy Bentham's Panopticon, a prison-like space that allowed "observers" to anonymously monitor (and so ensure good behavior from) prisoners, workers, or citizens.[17]

As the Mexican Revolution would demonstrate fifty years later, doña Ana's concerns were not baseless. The calpanería housed the people who were potentially the most dangerous of Acocotla's inhabitants. The architectural arrangement meant that, unlike their descendants in La Soledad Morelos who guard the privacy of their homes and domestic activities behind the walls of a compound, citizens of the calpanería enjoyed virtually no privacy—from outsiders or from each other. Anybody passing by on the road or emerging from inside the casco would immediately be able to see everything that the families living in the calpanería may have been doing. Given their size and layout, the calpanería's rooms offered little more than shelter from the elements. Most domestic activities would have had to take place in the field fronting the row of rooms in the company of friends, neighbors, bosses, and strangers.

Though lack of privacy and control over the household may have been the most important shortcoming of the living space, it was not the only way in which the calpanería and its inhabitants were exposed. Of all the people living at the Hacienda Acocotla, the calpanería's inhabitants were the only ones who did not benefit from the protection of the casco's five-meter-high walls. As we have seen time and again, Atlixco was a dangerous place in the middle of the nineteenth century. Surely the peones felt unprotected living outside the walls. Of course, this arrangement may also have served to allow the hacienda owners and manager, living behind those same walls, to feel safe not only from roving bandits but also from the hacienda's workers.

Feliciana glanced over at the gently snoring Petra. Though Rafaela was nearly hysterical at the girl's supposed illness, she didn't seem so sick to Feliciana. Her forehead was cool to the touch, and the little girl was sleeping soundly. Satisfied that she wouldn't be missed, Feliciana gathered up the pieces of her broken comal in her apron and, straightening her shoulders, marched resolutely toward the casco's main entrance.

Holding her apron with one hand, she pounded on the big, wooden door with all her strength. The guard peered out suspiciously. "What?" he demanded without preamble.

Feliciana looked down at her apron, trying not to feel the shame the man always made her feel. She held her apron out, showing the fragments of the shattered comal. "I need to see the hacendado's cook. If she doesn't have a comal to lend me, the peones will be without lunch or supper today."

She left the threat hanging in the air between them. She knew he didn't want to have to cope with hungry, angry workers, on the one hand, and a frustrated mayordomo, on the other, any more than she did. With a blank stare and a resigned set to his jaw, the man stepped back and unbarred the door. Feliciana stepped through and watched nervously over her shoulder as he barred it again. She knew she ought to feel a sense of security, but in fact she always felt a little trapped with the big heavy door locked behind her. The guard scratched himself rudely and said, "If you are going to need water, you might as well collect it while you are here. I don't need to be disturbed a second time." With that, he settled himself back in his shady spot on the ground, pulled his hat over his face, and, presumably, went back to sleep. Clearly, he felt she was of no importance.

She ducked her head and muttered something incoherent before scurrying toward the hacendado's kitchen. She hated coming into the casco. The first bit wasn't so bad. She passed the Patio de los Chivos on the right, where she came regularly to collect water, and the tienda on the left, where she and the peones bought household necessities and luxuries from the hacienda's guards. She walked down the hallway, passing through yet another arch. This area was where she came to be paid every Saturday. Nervously, she continued on. With each doorway and arch she passed through, she felt more and more like she was someplace she didn't belong.

Finally, she reached the stairwell. Setting her shoulders for what had to be the hundredth time in what felt like a very long walk, she climbed the stairs to the kitchen. Walking in, she found the hacendado's cook sleeping by the fire. The woman almost never had anything to do. The hacendado was rarely in residence. On the occasions when he arrived from town, fancy friends in tow, all the women would be pulled out of the fields to help the cook with the most menial tasks necessary to get food on the table. Feliciana begrudged Adriana her life; she was no better a cook than Feliciana herself. But Adriana had the luck of having been born cousin to the mayordomo.

"Adriana," Feliciana barked. The cook woke with a snort and a start.

"Oh, it's just you. What do you want?" Adriana glared at her. Everyone knew she didn't like being woken up when the sun was its hottest. Her look told Feliciana that whatever Feliciana was there for could have waited until the shadows were a bit longer.

Feliciana opened her apron one more time and explained the problem. The last comal was broken. She didn't know when the peddler would be by with more, and until that time, she needed something to cook the tortillas on. Could Adriana spare one of hers?

Adriana rolled her eyes in disgust. She waved her hand dismissively to where the cooking implements sat stacked and unused. "Take what you need," she said, less with generosity than disinterest. She leaned back against the cool wall and resumed her midday nap.

Dropping the bits of shattered comal in a corner, Feliciana eagerly swept up two of the nicer comales. She felt a brief stab of guilt before rationalizing that the comales would likely never be used here in the hacendado's kitchen. Given how intensively she used her kitchen tools, what was there to feel guilty about?

Hurrying out of the kitchen and back down the steps, Feliciana found herself wondering briefly what life was like on the other side of the wall.

Though she had been as far as the kitchen many times, she had never been allowed beyond it and into the Patio del Limón. Rumor had it that it was a beautiful place, but, other than the hacendado and mayordomo, few had seen it. Adriana dropped comments about it every now and again, but everyone disliked her so much, nobody ever asked her to elaborate. There was a woman in the calpanería who cleaned for the hacendado when he was in residence, and she told stories of the sumptuous luxury of the patio, but Feliciana could hardly believe the woman's uncorroborated tales. How could anybody live like that?

Her musings took her all the way back to the front entrance where she found herself having to fight a longing to kick the sleeping guard. She settled for nudging his ankle with her foot. He sat up, sputtering and confused, glaring at Feliciana as he remembered where he was. "All these people working in the casco do nothing but sleep," thought Feliciana, with no small amount of bitterness. "It must be nice to be related to the mayordomo."

As the door slammed shut behind her, Feliciana felt a surge of relief. Crazy, maybe, given how much more dangerous it was out here, but her trips into the casco always reminded her of just what her position in life really was. As she felt the tension melt from her shoulders, she trudged slowly back to the kitchen, weighed down by the pair of heavy comales.

By the time Feliciana and her friends and neighbors moved into the calpanería, the organization of the casco had been long established. Nobody would have questioned the design decisions made by doña Ana and her architect thirty years before; the arrangements would have become "natural." And what did doña Ana achieve through her redesign? One way to understand the arrangement of architectural space and its effect on people is to consider the ease or difficulty of moving through the space. The realignment of the casco so that it faced south and the placement of the calpanería flanking the main entrance was a design change that is hard to miss. More subtle, perhaps, is the way the casco's redesign created a structure that was very hierarchical in the same way that the bank in my earlier example is. In making access to certain areas of the casco difficult, doña Ana was reminding everyone of exactly where they belonged.

The casco's complexity allowed its owner to control access to private, domestic space, as well as to determine the movement of people through the space to control the ways in which workspace was defined and used—because, above all else, the casco was not a home but a business. The creation of this complex architectural structure with separate and defined areas dedicated to particular tasks was part of the intent to control the workers. Architectural compartmentalization and specialization like what we see at Acocotla have been shown time and again to be part of processes of modernization and embedded in the development of industrial capitalism.[18] By creating spaces with highly specific and clearly defined uses, doña Ana was creating an environment in which the ways individuals moved through the casco, used time, and completed tasks could be monitored. Similar patterns are seen elsewhere in Mexico. At the Hacienda Tabi in Yucatán, Allan Meyers and his collaborators have also found hierarchical architectural patterns that they interpret as a design intended to facilitate social control and to naturalize the social order.[19]

The connection between status and architecture is clear even in the ruins today, as is the dichotomy between public and private. The lowest-status peones were largely restricted to the outermost work areas, though they may have occasionally been allowed deeper into the casco to assist with animal care. The caporales, described as both "higher status" and "more trusted" by our informants, enjoyed housing behind the safety of the casco's walls and, thanks to their duties with the animals, would have been able to move freely through many of the casco's work areas. Both the peones and the caporales were allowed into the Patio Abierto, to the very edge of the hacendado's living quarters, in order to accept their payment for the week's work, an event that would have seemed ceremonious as they were handed their weekly salary and maize rations while the manager made notes of the exchange in his account books.[20] The manager's office was placed in the space between the "work" areas of the hacienda and the living areas of the hacienda owner. Administratively, the manager was the gatekeeper, controlling access to the interior living space of the hacendado and his family, and the architectural placement of the manager's office reflects this role.

The Patio del Limón is clearly the most restricted space in the casco and simultaneously the most self-sufficient. Once they had passed through the working areas of the casco, the hacendado and his family could lock themselves in the patio and live in uninterrupted luxury if they so desired. The few workers allowed into the Patio del Limón would have found themselves in a world wholly different from that occupied by the rest of the inhabitants of the Hacienda Acocotla (fig. 6.1). The informants who were able to describe the patio before its ruin did so with emotion approaching reverence. They described a quiet space filled with lime trees and flowering plants, dominated by an elaborate fountain in the center. The walls surrounding this patio show today the remnants of what must have once been impressive decoration, adding to the experience of those allowed

Figure 6.1. Reconstruction of the Patio del Limón. (Drawing by Lew Stevens.)

into the space. While we were able to gather two recollections of the patio space, not a single former worker was found who could describe the interiors of the rooms surrounding the patio; these spaces were even more restricted, something that must have heightened the architectural effect of exclusivity. In creating an area as sumptuously distinct and inaccessible to the majority of the hacienda's inhabitants as the Patio del Limón, Acocotla's owners confirmed their right to the position of power they held over the lives of their workers.

*   *   *

I paused for breath, and a hand shot up. "Yes?" I asked Guillermo. He was interested and serious. He always sat in the front row. He took copious notes and did the reading. I was glad to have a question.

"This is all very interesting, but what about Rafaela and Feliciana? I thought that we were doing archaeology at Acocotla and working in La Soledad Morelos to learn about people like them? I know that we have to understand the background in which they were living, but what about their day-to-day experiences in the calpanería? Isn't that what we are studying? How did the hacienda owner's decisions make it into Rafaela's bedroom and Feliciana's kitchen?"

The great thing about having students is that they keep you honest. It can be tempting to apply all sorts of social theory to our understandings of architecture and artifacts, but at the end of the day, Guillermo was right. I was working on this project to understand the lives of people like Rafaela and Feliciana, people whose lives were lost to history but who lived lives that nonetheless mattered. Luckily, when I forgot and got carried away, there was always a diligent student to look back through his or her notes and remind me of what I had promised them all on the first day of class—that we were in that room to spend a semester talking about the really mundane, material details of people's lives, and how we, as historical archaeologists, tease histories out of those details, turning bones and stones into stories that matter.

I grinned ruefully as these thoughts flew through my head. "Yeah, you're right. We are here to talk about people like Rafaela and Feliciana . . . "

Some of the students grinned back at me in triumph, others nudged each other, and some rolled their eyes as if I had just wasted an hour of their lives.

"BUT," I said, pulling their attention back to me, "We need to understand why people like doña Ana made the decisions they did to understand how those decisions affected the lives of people like Rafaela and Feliciana. Everything I've told you gives you the context in which Rafaela and Feliciana lived their daily lives. Imagine how Feliciana felt moving through spaces that were normally forbidden. How would you have felt? How would that have affected your work? If you had to do all your assigned readings for class on the bench in front of my office, would you be more likely to get them done than you are now?"

The class giggled.

"But Guillermo is right. Let's bring all of this back to the level of the daily experiences of Rafaela, Feliciana, and the calpanería's other inhabitants. Let's go back to the calpanería itself. What was it really like?"

✳   ✳   ✳

Experiencing the Architecture: Life in the Calpanería

And what was the calpanería really like? From the outside, we know it was a neat looking row of thirty-seven identical rooms (fig. 6.2). They would

Figure 6.2. Reconstruction of the calpanería, exterior. (Drawing by Lew Stevens.)

have been plastered in white and had doorways arched in brick. The entire row would have been roofed in red pantiles. In the mind's eye and artist's reconstruction, it is almost picturesque. Each room measured approximately three and a half by three and a half meters or just over 130 square feet. A room in the calpanería was probably not much larger or smaller than your bedroom. Though that might not sound too bad at first, and indeed doesn't look bad in a reconstruction (fig. 6.3), remember that each housed an entire family.

Each room had a single entrance—an arched doorway—in the southwest corner. Floors were either dirt or plaster. During our excavations, we found evidence, in the form of a few hinges and a lock, that some of the doorways might have had doors, but likely most did not. The rooms had neither windows nor chimneys. A small hearth sat in the northwest corner of each room where it would have drawn air from the open door. The fire in it would have filled the small rooms with smoke, making them dark, warm, and stuffy. There was, of course, no running water, but there was also no well. When water was needed for cooking or cleaning, the workers would have asked permission to enter the hacienda's stable areas to collect water from the animal troughs.

Oral history indicates that each family was assigned a single room; however, the size of some of the families as indicated by the censuses we found in the archives suggests that larger families may have been assigned an additional room (due to the seeming impossibility of housing as many as eight people in the same 130 square feet of space). In 1842, the average family size was 3.5 individuals.[21] Fifty years later, the average family size had risen very slightly to four.[22] Family sizes during both periods ranged

Figure 6.3. Reconstruction of the interior of a calpanería room. (Drawing by Lew Stevens.)

from two to eight individuals. Rather than trying to understand the calpanería as an "apartment building" of separate domestic households, we might be better off understanding it as a single domestic compound (in the style of those we saw in La Soledad Morelos in chapter 4) that was shared by anywhere from ten to thirty-four families.

During our research in the descendant community, the students and I had developed a model that described what we expected to see in the calpanería. We had come up with seven points that seemed important in the modern community. The first of these observations was the importance of exterior space, and this is central to our understanding of the calpanería. Though we can gasp at the horror (by US standards) of allotting only 130 square feet to an entire family, we have to remember what we learned during our studies in the village of La Soledad Morelos. Most of life there happens outdoors in patios, something that is true in communities in Mesoamerica and around the world today.[23] The field fronting the calpanería, measuring about 5,081 square meters, acted as the calpanería's patio space (though without the same level of privacy).

Though it must have regularly been swept clean, as are patios elsewhere, we were easily able to recognize work areas in the field fronting the calpanería by looking at spaces on the edge of the densest archaeological deposits.[24] For example, we were able to easily identify a kitchen, which sat in the middle of a circle of manos and fragments of comales (both fundamental tools of the Mesoamerican kitchen), but neither of these artifacts were found directly above the kitchen in great numbers. We found the kitchen by looking in places near, not under, kitchen artifacts.[25] The small rooms had hearths, though they likely didn't serve as cooking areas for anything more than simmering the occasional olla of nixtamal. Families would have relied primarily on that one kitchen space in the field in front of the calpanería for their food production.

The space in front of the calpanería was used for more than work, just as the people of La Soledad Morelos today use their outdoor space for both work and social gatherings. During interviews, we were told that the area in front of the calpanería was a space in which families gathered to share meals. One informant told us that after the workday was over, the peones would gather in the field, build a fire, share a meal, sing songs, and drink mezcal while the children would play nearby. He further explained that the rooms in the calpanería were too small to be of any use but for sleeping. Our informant's description paints a happy picture of cooperative domesticity, though it seems likely that the arrangements were not always amiable.

There is a significant difference, however, between conducting domestic activities in a compound in La Soledad Morelos and conducting activities in the field fronting the calpanería. In La Soledad Morelos, the vast majority of households have high walls surrounding the entire compound. The few that lack a wall have placed their houses in such a way as to interrupt the line of sight from public streets into the compound, giving them a measure of privacy. While the patio space of the domestic compound is used for "public" activities, members of the household have control over who is admitted and what activities the invited see while they are visiting. This control is analogous to the control exerted over parlors and living rooms in cultures where interior space plays this role. Take a walk down the street you live on after dark and look around. How many people in your neighborhood leave their shades up? In neighborhoods with low traffic, the blinds might stay up. But anybody who lives in a busy neighborhood on a traffic-heavy street draws their blinds. Why? Because otherwise passersby see everything that happens in the living areas of their home. In the case of Acocotla's calpanería, there were no blinds to be drawn.

In Acocotla's calpanería, families were allowed only 12.25 square meters of privacy. The majority of domestic activities would have taken place in the open field fronting the hacienda, easily visible to other members of the hacienda community and casual passersby. Rather than providing the peones with what we would understand today as culturally "appropriate" or "necessary" space, the calpanería was like the hacienda's window dressing.[26] The arrangement of space simultaneously allowed the hacendado a high measure of control over his employees while showing off the "possessions" of the hacienda to all who visited.

Privacy may not have been the only concern. Studies of modern architecture have noted, "Architectural design is driven not only by the functional needs of the inhabitants but also by a given society's culturally based ideals for 'appropriate' or 'necessary' space."[27] As we found in La Soledad Morelos, the smoke kitchen is the one architectural area that embodies the community's culturally based ideals. This pattern does not hold true at Acocotla, where there appears to be only one kitchen. This point of dissonance highlights the power dynamics at work in the construction of the workers' homes. The "culturally based ideals" evident in Acocotla's calpanería are not those of the inhabitants of the space but rather of the hacendado, his architect, and his manager.

Kitchen space provides the perfect example of the ways in which the hacendado dictated the use of domestic space and defined what was "appropriate." As discussed in chapter 4, kitchens not only are of fundamental importance to women in the descendant community but also seem to reflect a continuity of social practice dating to the Prehispanic period. Today, kitchen spaces act as the nucleus of domestic life. They are the domain of women, and every female head of household has her own space to cook, conduct other necessary domestic and agricultural activities, and entertain friends, neighbors, and family. This model seems to echo those identified by scholars working in both the early colonial and Prehispanic periods.[28] Excavations of a Postclassic household at nearby Chalcatzingo show evidence of dedicated food preparation areas with restricted access, which the author believes represents a room that is just for women.[29] In describing Aztec houses, Jacques Soustelle writes, "There was a tendency to reserve one or more [rooms] for the women."[30] Excavations at Postclassic Tula show houses that sometimes contain multiple kitchen areas, a pattern interpreted as signifying the presence of multiple families.[31]

We found the remains of a single smoke kitchen during our excavations, and while it is possible that other kitchen spaces existed, it is unlikely. Oral history is contradictory on this subject. Some people we interviewed indicated that kitchen spaces were in the rooms of the calpanería; others suggested that each family had their own small structure in front of the calpanería in which to prepare food, and some stated that only a single kitchen, shared by all the inhabitants, existed. Perhaps contradictory evidence signals the centrality of the kitchen space to domestic life. Though the people we interviewed agreed on a great deal, they disagreed in their descriptions of the kitchen structure (or structures). Why would we get three differing descriptions of the kitchen space if everybody remembered correctly and told the truth? In fact, oral histories that are at odds with evidence gathered from archaeological and documentary sources are as important as those that "tell the truth" because they tell us both what people expect should be true and what they think you believe is true because of unspoken social norms.

In the case of the kitchen, the majority of people we interviewed told us that either each family had a kitchen in the field fronting the calpanería or had one in a second calpanería room. Archaeological evidence suggests that these descriptions are incorrect. Were people living in one room and cooking in another as the informants suggested, we would expect that the artifacts would differ from room to room. This was not the case. If each family had an outdoor kitchen space, we would expect to see at least thirty-four kitchens scattered throughout the field. Though our test excavations were admittedly limited, they were judgmentally placed to find kitchen areas. We succeeded easily in one case out of five, suggesting that, had there been more than one kitchen, we would have found evidence of them. Finally, though oral history is contradictory as far as the details of the kitchen architecture are concerned, multiple informants told us that women from La Soledad Morelos were hired to come to Acocotla to prepare meals for the families inhabiting the calpanería. Under these circumstances, the female heads of household had no functional need for their own kitchens.

Why, then, the dissonance of memory, especially when most other details of life at Acocotla could be agreed on? Kitchens are of central importance to daily life among members of the descendant community, and throughout the world, a shared hearth defines the boundaries of a household.[32] Whether the kitchen is used to prepare food or not, every female head of household has her own, a pattern that has a long history. As such, these spaces are of fundamental importance to the community and family. Perhaps our informants remembered multiple kitchens because, in their understanding of the "normal" domestic world, there had to be multiple kitchens. Both archaeological evidence and oral histories collected on related subjects indicate that this was almost certainly not the case, and yet the idea of just one kitchen is seemingly incomprehensible to the people whose ancestors lived in the calpanería.

This example illustrates the clash of cultures inherent in the creation of a domestic space at the Hacienda Acocotla. In *Nahuas After the Conquest*, James Lockhart puzzles over the fact that the Nahuas had what they called a "woman house," which Spaniards called a kitchen.[33] Kitchen, to Lockhart, makes no sense, because the activities described by the Nahuas clearly exceeded the behaviors that one would expect to find in a kitchen, and yet, the Spanish insisted on calling this space a kitchen. The same confusion may be in play at the Hacienda Acocotla. To the Hispanic hacendado, a kitchen is an area to produce the food necessary to keep the peones alive and working. Therefore, a space in which this food is prepared is necessary. Functionally, having a single space staffed with enough cooks to prepare food for workers makes perfect sense.

To the indigenous worker, however, having a single kitchen staffed by outsiders is completely illogical. Today, the kitchen is not only the nucleus of domestic life but also the center of a woman's household. To deprive a woman of this space, to send her to the fields to work for money next to her husband, and to give this space to paid workers from outside the domestic unit is to completely turn the world on its head. In transforming the kitchen into an area of capitalist production, the hacendado attacked the meaning of domestic space held by his indigenous workers. The kitchen and its accouterments had been the symbols of femininity and domestic life for hundreds, perhaps thousands, of years. The "misinterpretation" of this particular architectural space illustrates the tensions inherent in life at the hacienda. Imagine how Rafaela felt when she was told by the hacienda owner or manager that everything her mother had taught her, had told her to expect, was worthless. She needed to forget about caring for her family and start earning money.

Rafaela hurried across the fields with her husband and five of her children. It had been a long day. She was tired, hungry, and, most of all, worried about Petra. She hadn't heard how her daughter was since Feliciana brought her lunch. The little girl had been so sick when she left that morning, and Feliciana had told her there was no change. Rafaela was worried that her youngest child would be worse, though she had tied a figa around Petra's neck that morning. One of her neighbors had borrowed the charm from the hacendado's house while she was cleaning. The charm had worked wonders for the hacendado's daughter the last time she'd been ill, and the girl, no longer needing the figa, had left it behind after the family's last visit. Though it hadn't been made specifically for her daughter, Rafaela hoped it would still work.

The calpanería finally came into view across the freshly plowed fields. Though they were still some distance away, she could see the peones rushing around, preparing to sit down to dinner. It was a sight that greeted her every evening, and she sighed with relief. Petra must be fine. If she weren't, the calpanería couldn't possibly look so normal. She saw the men building the fire; the women were grouped around the kitchen gathering items for the evening meal. Feliciana had left for home hours before, but she had laid out the food she had prepared, along with clean dishes and a comal to warm the tortillas, as she did every afternoon. As she and her family got closer, Rafaela saw Petra playing near the kitchen. The little girl looked up, brightening when she saw her mother returning. Petra dropped the bits of clay she was playing with and rushed to meet her family. Rafaela smiled as she crossed herself and silently thanked the Virgin. Petra was better—the charm had worked.

She swept her daughter up into her arms and carried her back toward the calpanería. Petra chattered happily about her day, telling her mother that Feliciana had promised to teach her to make tortillas. It stung a bit. Rafaela knew that she should be the one teaching Petra to make tortillas. But she was so relieved her daughter was healthy that she let go of her feelings of guilt as best she could.

The two-year-old's enthusiastic babble was incomprehensible to all except her mother, but the whole family smiled to see the little girl so completely recovered. As a family, they approached the kitchen area ready to help with meal preparations. Rafaela carried her daughter over to the kitchen to find out what needed to be done. Hipólita smiled a greeting and asked Rafaela to fetch the water. As the oldest woman in the calpanería, Hipólita was un-questionably in charge. Rafaela smiled in return and nodded her under-standing. She put her daughter on the ground with the other young children and lifted one of the large, heavy ollas used to store water.

She carried the olla up to the entrance of the hacienda and knocked hard on the heavy door. One of the guards opened the gate and glared out, prob-ably unhappy at having his evening meal interrupted. Rafaela explained what she wanted. He nodded, allowing her to enter the hacienda. As she

walked toward the Patio de los Chivos, she passed Miguel Hernández buy-
ing a couple of bottles of mezcal at the tienda de raya. Since his wife had
died the month before, he was drinking more and more, but she supposed
that at seventy-one years of age and after a lifetime working at the hacienda,
he had earned the right to drink as much as he wanted.

She quietly entered the Patio de los Chivos, offering a respectful greeting
to the caporales who were busy preparing their own meals. As she walked
past them toward the trough, she felt a pang of envy. She knew it was
wrong—the priest was always saying envy was a sin—but she couldn't help
it. There were rumors of bandits in the area again, and Rafaela would love
to live in this quiet, protected area with guards at the gate in front. Shrug-
ging in resignation, she went to the trough, fighting for space among the
goats, and dipped the olla into the water. She pulled it out, struggling with
the weight, and turned to leave.

She said goodnight to the caporales and made her way to the front gate.
She nodded her goodnights to the guards and passed through the gate. Ra-
faela paused nervously as they closed the doors behind her. She always felt
so exposed when she stepped back outside of Acocotla's walls. She scanned
the horizon but saw nothing. She carried the olla awkwardly back toward
the kitchen, her worries almost forgotten as she began to anticipate dinner
with her neighbors and family.

This chapter examined the role of Acocotla's architecture in shaping the
lives of the indigenous workers inhabiting the space. Though we cannot
know with certainty what drove the hacendada's decisions about the design
and remodeling of Acocotla's casco, or the impact these decisions had on
her workforce, certain points are suggestive. We do know that the nineteenth century was a dangerous, turbulent time. Hacienda owners had difficulty maintaining a stable workforce, and regular small-scale rebellions
threatened the established social order.[34] It seems reasonable to assume
that in this environment, the hacendada acted to stabilize her situation.

I used the stories of Rafaela and Feliciana to suggest the ways in which
architecture and the organization of domestic life may have affected the
individuals living in the calpanería. Their stories highlight a few aspects of
daily life that have come to light through an examination of both past and
modern patterns of the use of domestic space. Because the calpanería contained only a single kitchen space, Rafaela and her neighbors would have
been forced to live as a single, extended family. Families would not have
been able to maintain any level of independence because food preparation
and consumption, a central organizing factor for nuclear families in the

modern descendant community, would have to be communal. Further, either the hacendada's failure to understand, unconsciously, or disrespect, consciously, the importance of an independent kitchen to each woman and her family would have undermined and transformed the traditional family structure, an act that may have facilitated her control.

Arguably, this architectural pattern represents an attack on the peones' social norms. The use of kitchen space and arrangements for food preparation may be identified in the Prehispanic archaeological record and colonial historic record, and these same patterns remain evident today. In the modern community, the design of kitchen space reflects the mores of families and communities; kitchens are the material, architectural manifestation of the social role that women are expected to fulfill. The redesign of kitchen space instituted by the hacendada and her managers constituted a direct attack on families and the community, an act that must have left people feeling upset, angry, defensive, or simply uncertain.[35]

Rafaela's trip for water highlights the ways in which the hacienda's architectural spaces created an environment that naturalized the social order and her place in it. The goats, cows, and horses were housed behind the walls of the hacienda, protected and with free and easy access to water. In stark contrast, Rafaela and her compatriots occupied an exposed and unprotected location. Though they may have had the option of running for the shelter of the hacienda's walls at the approach of bandits or soldiers, they would have had to leave their household belongings unattended. Further, basic necessities like water could be accessed only with permission, and even then they had to be shared with the livestock. Rafaela certainly must have noticed the contrast in position between herself and the goats, and similar contrasts between life in the calpanería and life among the more privileged members of the hacienda community must have been equally noticeable. Just as kitchen architecture represents a dismantling of existing social mores among the peones, the redesign of the Hacienda Acocotla would have created a new behavioral norm, one that was based in power, control, and social roles dictated by economic class.

Scholars studying domestic architecture have argued that "residential architecture is perhaps the most visible symbol of the household as a whole."[36] What, then, does the architecture of the calpanería symbolize? As discussed previously, control over architectural space did not lie with the peones. Above all else, the calpanería was an architectural symbol to the hacendada, a symbol of power, control, and wealth, as well as of practicality. In spite of this, the calpanería was home to as many as thirty-four indigenous families. Though the hacendada controlled the space in which her workers lived, these families made the calpanería their home on a day-to-day basis, both with the help of the hacendada and in spite of her. As a result, the architectural remains are the product of a constant tension and negotiation between the needs of the hacendada and the peones. To understand this space and the lives of the people who occupied it, we have to acknowledge both sides of the equation, and we have to look beyond the architecture.

CHAPTER SEVEN

What You Eat

Life and Labor in the Calpanería

＊　　＊　　＊

I poured the next bag of artifacts out onto the table and groaned—another inestimable number of coarse redwares. When the cataloging was finally done, I would know that I had collected more than eighty-seven thousand artifacts during my excavations at the Hacienda San Miguel Acocotla. At that moment, I only knew that I had collected more than I wanted to catalog! My field lab was in my house, and bags and bags of artifacts were piled everywhere. The first floor of the house—dining room, living room, kitchen, and lab—was packed with bags and drying racks full of artifacts. I had cleared paths from the front door to the kitchen, lab, and the stairs that led up to the second floor; my couch and dining table were nothing more than a hazy memory.

I sighed, looking at the massive pile of redware in front of me. It was September, the height of the rainy season in Puebla. It was a great time of year for lab work. I began sorting the glazed from the unglazed, majolicas from redware. When this first step was done, I moved on to sorting the sherds into vessel forms—red polished comales in one pile, green glazed cazuelas in another. While I divided the ceramic wares up by vessel form, I also divided them by vessel portion. Rims from cups went into one pile, bases of *lebrillos* in another. This wasn't simply an exercise in organization. Identifying vessel forms would provide clues about what sort of food people were eating, how they were preparing it, and how they were arranging their mealtimes. Cataloging different types of ceramics and the locations in which they were found might hint at disparity in wealth between different households. The ceramics, when properly cataloged, would tell me a great deal about how life was lived in Acocotla's calpanería.

Though one would normally label every sherd, I had decided to delay that part of the process. Time was running short—I had to return to the United States in December. Because all artifacts excavated in Mexico must stay in Mexico, I needed to be sure that I had the raw data necessary to continue writing up the project when I returned to the States. Someday, I would get to labeling each and every sherd. For now, I was simply cataloging everything by provenience lot so that I would know what I had where. With that information, I would begin teasing out the material aspects of life at the Hacienda Acocotla.

✳   ✳   ✳

During the field seasons of 2005 and 2007, we collected a total 87,142 artifacts. After cleaning the artifacts in the lab, we cataloged them, entering them in a database. When the analysis was complete, I found that domestic artifacts, most of which were ceramic sherds, dominated the collection. This chapter is about foodways and relies heavily on those domestic artifacts, as well as the animal bones found primarily in the midden. Studying foodways is not just about food but about all the material culture and social interactions that come with it. Imagine any festive or celebratory meal. You have to plan a menu appropriate to the occasion, you have to get the food, you have to prepare it (for which you need equipment), and you have to serve it (which requires more equipment). After you've decided on the food but before your guests arrive, you have to decide what to wear and how to set the table (and the tone) for the meal to come. Every single step in this unconsciously complex process is culturally loaded.

Decisions made are based on culture, as well as a more specific social identity. Standing at the head of the Thanksgiving table, if that is where you belong, you have to decide who will receive white meat and who gets dark. For many, all the ritual associated with such a meal comes naturally. The manners drilled into us by our parents and grandparents during our childhoods come to the rescue. We know not to wipe our mouth on the tablecloth, and some of us even know which fork to use for the salad, but these niceties are not necessarily obvious to those outside our culture or even social class.

These rituals and their associated objects are important to more than just relationships among a handful of people. The material world we surround ourselves with, the way we organize it, and the way we use it all speak to who we are as a society and the grand historical processes affecting us. But how do the two connect when, by its very definition, daily life is mundane? French historian Fernand Braudel likens material (daily) life to the first floor of a three-story house.[1] Material life supports the two upper stories (for Braudel, economic life and capitalism) while remaining largely unexamined. Braudel writes, "Material life is often hard to see for lack of adequate historical documents," but, he argues, as the foundation for economic and capitalist processes, it acts to structure larger historical and economic events over the long term.[2] Braudel defined the practices of domestic life as one of the central facets of the *longue durée*, or aspects of life that change at painstakingly slow speeds and provide the undercurrent to brief periods of rapid change generated by historical events.[3]

Social meanings linked to the structures of everyday life manifest in the material world through *habitus*, an inculcated system defined by Pierre Bourdieu that functions as "principles which generate and organize practices and representations."[4] Habitus may be understood as a system of social habits or manners. These habits are socially learned behaviors instilled in members of a society from a young age that dictate such routine actions as the way one greets one's neighbor or the utensils one uses to eat a meal and may carry material correlates. For example, the number of forks set at your place for that Thanksgiving meal may dictate how you behave during that meal. For Bourdieu, structures of everyday life are generated and reproduced through habitus, and these structures, in turn, generate and reproduce habitus.[5]

Braudel suggests that the structures of everyday life may be difficult to study due to the lack of historical documentation. Bourdieu's habitus allows us to link Braudel's structures to the archaeological record explored in this and the next chapter. Because habitus dictates the material world, which in turn acts to reproduce a specific habitus in a new generation, we can "read" material culture as the physical manifestation of the structures of everyday life. But what does Acocotla's material culture tell us about the structures of everyday life in nineteenth-century Mexico?

* * *

Karime answered the phone promptly. She was expecting my call. Since returning to New York, I called every two weeks to check on the progress of the artifact analysis. Karime never missed my call, and this week, she was breathless with excitement. "I started reconstructing some of the vessels, Elizabeth!" she exclaimed.

"Great, find anything interesting?" I replied, giving her the opening she clearly wanted.

"Well," she said, "I was working in the lab, trying to put together some of the pieces of the coarse thin orange amphorae . . . "

I perked up. The presence of this particular ceramic was driving me nuts. Marta Adriana had initially identified it as coarse thin orange following our first field season, and all the experts had subsequently agreed with her. But it didn't make sense to me. In theory, coarse thin orange amphorae belonged to life in Classic period Mesoamerica, fully twelve hundred years earlier than anything else found on the site. When I pointed this out, people just shrugged and said, "Oh, it is everywhere. It probably just washed in to all sorts of contexts."

I was unsatisfied with this answer. Many of the pieces we recovered showed fresh breaks, not what one would expect of low-fired pottery exposed to the elements for one thousand or more years. Besides, the coarse thin orange ware amounted to more than 6 percent of our excavated ceramics—we had 3,741 sherds. The explanation of, "oh, there is just so much of it around . . . " was leaving me itchy—something didn't feel right. But since nobody has excavated a similar site in the region, there was nothing to compare it with. For now, I had to accept the idea that it was coarse thin orange.

So when Karime told me she'd found something interesting, I became, in turn, very interested. "What did you find?" I prompted eagerly.

Happy that she now had my full attention, Karime said, "Well, I was putting it together, and I found out that it is indeed an amphora, but it isn't anything like anything ever reported before. It is a completely new form of coarse thin orange."

"Good work." I said. "Put it aside somewhere safe. I'll see it when I get there next week. We can decide what to do with it then . . . "

When I arrived in Mexico a week later, I was eager to see the mysterious amphora Karime had pieced together. I'd been traveling for eighteen hours when she picked me up at the airport, but I didn't care. We had a quick dinner on Cholula's Zócalo before heading to my house. We dropped my bags just inside the door and went straight to the lab. Karime started rooting around through various boxes, muttering about the amphora being "here somewhere . . . " Finally, she found it and, with a triumphant, "Here it is," pulled it out of the box.

I took it from her carefully. She'd managed to reconstruct the rim, neck and shoulders of what was clearly a large amphora. It didn't look like any of the expected forms to me, but I was hardly an expert in Prehispanic ceramics. Trained as a historical archaeologist, I was at home with identifying pearlware, creamware, and transfer prints, but Classic period Meso-american amphorae? I needed to visit actual experts. Besides, I'd been traveling since long before dawn, and it was now approaching midnight. Exhaustion was beating intellectual excitement to an unrecognizable pulp.

Over the course of the following weeks, that amphora became my closest traveling companion. I tucked it into a commodious purse and took it everywhere. I pulled it out at dinner parties, in offices, in laboratories, and on street corners. Shoving it into the hands of Mesoamericanists, I would ask, "What is this?"

Most of those I inflicted my impromptu quiz on had seen the vessel when it was still in pieces. I had done just what I was doing now, but with a plastic bag full of fragments. At the time, every single one of my colleagues had replied without hesitation, "Coarse thin orange ware." With a certain amount of calculated duplicity, I didn't tell any of them that this was the same vessel but now reconstructed.

The results of my survey were split. About half of those asked said immediately, "Oh, this is just some sort of locally produced pot." I asked, "Is it coarse thin orange?" "No," they would respond emphatically, "It looks nothing like coarse thin orange." The other half of those I put, rather unfairly, on the spot with my ceramic query said, "Oh my! That is coarse thin orange, but I've never seen a vessel like it before. This is very exciting." These conflicting responses were intriguing and said much about our understanding (or lack thereof) of historic ceramics.

A few weeks of this back-and-forth did nothing to give me clarity. I sat in my lab, glaring at the chunk of amphora that Karime had so carefully reconstructed. Was it a fourteen-hundred-year-old amphora that had accidentally found its way into a nineteenth-century context? I doubted it, but if not, where had it come from? Why did it look so much like ceramics that had been made twelve hundred years earlier? Did the people who used it have a sense of the heritage of the object they held in their hands? What did this hunk of clay tell me about life in rural Mexico during the nineteenth century?

*　　*　　*

Making Ceramics

Few nineteenth-century hacienda sites have been excavated in Mexico, making the analysis of ceramics especially complex. The study of colonial-period ceramics, almost exclusively majolicas, has been steadily gaining ground over the course of the last thirty years.[6] In comparison, nineteenth-century material culture, and ceramics especially, has been understudied in Central Mexico, as have the production and consumption of locally produced wares.[7] Though we were able to identify some ceramics from published sources, Karime, Marta Adriana, and I faced the difficult task of describing and cataloging many previously unidentified ceramic types.[8] The majolicas were by far the easiest, but with only 5,215 sherds (7.5 percent of all ceramics), they were also, by number, less important than many of the other artifacts. Furthermore, majolica appeared in Acocotla's calpanería only as vessels such as bowls and plates, vessels that a person would have used while eating a meal, but what, I wondered, about the rest of the process? As hard as I tried to focus on the pieces that were well documented, I just couldn't forget the "uglier" pieces, pieces like the "coarse thin orange" that had been used for storage, preparation, and serving the meals. What were their stories?

Bonafacio squinted across the sun-drenched landscape. The burro nudged his shoulder impatiently. It was a hot, dry day. The burro didn't want to be

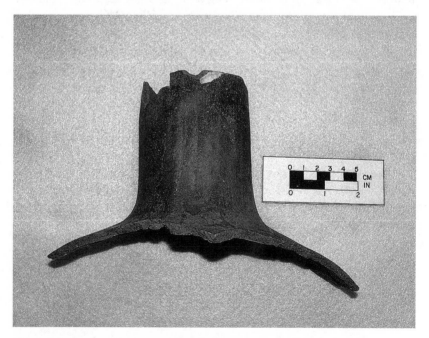

Figure 7.1. "Coarse thin orange" amphora.

out in the sun any more than Bonafacio himself, but Bonafacio didn't want to rush and get clay from the wrong place. Rosa was very particular. She had come out with him last Sunday to show him the new source she wanted him to use. Though Bonafacio helped with the ceramics business, it really was his wife's expertise that allowed them to be so successful. Rosa's family had been making comales and ollas as long as anyone could remember, longer probably. Even now, with the ready availability of fancier ceramics like they made in the big cities, traders came far and wide for ceramics from their village, and for Rosa's especially. The grandmothers claimed that people had been coming to the village for its pottery since before the Spanish arrived in Mexico. Though Bonafacio always showed them the respect due their age, he secretly shrugged this claim off. Maybe it was true, but what did it matter now?

Bonafacio shook off his musings and, as he finally located the pit that Rosa wanted him to use, dragged his burro forward. Reaching the pit, he unloaded his pick ax, shovels, and the deep, wide-mouthed baskets he would load the clay into. Quickly, he began to dig. The sooner he filled the basket, the sooner he could get back home for his lunch.

The ceramics found at Acocotla can be assigned to four broad ceramic types: coarse earthenwares, earthenwares, refined earthenwares, and porcelains. The difference in these types is primarily the extent to which the clay has been processed (in this list, from least to most) and in the temperature at which they are fired (from lowest to highest). The last two types, refined earthenwares and porcelains, were both the rarest we encountered and the easiest for us to identify. In Puebla, porcelain is a common artifact (and a common inspiration for majolica decorations), though only forty sherds of it were recovered at Acocotla. Chinese porcelain was widely available in the Latin American market after 1573 when the Manila Galleon began trade between Spain and the Philippines.[9] The trade route ran from the Philippines to ports in Acapulco and then overland via Puebla to Veracruz, where it was loaded onto ships bound for Spain. Initially, porcelain flooded Puebla's ceramics market and was sold at prices lower than ceramics produced both locally and in Europe, forcing local potters to attempt to compete with the newly popular style.[10] Artisans in Puebla, a center of ceramic production in New Spain, were influenced by Chinese designs because of the trade route, resulting in many of the blue-on-white majolica patterns still seen today.[11]

In spite of the ready availability of porcelain in nearby Puebla, its presence is limited at Acocotla. The forty sherds of porcelain were recovered during both survey and excavations. Though limited in quantity, the porcelain came from a variety of places. One piece of brown-glazed Chinese porcelain was recovered from above room 22's collapsed roof. This porcelain type dates to the eighteenth century, and thus it was presumably out of place above the roof.[12] It may have washed out of the adobes in the wall (which are full of fragments of ceramics) or been picked up elsewhere and dropped in the calpanería long after it was first thrown out. In the midden, we found the base of a French porcelain cup immediately below the plow zone. Using the maker's mark, we were able to date the production of the little cup to the last decade of the nineteenth century and first decade of the twentieth, a date that agreed with other artifacts found in the same level.

Refined earthenwares, in this case whitewares, were slightly more common than the porcelains recovered in the calpanería. In Mexico, whiteware vessels were imported from both the United States and Europe until the period following the Mexican Revolution, when Mexico began producing its own whitewares for the first time (though failed attempts at its production had been attempted in Puebla as early as 1837).[13] With the exception of sherds from recently produced vessels found during the surface survey, most of those we recovered seem to have been imported from abroad.

After about 1800, documentary and archaeological evidence suggests that whitewares dominated the Mexican market, largely because the establishment of Mexican independence led to the end of the tight trade restrictions that had been in place throughout the period of Spanish rule.[14] Some authors have argued that these imported whitewares dominated the ceramics trade in Mexico throughout the nineteenth century and identify the imports as the leading cause in the decline of Mexican majolicas, while others suggest that locally produced majolicas remained an important commodity.[15] This dominance of whitewares is not evident at Acocotla. A total of only 339 whiteware sherds were recovered. All of these were whitewares most commonly associated with the nineteenth century, including transfer-printed, flow blue, and annular wares. Some studies have suggested that access to this new elite good was indicative of social status, a suggestion that might explain the virtual absence of this ware type at Acocotla.[16]

Rosa smiled in satisfaction as she sunk her hands into the clay. Though making ceramics was hard, dirty work, she loved the feel of earth in her hands. Bonafacio had done the heavy work for her already, mixing the different

clays and her special temper—a blend of quartz and calcite. He had done
an excellent job; there were few air bubbles in the clay. Slowly, she began to
fit the clay over the bottom half of the mold for the large olla she was build-
ing. Someday, water would be collected in it. The olla would be kept near a
kitchen, ready for cooking, drinking, washing, whatever a family needed.
Rosa found a great deal of satisfaction in making something that no family
could survive without here in the highland desert environment. Though
many of her compatriots yearned to make things that required more creativ-
ity—pretty, decorated ceramics that wealthy patrons would display with
pride on their dinner table—Rosa loved making things that were necessary
to survival. As she molded her boring, utilitarian pot, Rosa dreamed of the
lives it made possible.

She finished molding the base of the olla and set it in the sun to begin
drying. This part of the construction was a careful balancing act. The base
had to be dry enough to support the top half of the pot while remaining wet
enough to accept the addition of the coils that would form the shoulders,
neck and rim of the olla. She turned her attention to the bases she had
formed earlier. The first she inspected was still too wet. It would collapse on
itself if she tried to build anything on top of it. The next was perfect, though.
She took it back to her place under the tree and began to roll the coils out.

Earthenwares and coarse earthenwares make up the bulk of ceramics
found at Acocotla, and these ceramics have some of the most mysterious
origins. Some are painted, some are glazed, some are slipped and polished, almost all are understudied and misunderstood. My "coarse thin
orange" amphora is an example of this problem. During the 1960s, historical archaeologists in the United States were electrified by the discovery of
Colono-Indian ware.[17] The debate about who was responsible for the production of the ware, indigenous or African peoples (or both), continues to
this day.[18] Mesoamerica lacks a similar discovery for the simple reason that
nobody has any doubt that indigenous potters continued their work long
after the arrival of Europeans; however, the omnipresence of the earthenwares also meant that nobody bothered recording or regulating it, and few
people have since bothered studying it.[19]

Still, we know a little about earthenwares like my "coarse thin orange."
Archaeologists have identified unglazed coarse earthenwares as a continuity of Prehispanic ceramic traditions. All assign dates ranging from the
sixteenth through the eighteenth centuries, and our findings at Acocotla
suggest that the tradition extends through the nineteenth century and into
the early years of the twentieth century.[20] The heritage of these vessels

seems to be long, as shown by the confusion surrounding the identification of the "coarse thin orange" amphorae. Gonzalo López Cervantes and
Florencia Müller both suggest that dates for the similar but lead-glazed
coarse earthenwares also range from the first half of the sixteenth century
through the beginning of the nineteenth century, though in reality manufacture of these goods continues today.[21] Many vessels indistinguishable
from those found in the archaeological record are available for purchase
in markets throughout Mexico.

Coarse thin orange is a well-known ware type found most commonly
on Classic-period sites throughout central Mexico. It is usually dated to
after AD 200, though research throughout the state of Puebla suggests its
production is more ancient.[22] In 1990, Evelyn Rattray published the results of excavations conducted in the Tepexi de Rodríguez region of
Puebla. There, she found ceramics workshops dating to the Classic period
that were producing a number of ceramics that are similar to those excavated at Acocotla, including my "coarse thin orange" amphora.[23] Today, in
the same region Rattray explored, the potters of Acatlán are famous for
continuing to produce ceramics that, again, are quite similar to those
found archaeologically.[24] It may be that potters from this region, just over
seventy kilometers from the Hacienda San Miguel Acocotla, supplied the
calpanería's inhabitants with much of their utilitarian pottery, as they had
supplied the needs of people in the region for centuries.

*The sun was hot already; it was going to be another dry and dusty day. Rosa
wondered when the rains would start as she spread her mat in her usual spot
in the main street in front of the market. She preferred a place in the middle
of the street, flanked by others on both sides selling their wares. Rosa knew
her ceramics stood out among the surrounding vendors—they were of much
higher quality than most. She settled comfortably on her heels, glad for the
few moments of peace that filled the market early when everyone was still
setting up shop. Later in the day, she would have to be focused as crowds
pushed and pulled. She would negotiate with multiple buyers while watching to make sure no one made off with any of her smaller cazuelas. It was
exhausting, but she enjoyed the weekly chance to be social. The gossip and
news she collected today would give her lots to think about over the next
week in front of her molds and kiln.*

*Rosa watched with bated breath as a few of the itinerant traders wan-
dered out of the bar down the street. They lived hard, lonely lives, and most
began their days with a beer and shot of tequila. But the traders knew it was
best to come to market early and have their pick of the best wares. When the*

sun and temperatures in the market rose higher, the traders would return to the cool shade of the bar, goods purchased. They'd share a few more hours of jokes, stories, and gossip before heading back on the road later that evening. Rosa stared down the street, nervous, but hoping that she would see him with the rest. Her racing pulse calmed as she saw Miguel stumble out of the bar and squint down the street in her direction. She never knew when he would appear, but his arrival boded well for her day at the market. He favored her ceramics above all others, knowing that his customers remained loyal to him thanks to Rosa's skill at producing high-quality vessels. His presence in the market meant she would make enough money to replenish her dwindling supplies. She desperately needed more firewood for the kiln. Maybe, if Miguel brought along a friend, there would be enough money left over to buy her family a bit of meat to have with lunch tomorrow.

She watched him stop in front of someone selling some cheap, hand-painted bowls. They were intended to look like the fancy Talavera that was sold in places like Puebla and Mexico City. She'd only ever seen a few pieces of the ceramic, but still she knew that what was for sale here didn't compare. Though they seemed popular enough, anyone who knew anything about pottery knew that these pieces were poorly made and wouldn't last long. Miguel asked the vendor a question, and Rosa smiled to herself when she saw Miguel roll his eyes and grimace at the vendor's response. He continued on his way toward Rosa. As he came closer, Rosa put her head down and began to rearrange her vessels, hoping not to look too desperate.

Trading Ceramics

Today, kitchen and tablewares find their way to La Soledad Morelos in one of two ways. People purchase mass-produced items such as aluminum cooking pots, redwares, and machine-decorated ceramics at the market and in stores in Atlixco during their shopping trips. Local, hand-made ceramics such as comales are brought to the village by vendors. These vendors carry the comales in and set up shop on a street corner. News of the vendor's arrival spreads via word of mouth, and women leave their kitchens to replace necessary equipment. We have no evidence for how, exactly, goods arrived at the Hacienda San Miguel Acocotla during the nineteenth century, though one imagines that both of these methods would have been employed then as now. Historical records also tell us that the tiendas de raya at some of Atlixco's haciendas seem to have carried household goods such as manos and metates.[25]

While we do not know exactly which route household goods took to arrive in Acocotla's calpanería, the homogeneity of the archaeological deposits suggests that the hacienda owner or manager may have provided the goods. Using minimum vessel counts,[26] I compared the relative abundance of ceramics in private (the individual calpanería rooms) and public (the midden) areas of the hacienda. With the exception of room 11 (which had a significantly smaller number of artifacts than the rest of the rooms), the relative abundance of majolicas and common redwares was matched in both public and private areas.[27] This even distribution of goods across the site makes it unlikely that people were buying their own household goods. Had individuals been responsible for acquiring their own ceramics, we might expect to see some differences in quality or quantity of various types of goods from home to home.

Feliciana leaned on her heels, stretching against the ache in her back. Every woman knew that making tortillas for her family was backbreaking work, and here she was making tortillas for two dozen families. Her children would starve without the work, but still she resented having to do it. She glanced over at Petra, who had been sound asleep in the shade of the smoke kitchen but was now rubbing her eyes. The little girl had seemed so much better the afternoon before, but her fever had risen overnight. Feliciana fought her rising feelings of jealousy. She knew it was an ugly feeling. But as sick as Petra seemed, Feliciana knew that the hacendado would send a doctor to check on her. The half-full bottle of medicine sitting next to the girl was proof of that. Feliciana had seven children at home. Nobody would send them a doctor. She knew from bitter experience. She had lost four other children before their third birthdays. She picked the mano back up again, ignoring the pain, and began to furiously grind the corn for the tortillas. She knew her anger was misdirected, but her children had to cope with much more serious dangers than faced Petra. Illness was really an inconsequential worry compared with the threat posed by her husband. His hangover would have him waking up in a foul mood by midday. She hoped her children had listened to her and gotten out of the house early.

Sniffing the air, Feliciana realized it was past time to add the meat to the mole. She put down the mano and turned, reaching for the chicken she'd plucked earlier and the old nail she kept handy. As she thought about her husband, Feliciana grimly pounded the nail into the chicken, and Petra sat up, giggling. Feliciana supposed the medicine had done its job; the child seemed better again. Feliciana tried to focus on the meal preparations. The chicken was a tough old bird, but her mother had taught her the trick with the nail—Feliciana could hear her voice, "Pounding the nail into the bones of an old chicken makes the meat younger tasting and more tender." She tossed the chicken into mole simmering in the big cazuela over the fire. It was very little meat considering the stew would serve more than eighty people. Only the calpanería's oldest inhabitants would actually get any, but the rest might enjoy a bit of the flavor. Feliciana smiled grimly as she went back to her work at the metate. At least Acocotla's peones didn't eat any better than her family.

Suddenly, she heard someone, somewhere out of sight, singing loudly. Feliciana looked up nervously as she heard the man approach. She watched the road where it curved out of sight around the casco until she saw Miguel trudge into view. She smiled, as glad of the bit of company she was about to receive as she was for the opportunity to replace some of her broken kitchen ceramics. The comales especially broke so often; having a couple more would allow her to make tortillas more efficiently, and the ones Miguel brought were especially good. They were as durable as they were pretty, their deep red slip polished nicely. Feliciana wiped the nixtamal off her hands with the hem of her apron and reached for a cup. Miguel would want a drink of water after his long walk and, after he'd cleared the dust from his throat, probably something stronger.

Filling the Pot

Feliciana's kitchen would have been stocked with the nineteenth-century versions of many of the things we see today in La Soledad Morelos. Her kitchenware would have included a mix of glazed and unglazed coarse earthenware vessels such as amphorae, cazuelas, comales, and ollas (fig. 7.2). She may have had a few *molcajetes* (mortars and pestles) and a colander or two. Feliciana's kitchen would also have been equipped with at least one basalt mano and metate for grinding corn to make tortillas. If today's diet is taken as representative, the inhabitants of the calpanería would have depended on tortillas for the bulk of their diet. Anybody responsible for preparing food for the peones would have needed to make mountains of tortillas, which would probably have been complemented by something to give them flavor, such as plain, unprepared chiles from the can (as is often done today) or some sort of salsa or mole, as the people of La Soledad do for special occasions like birthdays. Though the workload suggests there must have been multiple cooks in the calpanería, oral history tells us of only one.

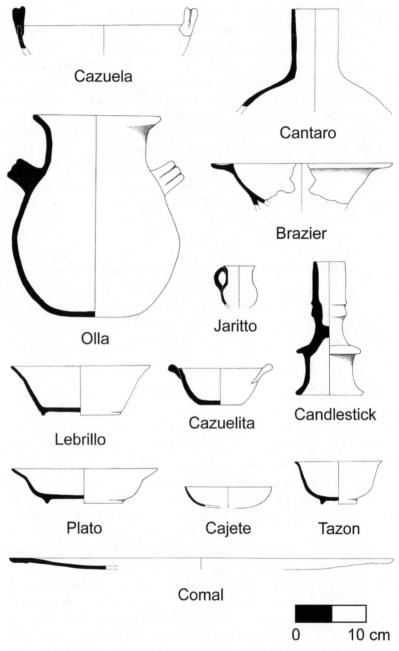

Cazuela

Cantaro

Brazier

Olla

Jaritto

Candlestick

Lebrillo

Cazuelita

Plato

Cajete

Tazon

Comal

0   10 cm

Figure 7.2. Vessel forms found at Acocotla. (Drawings by Karime Castillo Cardenas.)

Feliciana's first task in preparing tortillas would have been to boil dried corn (preferably white corn, though whatever was available would have served the purpose) in water with a bit of slaked lime and then let the mixture soak overnight—a process known as nixtamalization. Boiling the corn in water with lime makes it easier to remove the hulls, softens the corn for grinding, and adds significantly to the nutritional value of the tortillas.[28] Feliciana would have used some of the ollas we discovered for this part of the task. During excavations, we found 2,994 ceramic sherds that could be identified with complete certainty as ollas of many different sizes. Some of the ollas had been built on a potter's wheel or on molds and glazed with a lead glaze, while others followed the more traditional pattern of hand building, slipping in bright red, and burnishing. Of the nearly three thousand fragments we discovered, 6 percent showed evidence of burning on the outer surface. It is likely these 6 percent would have been used over a fire to perform a task such as nixtamalization.

With the corn softened, Feliciana would have rinsed the corn and removed its hulls. Under ideal circumstances, she would have used a colander for this task, an artifact that predates the arrival of the Spanish, though at Acocotla, we only found two sherds that might have come from colanders.[29] With the corn rinsed and cleaned, Feliciana would have then begun the very hard work of grinding enough corn to feed her family (or families in the calpanería) on a basalt metate. Manos and metates are indispensable parts of any Mesoamerican kitchen, but we found only nine fragments of metates and sixty-six whole or fragmentary manos at Acocotla. Because these items were made out of basalt, one imagines they rarely needed to be replaced, and women may have traveled with their metates, taking them from kitchen to kitchen when they moved.

Grinding corn for the tortillas would have been the most labor-intensive and time-consuming part of Feliciana's day. Indeed, grinding corn with these tools is such hard work that bioarchaeologists are able to identify evidence (such as malformed toe bones and osteoarthritis in the hips, spine, and shoulders) of this task in human remains.[30] One researcher even coined the term "metate elbow" to describe the osteoarthritic damage he saw in female skeletons.[31] When Feliciana finished grinding the corn, she would have set to work mixing the dough made up of the ground corn, water, and a bit of lard before forming the tortillas by hand. Finally, she would have grilled the tortillas on a comal, the other indispensable part of her kitchen equipment. Comales are large, flat, round ceramic griddles, and they were the most common ceramic vessel form found at Acocotla.

We found 16,999 comal fragments spread across every surveyed and exca-vated context at Acocotla. All were large, with rim diameters measuring fifty centimeters or more. They were hand-built vessels and had been slipped with a bright red clay and then either smoothed or polished in the traditional fashion. Some of the comales were thicker and had a more highly polished surface, while others were significantly thinner and had a less polished surface. All had a rough, sandy underside, an attribute that probably helped hold heat and made them better to cook on.

Tortillas would certainly have been the most important part of the meal, a staple that the peones would have filled up on. They would have sometimes been complemented with a stew of sorts, or mole. Depending on the type, Feliciana would have used a variety of spices, nuts, and seeds in her mole and, when possible, would have added some meat to it. She would have used either her mano and metate or a molcajete to grind up the ingredients for the mole, which would have gone into cazuelas. Cazu-elas are large, open-mouthed ceramic stew pots. At Acocotla, they varied in size from tiny (with a ten-centimeter rim diameter) to large (measuring more than fifty centimeters across). One thousand four hundred and forty sherds could be identified as having come from cazuelas, and about 13 percent of those were burned on the exterior surface. They were made out of a coarse earthenware and often had lead glazes on the interior surface. Many were decorated with dark brown lines, and they often had scalloped rims (creating an easy place to rest a spoon while cooking). These stew pots would have sat on hearths in the kitchen, bubbling away and scenting the air with eye-watering spices, but exactly what was in those stew pots?

*   *   *

"You want us to do what?" Adrián couldn't contain himself. Most of the other students were silent—probably with horror.

"I need you to go and interview some butchers."

"Butchers?" Evidently, Adrián was the self-appointed spokesman for the class.

"Yep. Butchers." The students all looked at each other in confusion. "How many of you read the article by Schulz and Gust that I assigned as part of the homework?" I continued.

A few of the students summarized the article for the rest of the class. I was teaching a course in historical archaeology and incorporating actual anthropological projects. I hoped the real projects would help the students make sense of the lectures and assigned readings while helping me with my own research.

I waited until the students finished outlining the article, and then I took over. I wanted the students to develop, as a class, a research program that would mirror that of Peter Schulz and Sherri Gust but with modern butchers. They were going to take the lead and develop questions and a methodology with my guidance. Then, they would go out in teams and interview butchers in a variety of places—stand-alone stores, city markets, and supermarkets—so that I could develop a baseline for the relative prices of different cuts of meat in the region. Comparing these with Schulz and Gust's rankings, I could get an impressionistic idea of the relative value of cuts of meat found at Acocotla.

After explaining this to the students, I turned to the chalkboard and wrote "1." Turning back to them, I said, "O.K., what is the first thing you need to find out?"

✻   ✻   ✻

For many, animal bones are just animal bones. For a zooarchaeologist, the food part of foodways represented by the animal bones is a window into the ethnic and socioeconomic identities and health conditions of the past.[32] During excavations in the winter of 2007, we collected 3,263 bone fragments and teeth. Of these, 142 could be identified only to the level of vertebrate; the rest were put into the broad categories of mammal, bird, reptile, and fish (no amphibians were identified). With as much specificity as possible, I identified species and skeletal part for each of those more than three thousand fragments of bone.[33] I also examined patterns of butchering and the condition of the bones—focusing on things like marks left by humans, such as burning; marks left by animals, such as gnawing; and weathering caused by extended exposure to the elements.[34]

When I was done, I had a comprehensive picture of the animals used for food by the calpanería's inhabitants. Mammals made up more than 90 percent of the collection. Of these, domestic species such as cows, pigs, sheep or goats, and dogs dominated the collection. Wild animals were diverse in species but few in number and included animals like the ringtail (a member of the raccoon family), opossum, nine-banded armadillo, rabbits, and marmots. We also found evidence of birds (primarily chicken and turkey, along with one duck bone), reptiles (turtles and/or tortoises), and, finally, a single fish bone.[35]

Of the animals that could be identified as either wild or domestic, only thirty-seven bones came from wild animals, compared with 850 bones from domestic species. While people were consuming primarily domestic farm animals, the pattern of exploitation of wild fauna hints at some interesting aspects of life in Acocotla's calpanería. A few of the animals may have been brought to the site for religious or ritual reasons. Regional stores and market stalls near the site now sell ringtails (*Bassariscus astutus*) for ritual/shamanistic purposes. In Atlixco, these animals are sold dried (and inedible) to shamans, who place them on altars when seeking specific aid in the spirit world.[36] Some of the bones in the collection speak to the use of pre-Columbian food animals, such as deer, turkey, armadillo, turtle, and dog—which may have been either purchased at a local market or hunted. Altogether, the remains suggest that the inhabitants of the calpanería were provided with or acquired cuts of meat or whole animals from the owners of the hacienda or local markets, or raised small domesticates themselves, but supplemented these foods with a limited supply of animals that were hunted or scavenged. The shift to a reliance on domesticated animals is something that is seen elsewhere in Mesoamerica and quite early following the arrival of the Spanish. Researchers have linked this narrowing of consumed species and increase in domesticates to the transformation and industrialization of local economies throughout New Spain, and so at the rapidly modernizing Acocotla, the results are no surprise.[37]

Butchering and burning marks on the bones tell us about the methods of food preparation used by the calpanería's cook. Six hundred and forty-nine of the bones had evidence of butchering on them, and those bones had, on average, 2.05 marks per bone. The majority of the identified butchering marks were shears, which would have been caused by the bones being broken down into manageable pieces with a sharp instrument like a machete. While butchering was reasonably common, burning appeared on only 160 bones. These two sets of data taken together suggest that meat was prepared in soups or stews (roasted meat would have resulted in more burned bones).

Though how people were preparing their meat was interesting, I wanted to know more. I calculated high- and low-utility percentages for all identifiable body parts to look at the economic and nutritional value of the food remains.[38] Utility percentages are calculated by dividing the body into the low-utility parts, or the head, tail, and the feet including the carpals and tarsals, and high-utility parts, or the remaining parts of the body. The low-utility parts offer the least nutrition and the least amount of meat. They also tend to be the least expensive pieces. The high-utility parts are the opposite, offering the most meat but at the highest prices. This calculation of utility is useful in two ways. First, it provides clues to how food is obtained. If animals are raised, butchered, and consumed entirely on site, we would expect that the actual high- and low-utility percentages of the collection would be close to the expected percentages for a single animal (because one doesn't cut the feet off of a cow and then send it back out to pasture). If, on the other hand, the meat were market bought, one would expect that high-utility parts (or low-utility parts, depending on economic access to goods) would be overrepresented.

Second, the calculation provides insight into any potential differential distribution of the carcasses across the site and/or socioeconomic access to purchased meat cuts. Some have identified high-utility cuts as being high in nutritional value and low-utility meat cuts as having less nutritional value.[39] Schulz and Gust took this observation to the next level and developed an economic correlation of beef cuts (and the bones they would be associated with) for Sacramento using newspapers from the nineteenth century.[40] The authors examined advertisements for meat prices, correlated those prices with the body part that would be represented in the archaeological record, and created a ranking (1–9) of the prices of cuts of meat and the part of the body they had come from. They then applied this analysis to archaeological remains and used the results to discuss socioeconomic status on four nineteenth-century sites in California.

Because the value of different cuts of meat is culturally dependent, I decided to test the applicability of this study to Mexican collections. Along with my students in an upper-level seminar on historical archaeology in Latin America, I developed an ethnoarchaeological study of meat prices in contemporary Mexico. The students went out and interviewed twenty butchers in Puebla, Cholula, and Atlixco, collecting information about the types of meat cuts sold, the popularity of the various meat cuts and species, the prices of each cut of meat (per kilo), and the tools used for butchering. The butchers worked in a variety of settings: city markets, neighborhood butcher shops, and chain supermarkets.

While I asked the students to collect data on all types of meat the butchers handled, only the beef cuts were comparable to Schulz and Gust's work, and so I focus on those here. The twenty interviewed butchers identified thirty-two cuts of beef, though not all twenty sold all thirty-two cuts. Prices varied among types of shop. At the chain supermarkets, prices for cuts of meat were as much as twice as high as the prices of the same cut of beef at a neighborhood butcher shop or city market. For example, rib eye was identified as the most expensive cut of beef. At the supermarkets, the price for rib eye ranged from 170 to 219 pesos per kilo (about $7 per pound).[41] At a neighborhood market in a well-to-do section of Puebla, however, that same cut of meat was priced at seventy-eight pesos per kilo. The differences in prices, while dramatic, did not affect the rankings of meat cuts. While the price of rib eye varied by vendor, it was, without exception, the most expensive cut of meat at all of the butcher shops that offered it for sale. Using the data collected by the students, I calculated average meat prices for each cut of beef and then ranked each cut by its average price. The prices at each butcher shop accurately reflected the rankings of the average prices.

I compared my rankings with those assigned by Schulz and Gust in their study of nineteenth-century beef cuts, as well as the high- and low-utility rankings proposed by Lee Lyman and applied to value-ranking on historic sites by Walter Klippel.[42] There were a number of minor differences in monetary rankings. For example, what Schulz and Gust identified as the second most expensive cut was first in my rankings, and the most expensive cut identified by Schulz and Gust was my second most expensive cut. When examined in terms of high and low utility, I found only one exception to this system in my rankings. A cut of beef, known in Mexico as *aguja*, was priced in my rankings as the third lowest, averaging 40.67 pesos per kilo. Aguja is a cut that comes from the middle of the rib cage (the midportion of ribs 6–10). It is comparable to the rib cut ranked second in price by Schulz and Gust and falls firmly into the category of "high utility" as ranked by Lyman and others, yet in modern-day Mexico it is one of the most inexpensive cuts available. What my students and I found was just how culturally contingent value placed on food can be. When we came back to the classroom to analyze the results together, we realized that while a suggestion of value may be made impressionistically, we should make it (and read it) with care.

High- and low-utility percentages are still informative, however, and tell us about more than just value. Figure 7.3 shows the expected and actual high- and low-utility percentages for cows, sheep and goats, and pigs. Expected utility percentages are based on the percentage of bones in a single animal that are categorized as either high or low utility. The actual utility percentages are based on a comparison of the total identified skeletal elements in each taxon that fit one category or the other. At Acocotla, both cows and pigs are overrepresented by low-utility elements, while the goats and/or sheep are overrepresented by high-utility elements.

Although it is likely, based on these data, that all these species of animals were butchered and consumed as whole animals on site by Acocotla's

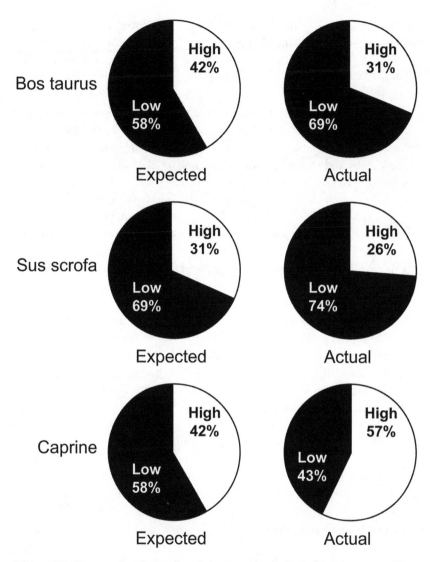

Figure 7.3. Expected and actual utility percentages for beef (*Bos taurus*), goat (caprines), and pork (*Sus scrofa*).

inhabitants, it appears that the peones either did not always have access to whole pigs and cows (perhaps the hacendado kept the best pieces for himself) or supplemented their diet with additional cuts of meat purchased and carried to the site. The possibly supplemental meat cuts were the most inexpensive by modern standards and often the least nutritious cuts, indicating a possible economic disparity in access to food. In contrast, sheep and goat meat is overrepresented by the high-utility cuts. Perhaps the indigenous peones liked sheep and goat better than other species. Maybe the hacendado liked them less. Research shows that Spaniards had a clear preference for beef and pork over sheep and goat during the colonial period.[43]

Archival research showed us that both cattle and goats were raised at Acocotla, but documentary and archaeological data from other parts of Mexico suggest that cattle ranching and access to beef products were largely restricted to the Spanish, while natives controlled sheep and goat ranching.[44] In fact, in the seventeenth century, the price of sheep was so low that it wasn't considered worthwhile to send them to market for sale.[45] The overabundance of high-utility body parts belonging to sheep and goat at Acocotla may reflect a greater control over these resources by the indigenous inhabitants of the calpanería, the hacendado's distaste for these low-status animals (and thus willingness to feed them to the peones), their lack of market value, or a combination of the three.

During interviews in La Soledad Morelos, we found that indigenous inhabitants of the hacienda did seem to have greater access to goats. During our architectural tours during the summers of 2004 and 2005, people who had lived at the hacienda as children identified one area as the Patio de los Chivos (or Patio of the Goats). When asked why this area was so identified, the people told us that the higher-status peones, the ones who worked directly for the hacienda manager, had lived in this area and had controlled the goat herds. Based on the bones we found during our excavations, the lower-status workers in the calpanería may have had equal access to these animals (but perhaps the inhabitants of the Patio de los Chivos were willing to share their meat or trash). Regardless, a variety of cuts of meat from various domestic species would have been regularly, if not abundantly, available to inhabitants of the calpanería as part of the meals provided by the hacendado.

Rafaela struggled back to the kitchen area with the olla full of water. Setting it down on the ground next to Hipólita, she looked around questioningly, ready for her next task. The cazuela was bubbling away on the fire, and the tortillas, warm and moist, were wrapped in their colorful towels. Rafaela's mouth began to water at the smell; she was so hungry lately. A pile of bowls sat on the ground nearby waiting for the women to begin serving the food. The bowls were a jumble of styles and sizes, some small, some large. Some were the pretty painted ceramics that Rafaela liked so much; others were the old-fashioned kind with no glaze, just a red-painted surface, shiny like the olla she had just filled with water. Hipólita caught her looking around for something to do and smiled, "I think we are ready. Why don't you call the men."

The men were standing close by, gathered in knots, joking and passing a bottle of mescal. Rafaela gave a quick shout and waved them over. Putting the bottle down, the men walked over and helped themselves to empty bowls. The hungrier grabbed the larger bowls, others thrust the smaller ones into the hands of their children. They moved slowly past the bubbling cazuela, and Hipólita doled out a bit of stew to each person, saving the bits of meat for the elderly, the pregnant women, and the sick. Nobody resented the way things were divvied up, knowing those who got the meat needed the strength. "Besides," thought Rafaela with a wry smile as she watched the familiar proceedings, "nobody would dare complain about anything to Hipólita."

With bowls filled, the men moved along and grabbed big handfuls of tortillas. Those so inclined picked up a mug and filled it with water from the olla that Rafaela had just brought from the patio. The rest would continue to share the mescal. Seeing that the men now had their food, Rafaela joined the women and remaining children in line. Though most people preferred to have their main meal of the day at noon, the peones' work schedule didn't allow much time to take breaks while it was light enough to work in the fields. Rafaela was surprised at how quickly she had adapted to eating her biggest meal in the evening, but given how much more she was able to eat thanks to the hacendado's generosity (they even got beef sometimes), and given how hungry everybody was after a long day in the fields, she supposed it made sense.

As Rafaela reached the front of the line, Hipólita slipped a bit of meat into her bowl with a quick wink. Rafaela blushed and looked around, wondering if anybody had noticed. She hadn't even told her husband about the baby yet. It was too soon. Rafaela never could figure out how Hipólita knew these things. She smiled her thanks at the older woman and quickly went to grab tortillas and some water. She wanted to join her family before anyone noticed or commented on the bit of chicken floating in her mole. Living in the calpanería was like living in a very large family, and gossip spread faster than anywhere she'd lived before. Reaching the spot her husband had chosen for their evening meal, she sat down on the ground with her family, carefully tucking her skirts around her legs. Her husband was trading jests with the family sitting closest, and the children were busy laughing with their father. Rafaela reached into her bowl with a tortilla and furtively grabbed the piece of meat. She ate it before anyone noticed and, with a sigh of relief, settled back to enjoy an evening in the field with friends and neighbors.

Setting the Table

Unlike the complex table settings many of us rely on today, Rafaela and her family, friends, and neighbors would have had very simple tableware for their evening meal. A few mugs would have supplemented what we recognize today as bowls in a variety of shapes and sizes, including some small enough to serve as cups. People may have poured their drinks into these cups and mugs, or they may have drunk directly from the bottles that we found during our excavations. Spoons, forks, and knives were virtually nonexistent. Then, as now, people would have eaten their meals with tortillas and their hands.

Ceramic tablewares came in a variety of shapes and sizes, all of which we would classify as bowls today (fig. 7.2). The bowls would, of course, have been ideal for eating the soups and stews that, along with tortillas, would have made up the peones' meals. Some bowls were traditional-looking wares—locally produced, hand built, slipped in red, and polished like many of the cooking vessels (fig. 7.4). Others were coarse earthenwares that had been lead glazed and were sometimes painted with decorations in brown, yellow, or white. Finally, a substantial proportion of the tableware was made out of majolica, the only class of vessels to be made out of this traditionally elite and expensive ware.

Majolicas are truly a "mestizo" product of Spanish colonialism. The techniques of tin enameling (which gives majolica its white background upon which designs are painted) were brought from Spain, where they had been developed with influence from Italy and the Arab world. Puebla became a center for the industry, and an industry it truly was. Production was tightly regulated for the high-priced, high-status vessels mass-produced in factory-like workshops.[46] Majolica is found on archaeological sites throughout Hispanic America, though only 5,215 sherds of it were recovered at Acocotla. In fact, the presence of any majolica in the calpanería is surprising, but access to elite goods like it may have been one of the things that drew workers to Acocotla. Similar contexts from the colonial period show many fewer fragments of this elite ware than the 7 percent of the 82,147 artifacts recovered during excavations at Acocotla, and today such goods are not present in La Soledad Morelos.[47]

With the establishment of independence in the early years of the nineteenth century, regulation for majolica production disappeared.[48] The majolicas found at the Hacienda Acocotla were not the well-made, regulated elite wares of an earlier century but were "seconds," which would have been significantly less expensive than those produced during the earlier

Figure 7.4. Polished coarse earthenware bowl.

era. Some of the vessels were produced by inexperienced potters who seem to have been uncertain about how to throw a pot and were unsteady with a paintbrush (fig. 7.5). Other fragments showed mistakes in production such as pots that had stuck together during firing. It seems likely that these seconds were made by untrained potters and sold at prices lower than those of the more "professional" majolicas. Interestingly, this pattern of poorly made ceramics is limited to the majolicas. Utilitarian wares were well-made, solid vessels. Not one of these locally produced vessels showed a single mistake in production. Though the majolica found in the calpanería would have been cheaper and clumsier versions of those that appeared on the hacienda owner's supper table, inhabitants of the calpanería were still given access to "elite" goods that inhabitants in surrounding villages would have had less access to.

Nineteenth-century majolica is characterized by a proliferation of patterns, something that is reflected in the archaeological materials at Acocotla.[49] When Rafaela and her family sat down to dinner, they would have been eating out of bowls in a variety of shapes and patterns. The designs were often poorly executed in unexpected color combinations. The design

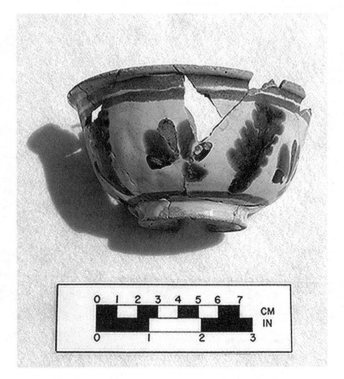

Figure 7.5. Tazón/taza, nineteenth-century majolica.

found on Oaxaca Polychrome (fig. 7.6), a ware that would become dominant during the twentieth century but was already being produced in the early years of the nineteenth, was described by one archaeologist as "splotchy efforts of an unknown nature in a variety of colors—blue, purple, green, and yellow—carelessly running over each other."[50] Though many of the ceramics found today seem quite ugly, especially compared with finer, more expensive types of majolica, they may very well have been a source of pride for inhabitants of the calpanería.

Other than the ceramics, little tableware would have been present at mealtimes—unsurprising given the absence of tables. We found a few cups and mugs made out of the wares already described, and some inhabitants of the calpanería may have drunk out of these. Alcohol consumption was also an aspect of life in the calpanería. During our excavations, we recovered more than one thousand bottle fragments, and more than half of those were olive green, brown, or dark amber, all colors used most commonly for liquor or beer bottles.[51] Flatware was limited to three fragments

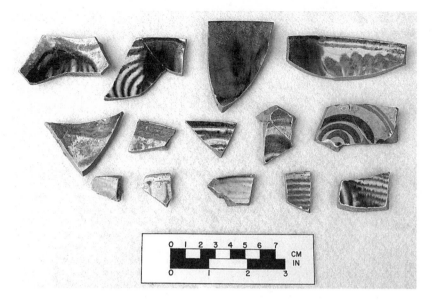

Figure 7.6. Oaxaca Polychrome.

of a single iron-alloy knife blade and the handle from either a knife or pocket knife. Bottles, mugs, and bowls, then, constituted the bulk of items that would have appeared at mealtime in the calpanería.

☆   ☆   ☆

I looked down at the bright red plastic bowl in front of me with what I hoped was a reasonably accurate expression of delight. A chicken head was floating in my green mole. Some effort had been made to pluck it, though feathers still clung to its neck and head. Its eyes had clouded over some, so I didn't feel too much like my meal was anticipating my every move. The beak looked . . . crunchy.

Somebody thrust a basket of tortillas into my hands, and I looked up. We were sitting around a long wooden table that nearly filled the space. The building we were in was a single room made out of cinder blocks with a corrugated tin roof. A bed had been tucked into the end of the dimly lit room. A variety of pots, buckets, colanders, and other necessary cooking implements hung above the bed. An unplugged fridge sat next to the bed, acting mainly as a stand for the tiny black-and-white TV that blared from its top. There were no windows and just one open doorway at the end of one wall. All of the available light in the room streamed through this doorway. Looking back at the chicken head floating in my bowl, I was grateful for the lack of windows.

I glanced up. Everybody, my students and our hosts, was watching me in anticipation. They all rushed to assure me that the chicken head was the best part and saved for the most honored guest. One of my students giggled. Someone elbowed her into silence. I smiled a big smile, expressed my thanks, picked up a tortilla, and reached for the chicken head. I took a big bite. I'd been right; the beak was, well, crunchy.

I heard everybody sitting around the table let out the breath they'd been collectively holding, and the chatter and laughter began again. I had no idea whether I was really eating the "best part" gifted to me as a guest of honor, or whether a joke was being perpetrated on the only gringa in the room. No matter. I had received the gift with the grace it required, or I had given everybody lots to laugh about after I left. Either way, they'd be delighted to welcome me into their homes again. As attention shifted away from me and toward the food in front of us, I let my mind wander from the chicken neck I was trying to swallow and back to the mental catalog I was compiling of the cooking and eating implements that filled the room. As I chewed, I compared them with those I'd found at the hacienda.

✼ ✼ ✼

An archaeologist excavating a house compound in La Soledad Morelos 150 years from now would find many similarities to the remains we see in the calpanería. Today, almost every kitchen in La Soledad Morelos has at least one mano and metate, though some women have their corn ground at a mill. Tortillas are made, now as they were then, over an open fire on a comal resting on three or five rocks. Some women use ceramic comales like those we find at Acocotla, while others have switched to the more modern metal version of the same form. Ceramic and metal cazuelas are still used to make moles for parties and holidays, though on a day-to-day basis, women often cook in smaller and less fragile aluminum or enamel pots. Though flatware is occasionally brought out for guests (especially gringas like myself), the villagers use tortillas and their hands to consume their meals.

On the other hand, what people eat out of and what fills those vessels are quite different. Ceramic bowls are nearly absent, and most people eat out of small plastic bowls, some decorated, some not. Though red is still the favorite color, the gaily painted majolicas of the last century are missing.[52] By today's standards, the calpanería's inhabitants had nicer tablewares.

The most significant differences between today and the past, though, are found in the faunal remains. Acocotla's peones had access to a diverse array of animal proteins. Though access was probably limited, many of the meats consumed in the calpanería are unheard of luxuries in the village. Today, chicken and turkey are by far the most common meat, supplemented by a pig slaughtered for community celebrations. It seems, then, that people would have had nicer tablewares and, sometimes, better food.

I began this chapter with a discussion of the ways in which material goods may speak to grand historical processes. The "coarse thin orange" amphora that plagued the analysis phase of my project is a testament to how little historical processes affect people sometimes. Though the form has altered slightly, the production process for this ware is little changed since before the birth of Christ. Empires have swept through the Valley of Atlixco—Teotihuacán, the Aztecs, the Spanish—but the people there continue to produce items necessary to their survival as they always have, in spite of tragedies such as the 90 percent mortality rates in the wake of the Spanish conquest.

One day during our excavations, a frustrated student shouted, "This is a waste of our time, its garbage. It looks just like what people have now!" She was correct in her identification of similar garbage but wrong in her suggestion that finding similarities was a waste of our time. Many of Acocotla's artifacts related to food and its preparation and consumption have a clear, Prehispanic Mesoamerican heritage, and that heritage persists to this day. The fact that it does persist in spite of wars of conquest, death, oppression under a new ruling order, wars of independence, processes of modernization, and wars of revolution is a testament to the strength of the people who endured the regular upheaval and destruction brought with each new world order. This persistence suggests that these artifacts, the processes by which they were made, and the activities for which they were used were of such importance to people that they did not relinquish or forget them in the face of the worst possible experiences.

Not everything remained the same, though. For example, majolica became available to Acocotla's workers during the years between independence and revolution but is completely absent in the descendant community today. Why this century-long blip on the millennial radar? The nineteenth century was a spectacularly important time in Mexican history, and the majolica anomaly highlights its importance. As discussed in preceding chapters, Mexican independence threw the country into a period of turmoil. Society had to be reordered. Regulations governing the production of goods like majolica disappeared, as did regulations governing the use and control of indigenous labor. By the last quarter of the century, President Porfirio Díaz was instituting drastic policies of modernization. As contemporary ideas about modernity, efficiency, and management filtered into Mexico, labor organization on the hacienda was redefined. We have already seen the impact of these ideas on architecture, living arrangements, and labor in the hacienda's calpanería. The presence of majolicas, the quality and diversity of the available food, and even the single piece of French porcelain found in the midden are other aspects of these processes. People were given access to goods that they otherwise would not get and food they could not otherwise have afforded to eat in return for their labor. After the Revolution, in which people were revolting against these very processes, the goods that were used to co-opt their labor disappeared along with the larger social structure.

For the most part, though, the foodways part of people's lives has remained largely unchanged. But people tend to be conservative about things like food. While food and foodways tell one story, other artifacts recovered at the Hacienda San Miguel Acocotla offer another, nuanced, tale of conquest and revolution.

CHAPTER EIGHT

Small Finds

*　　*　　*

"¡Ellie! ¿Una bolsa especial?"

I looked up. Ramón was jogging across the field holding something in his closed hand. As he approached me, he asked again for "a special bag" and opened his hand to show me what he'd found. I took the little earring and pretended to weigh the merit of using one of my small bags for the item. Ramón's eyes glinted hopefully while he tried to look too cool to care for the benefit of his digging buddy Jaime. My habit of putting notable artifacts, or small finds, into their own bags (so the artifacts wouldn't get lost) had turned into something of a competition between the two young men. Whenever either of them found something that was the slightest bit out of the ordinary, he would come running to ask if it deserved its own bag. Every time I answered his query with a nod, the finder would puff up and hold the find over his friend's head until the other was able to "catch up."

Putting aside the paperwork I had been filling out, I nodded, "Sí, una bolsa especial." He grinned as I reached into my toolbox for one of the little bags. I double-checked the provenience designation for Ramón's excavation unit on my log sheet and began filling the pertinent information out on the bag with my permanent marker—provenience designation, date, my initials, the bag number, and a brief description of the contents. I added the bag number to my bag log and the little bag before handing it back to Ramón, telling him to keep it with the other artifacts. He went off, proud but cool, to show Jaime what he'd found. I flipped through my note-book to the paperwork for the unit where Ramón was working and added a note about the earring he'd just discovered.

As I mechanically completed my paperwork, I thought about the woman who had lost the little gold earring 150 years earlier and found myself smiling in sympathy. I knew that particular frustration well. My jewelry box is full of unmatched bits of jewelry, each lone earring offering testament to my optimistic personality. I know the other isn't turning up, but discarding its match would mean admitting failure. As I stood in the hot sun updating my paperwork and keeping an eye on the competitive antics of Jaime and Ramón, I found it easy to imagine that the particular emotional experience of loss, regret, and frustration linked to the little gold earring I weighed in my hand crossed the boundaries of time and culture.

✳   ✳   ✳

When someone discovers that I am an archaeologist, *the* question pops out in short order. "What is the most interesting thing you've ever found?" they ask, eyes alight with excitement, visions of King Tut's tomb dancing in their heads. Like most archaeologists, it is the question I hear most of-ten. I don't want to disappoint the person looking at me so eagerly—over the second course or the grocery cart—but, truthfully, the most interesting discoveries are often the most mundane. The small finds that I carefully tucked away, to the delight or dismay of Ramón and Jaime, in my "bolsas especiales" were rarely earth-shattering discoveries worthy of a magazine spread, but they almost always gave me a bit of a thrill. And so, when asked the dreaded question, I answer, "My favorite finds are the little things that connect me to the experiences of the people I'm studying." And then I explain, trying to entice and entertain my listener with descriptions of life's detritus. Archaeological finds do not have to be worthy of a blockbuster museum exhibit to be magical.

There is a tendency to think about the artifacts we find in functional terms. We delicately hold an item in the field or lab and think, "What was *this* for?" We look at the pictures of artifacts in books, magazines, or the newspaper and wonder, "What did they do with *that*?" But our lives are filled with functional objects that are also imbued with meaning. The mug sitting on my desk serves the purpose of holding my coffee, but it also re-minds me of the vacation I bought it on. As I take a sip of my coffee, I remi-nisce about that long-ago trip to Florida's Everglades with a dear friend.

The mug's meaning is the link it gives me to that trip, that time, and that friend.

Not all connections are so obvious. Some things are purely functional until an action gives them meaning. A button on a shirt is a very functional item until it is lost. Then, that button becomes a source of irritation or embarrassment. Regardless of time, place, or culture, the human emotion linked to the lost button is easily understood. On the other hand, the meanings of some things are more profound and harder to interpret. These latter are often things whose function is based solely on the meanings we've assigned them. A rosary's function is defined by the meaning given it by the Catholic Church and the worshipper who holds it as he or she kneels in a pew. For those outside the Catholic faith, however, the rosary may be nothing more than an enigmatic religious symbol or even just a piece of jewelry.

Chapter 7 was about the things with which we set our social stage. The artifacts linked to food and foodways carried personal meaning, but their primary purpose was to communicate meaning to others and mediate social interactions. Though many of the small finds discussed in this chapter do convey meaning to others and some, like perfume, mediate social interactions, the primary importance of these things, these small finds, was to their owners.

When we gather around the Thanksgiving table, the setting and food control the ways in which my family and our guests act, defining who we are and how we treat each other. The porcelain and crystal, or paper plates and plastic cups, on the table in front of us tell us how to behave. But before dinner, as I stand alone in my room dressing for the meal, my hands reaching for makeup, jewelry, a favorite top, I have the opportunity to decide who I am going to be that night. While the artifacts I select will ultimately serve a purpose similar to those I earlier placed on the dining room table, my choice of jeans and an old sweater over cashmere and pearls allows me to introduce my personality and moderate society's definitions of who we should all be at that table.

When we encounter small finds in our excavation units, we are connected directly to their owners. These beads, buttons, and toys illuminate facets of people's lives—from leisure activities to religious beliefs—in the same way that my rejection of cashmere and pearls tells everyone invited to eat who, exactly, I am not. The artifacts discussed in chapter 7 tell us about social structure and historical processes. The small finds in this chapter hint at those things in the whispered voice of the woman who carried a thimble in her pocket, the man who cursed when he lost a shirt button, and the child who dreamed of the future while galloping a clay horse across a dirt floor. Because the small finds I tucked into my "special bags" are so connected to their former owners, they provide us with a glimpse of lives that often went unrecorded. These artifacts intimate, for example, the ways in which women and children spent their days, helping fill the gaps left in the historical record and feeding our imaginations about lives otherwise invisible.

Nicolás rode slowly, thinking about his wife. Everybody knew she was pregnant again, even though she hadn't told him or anyone else yet. Losing the last child so young had shaken the entire family, and his wife was still having nightmares. He had spent many nights holding her close while she cried silently into the dark, both of them trying not to wake their children in the calpanería's close quarters. His wife's waking behavior was just as troubling. She checked on the children constantly, dosing them with the medicines sent by the hacendado at the slightest hint of real or imagined illness. Perhaps she was too scared to acknowledge the baby growing inside her. He hoped he could coax her into a more relaxed frame of mind. All this worry couldn't be good for the new child.

Balanced on the burro, Nicolás awkwardly shifted the rifle in his right arm so he could settle the flowerpot more firmly between his legs. He hoped that the sentimental offering of the pretty flowering plant would help raise the spirits of the whole family. At the very least, the red flowers would brighten their little room a bit. If the flowers failed to do the trick, then perhaps the gaily-painted clay mug he'd bought from the bruja would help. The witch had sworn that Rafaela would cheer right up if she drank from it regularly, and Nicolás was ready to try anything. Besides, it was supposed to help the baby grow strong in her belly, something that would improve his wife's spirits more than anything else.

Shifting the heavy rifle yet again, Nicolás looked around nervously. The trip was long, but Nicolás was proud that the mayordomo trusted him enough to send him to the hacendado in Atlixco with the account books. He got to make the trip every month, and he always brought something back for the family. He used to look forward to the monthly break in his routine, but things had become so dangerous in the valley. He was nervous. He hoped the rifle provided some sort of deterrent. He couldn't imagine having to take on an entire pack of roving bandits himself. Still, the greatest danger would have been on his trip into town that morning. Surely everyone would know he was returning to the hacienda with no money left.

On Being a Father

Nicolás's life would probably have been slightly better recorded than most of his immediate family members. Like other male heads of household, Nicolás had his employment at the hacienda, and perhaps the wages he received for that work and any debts he incurred, included in the historical record. Thanks to a particularly detailed census taken in 1893, we know the same things about Nicolás that we know about his wife, Rafaela, and their six living children—age, religion, health, literacy, language, and race.[1] But as far as history is concerned, that encompasses all that was significant about Nicolás's life. The story of an Indian and a peon just wasn't worth telling.

None of the artifacts we find can be linked directly to Nicolás, but the small finds that can be dated to the same time that he occupied the hacienda tell us something about the lives of all the men living in the calpanería during the last quarter of the nineteenth century. Though this chapter separates the stories of men, women, and children, in reality assigning artifacts to one group of residents or another is difficult. The decisions inherent in this process require us to make a few assumptions about life in the past that may or may not be valid. For example, the historical records would have us believe that the scythe found on the floor of the calpanería's room 11 belonged to the man who lived in that room (fig. 8.1). There is a good chance that it did, though oral history tells us women and children worked in the fields alongside husbands and fathers. Perhaps Nicolás or one of his neighbors owned the scythe, but it is possible that Rafaela was the one to wield this particular tool. Today we can only guess as to the gender and age of the scythe's owner, but our guess is an educated one. In La Soledad Morelos, women and children go to the fields, but their role is planting and gathering. A scythe like the one pictured here is a tool used by the men of the household, and so, rightly or wrongly, I include it as part of Nicolás's life.

Nicolás's story puts other items into his hands that may or may not belong there. We know that the peones must have had access to firearms, as attested to by the seventeen bullet casings and three complete bullets found during our survey and excavations. The bullets and casings belonged to a variety of calibers and would have been used in anything from pistols to rifles. Two bullet casings have dates on them (1901), and both were recovered from immediately below the plow zone in the midden. Bullet casings with inscriptions tell us that the ammunition was produced in

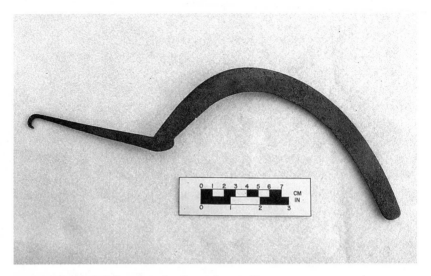

Figure 8.1. Scythe, found on the floor of room 11.

England and the United States. Though we do not know exactly what the pistols and rifles would have been used for, the dearth of wild animals found in the faunal remains suggests their primary purpose was not hunting. Historical records from Atlixco's archives document the dangers of rural life. During the nineteenth century, roving bands of outlaws attacked lone travelers and small settlements throughout the Valley of Atlixco. Given the exposed nature of the calpanería's architecture, pistols and rifles may have been necessary for protection.

We can also guess what Nicolás was wearing as he rode across the plains of Atlixco. An early twentieth-century photographic register found in San Jerónimo Coyula shows men, young and old, dressed in the white cotton shirts and pants that would later be associated with the rural Mexican peon. At Acocotla, clothing appears in the archaeological record primarily as buttons, fifty-one of which were recovered. Almost all were small, molded china or "Prosser" shirt buttons with either two or four holes.[2] We found a variety of colors, including white (the most common), turquoise, brown, orange, and black. One white shirt button was decorated with green transfer printing, a style known as "calico."[3] The shirt button may have been what the hacendado made available to his workers in the hacienda store (either as clothing or as goods for repairing clothing), or it could have been selected deliberately by someone looking to add something different and unique to their garments on a rare trip to the market. While the majority of buttons we found at Acocotla were small, china shirt buttons, a few other, less common types were found. Similar in design to the glass buttons, we found one carved bone button that was plain and undecorated with four holes through the center, like a clumsily handmade copy of the more common, industrially produced styles. We also found two copper alloy buttons with shanks. Both were undecorated, domed buttons with a single-hole shank, both, perhaps, lost from a man's coat.

A silver cuff link that we found in the midden was more out of place. The cuff link is decorated with a shell or floral pattern and has a straight shank with a quarter-moon fastener attached. It is difficult to imagine one of the peones headed out to work in the fields with sliver cuff links fastening his clothing. Perhaps it was lost by the hacendado or one of his visitors. It may have ended its useful life in this way, or, being made of a valuable material, it may have been picked up and kept or reused by one of the calpanería's inhabitants before finding its way into the midden.

Nicolás stood in line, looking nervously around the Patio Abierto. He came here every week to collect his wages, but he never got used to this normally forbidden space. He hated the mysterious ritual of it all. The space, the mayordomo, the damn account book. . . . The written word held so much power and, in the hands of someone he trusted as little as the mayordomo, made him uneasy.

The line moved forward slowly, but Nicolás found himself at the front facing the mayordomo and his account book across the big table all too soon. The mayordomo showed him the books, pointing to letters and numbers that were illegible to Nicolás. He knew how much money he ought to receive in exchange for his labor and the labor of his wife and children this busy harvest week, but there were always deductions—a bit of money off for something bought from the store, the cost of their housing and food, a reduction in pay for the day his son had not been ready to work in the field at the exact moment the sun crested the eastern horizon. Nicolás struggled to keep track of these things in his mind; he just couldn't bring himself to trust the mayordomo. But the weeks ran together, and it was so hard to remember if his son had been late this week or last. Nicolás shrugged and just held his hand out, waiting for whatever the mayordomo chose to drop into his palm. It felt like so little, but it was more than his neighbors back in his home village of Huexocuapa were able to bring to their families.

We found six coins during our excavations at Acocotla, three of which had readable dates and text. All three are one-centavo pieces dating to 1864,

1884, and 1906. Finding coins of any sort was a bit of a surprise given the presumed poverty of the calpanería's inhabitants, but perhaps the very few coins in the very small denominations we found underscores the lack of disposable income. In 1910, adult males were paid thirty-three centavos for a day's labor.[4] Assuming a (reasonable and conservative) twelve-hour workday, each lost centavo represented about twenty minutes of labor. Oral historical accounts tell us that women and children made substantially less. One coin may have represented more than an hour's labor for a child.[5] We do not know how much women were paid since no record of women as workers was kept.

The other three coins we found were made of silver and much larger in size, but the surfaces were completely abraded. With no identifying marks, it is impossible to say whether they were larger denominations or even coins at all in our modern understanding of state-issued currency. On some haciendas, workers were paid in tokens to be used in the hacienda store rather than in actual money, forcing the workers to patronize the tienda de raya, regardless of price or availability of goods.[6] Under this system, the workers would have been further and more effectively locked into the hacienda economy and its employment. Unlike the tokens found at other haciendas, however, these silver pieces have no markings at all.

The experiences recounted thus far paint a bleak picture. But if life was so dreary and controlled, why did anyone live in the calpanería and work for the hacendado? The money is one answer. It may not have been much, but the wages represented a steady income and an entrée into the cash economy. Today, descendants of Acocotla's workers struggle to live above a bare subsistence level. In the modern world, the farmers cannot make do with just enough to feed their families. Money from the jicama and peanut harvests is quickly spent at the end of the season, but cash is needed year-round to buy seeds for next year's planting or a graduation costume for a child finishing elementary school. To meet these expenses, men leave, permanently or seasonally, for the United States so that they can earn money to send home to an otherwise largely cashless village. One hundred and fifty years ago, their ancestors made a similar choice to accept the costs of hacienda employment in hopes of bettering the economic position of their families.

Money was not the only reason to sign on for residential employment at the hacienda. Though Nicolás's little calpanería room looks uninviting to us, it may have been palatial to him and his family. The architecture was nicer than anything he would have inhabited in his home village. We know from the archaeological remains that the small rooms were not barren; people made an effort to transform the shelter into a home. The remains of a flowerpot may have held a flower that brightened the room, and a small black pitcher, incense burners, and candlesticks hint at the presence of a family altar.

Rafaela looked at the Day of the Dead altar in the corner of their little room. Nicolás had built the crude table at her urgent request. He had complained that they didn't have the space; they were sleeping on top of each other as it was. She knew his complaints were legitimate, but she couldn't let the holiday pass without making sure her little boy was properly fed.

She fingered the tiny, black pitcher and remembered watching José's struggle to keep breathing. He'd been so small, not even a year old, when the epidemic swept through the countryside. She supposed she was lucky. Many of her neighbors and friends had lost two or three children, some in the space of just a few days. She'd only lost one son, but she still felt the emptiness. He'd been such a sweet little boy. Even Feliciana hadn't complained about having to watch him while she made the tortillas.

Rafaela gently placed the pitcher back on the Day of the Dead altar while she rubbed her growing belly with her free hand. Though she knew it worried her husband, she couldn't shake the fear that filled her. As if in response, the baby kicked her hand hard, drawing her out of her melancholic reverie. She reached for a bit of clay and put it in her mouth. As she let it dissolve on her tongue, she smiled ever so slightly. The new baby would be a handful, and she was glad. Perhaps he would have the strength to fight his way out of childhood.

On Being a Mother

We came across a small pitcher made out of black glazed redware in the field one day. One of the workers from La Soledad Morelos shrugged, "This is from a Day of the Dead altar. It's small because it is for an offering to a child." The other workers nodded in agreement, making comments about how sad it must have been for the family when the child had died. In their minds, there was no doubt as to what the pitcher symbolized today, though its meaning could have changed over the course of the last 150 years.

While digging at Acocotla, we found more than seventeen hundred fragments of black glazed redwares like the miniature pitcher. This locally produced ware gets its name from its deep graphite-colored surface. Archaeologists working in Mexico find the ceramic in contexts dating to between 1850 and 1930, but in Florida and the Caribbean, it appears on eighteenth-century Spanish sites and seems to come from Mexico (suggesting its antiquity is greater than we suspect in Mexico).[7] By the second half of the nineteenth century, Rafaela would have decorated her Day of the Dead altar with ceramics made from this ware type. The little black pitcher would have been joined by candlesticks and incense burners made out of the same ceramic. Indeed, candlesticks and incense burners together accounted for more than 80 percent of the black glazed redware we found at Acocotla.

In Mexico today, black glazed redware is still commonly produced and used for religious events and holidays, especially Day of the Dead and funerals (fig. 8.2a,b). Archaeologists have suggested that the ware was used for the same purposes in the past, and given the fact that incense burners and candlesticks are common parts of the ritual kit, it seems likely this inference holds true.[8] Informants in the descendant communities of La Soledad Morelos and San Jerónimo Coyula say that each vessel may only be used once, and after the ceremony is over, the vessel must be discarded or packed away in storage. One older and delightfully practical woman, recognizing the financial infeasibility of this practice, clarified. She explained that the vessels may only be used by an individual or family once, but that afterward, they were frequently passed down to other members of the community who could not afford to buy new vessels every year. She also said that courting couples often exchange old black-glazed redware vessels in the period leading up to their engagement as a way of, as she put it, flirting.

Black glazed redware was not the only ceramic we found that may have had special meanings and purposes. We also found three sherds of Guadalajara Polychrome, also known as Tonalá Bruñida ware. This ware type was produced near Tonalá, Mexico, between 1650 and 1810.[9] Guadalajara Polychrome is a burnished ware with a gray-cream ground upon which designs are hand painted in black, brown, rust, and red.[10] The three sherds recovered at Acocotla are painted in red and may be from one small mug. During the eighteenth century, it was believed that vessels made from the clay used for Guadalajara Polychrome had beneficial cosmetic and medicinal purposes, including "inciting women to eat clay and the dropsical to drink."[11] The fame of these vessels extended well beyond Mexico's borders, and Guadalajara Polychrome was exported to Spain, where it was understood that the vessels had "been created for the ladies who enjoy drinking the water and eating the clay."[12]

The little mug traveled a long way, more than five hundred kilometers as the crow flies, to get from the place it was made near Guadalajara all the way to Acocotla's calpanería. Perhaps someone brought it into the

Figure 8.2*a*. Day of the Dead, San Jerónimo Coyula, November 2007: black glazed redware on a family altar.

calpanería because of the ceramic's famed medicinal properties. The description of the mug as being something that encourages women to eat clay sounds a bit odd to our ears, but geophagy is widespread. Pregnant women are the most common eaters of earth, evidently because certain types of clay act as a primitive sort of prenatal vitamin, and it is a common

Figure 8.2b. Day of the Dead, San Jerónimo Coyula, November 2007: black glazed redware on grave.

practice among poor women in Mexico today.[13] The little mug may have found its way all the way from Guadalajara and into the calpanería to treat a woman battling a difficult pregnancy.

During our excavations at Acocotla, we found many other artifacts that would have carried religious or ritual meaning. We can easily understand the significance of two crosses that we dug out of the midden (fig. 8.3). They tell us that the 1893 census that defined the peones as Catholic was not untrue; some form of Catholicism must have been practiced. A delicate copper cross found just above the floor of the midden structure was probably part of a rosary or a pendant (fig. 8.3, right). The other, more curious, is a small, carved bone cross that has a design vaguely reminiscent of Celtic art (fig. 8.3, left). Its actual meaning and design are unknown. The cross carries a design that is certainly not commonly found on Spanish colonial sites, but it is evocative. One potential association comes from the number of concentric circles carved on both faces of the cross. Including the central hole, the number of sets of circles totals seven. Seven is a significant number on Franciscan rosaries.[14] The Franciscan rosary involves prayer dedicated to the contemplation of the Seven Joys and the Seven Sorrows of the Virgin and is an alternative method of praying the rosary. It is easy to imagine that Rafaela and her neighbors felt a particular connection to and deep understanding of the prayers associated with the Seven Joys and Sorrows and that one of them may have clutched just such a rosary while she prayed for her sick child to survive whatever epidemic was making its way through the calpanería.

The crosses are obvious symbols of devotion, but they are not the only ones we found. Twenty-seven beads—the remains of jewelry, clothing

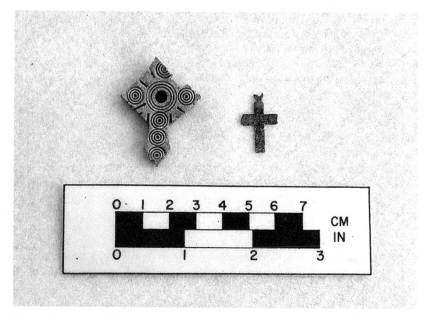

Figure 8.3. Carved bone cross (left) and copper rosary cross (right).

decoration, or religious amulets—were recovered. Beads are common on postconquest sites throughout the Americas and were imported in huge quantities during the colonial period to be used for rosaries and jewelry, as well as in trade with local indigenous groups. During the sixteenth century, more than three million beads were exported each year to Mexico and the Caribbean from Spain.[15] The majority of beads recovered at Acocotla were glass, though two stone, one bone, and one plastic bead were also recovered.

What did the calpanería's inhabitants use these beads for? It is impossible to know for sure. Perhaps they are the remains of costume jewelry, maybe some of them dropped off a beaded blouse, some might have been strung on a rosary with one of the crosses we found, and a few could have been used to heal or protect one of the calpanería's inhabitants. Two of the beads were made out of natural materials, one of jet, one of amber. During the colonial period, many Europeans believed jet and amber had beneficial properties, beliefs that may have been adopted by indigenous peoples, and the two beads we found may have been part of amulets. Europeans believed that jet would protect its wearer from evil, most especially from the evil eye, and would cause demons to flee, could cause abortion, and was a detector of virginity.[16] Amber had its own magical properties. It was believed to aid in gestation, birth, and lactation for women, aid in teething of infants, protect from poisonous things, and protect against witchcraft and spells.[17] Rafaela may have worn an amber bead to help with her pregnancy, much like she could have sipped from the cup of Guadalajara Polychrome in hopes of strengthening her unborn child. Maybe she gave the bauble to one of her children, tying an amber bead around Petra's neck or wrist, for example, in hopes of protecting her from the evils that took the life of one of her other children.

Some of the beads represent nothing more than a bit of common vanity. Many were probably part of the mostly cheap costume jewelry that was worn by the women and girls in Acocotla's calpanería. During our excavations, we found both earrings and rings. With the exception of a single earring, most of the jewelry was made of a copper alloy with glass bead accents. We found two small copper rings in the midden; both were very plain in design (fig. 8.4c,d). One of the rings has a wide copper band fronted by a copper disk with the initial "C." The other was similar in manufacture but has a cobalt blue glass bead mounted in the center in place of the initial.

Earrings were the most common jewelry item recovered at Acocotla (fig. 8.4a,b). We found seven unpaired earrings during our excavations in

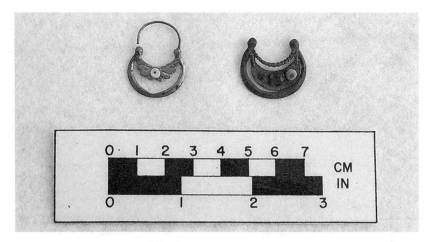

Figure 8.4a. Earrings: gold with coral and copper with glass beads.

the calpanería rooms and the midden. Most of the earrings were simply made, of copper and glass, but one was made of gold with a coral bead in the center (fig. 8.4a). The similarity in design but difference in materials and workmanship between the earrings pictured in figure 8.4a is striking: one of the two is a delicate, hand-worked bit of art made out of precious

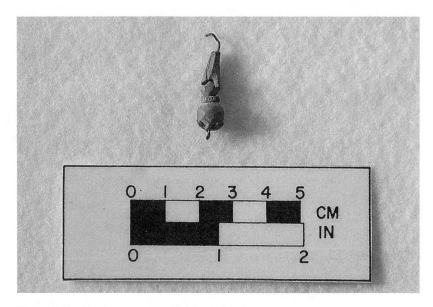

Figure 8.4b. Earring: copper with plastic beads.

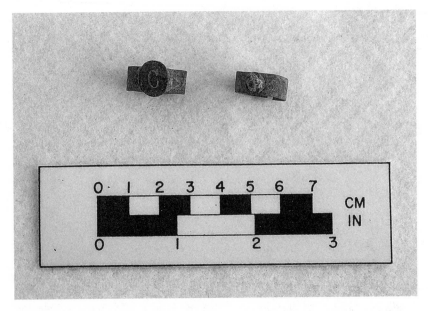

Figure 8.4c. Copper rings, monogrammed and beaded.

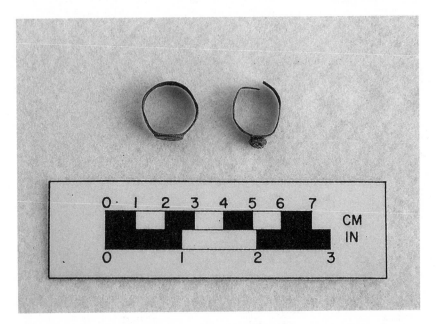

Figure 8.4d. Copper rings, monogrammed and beaded.

materials; the other is a cheap, machine-made imitation punched out of inexpensive materials. Maybe Rafaela was given the fine earrings as a gift, a gift that generated a certain amount of envy among the other women of the calpanería. The envy they felt could have encouraged one of the women to buy the cheap copy in an attempt to capture a bit of the glamour that came with Rafaela's earrings. Or maybe Rafaela lost one of her pretty gold earrings, as women often do, and sadly bought a cheap copy to replace the prettier but more expensive ones she had previously worn.

Pieces of jewelry were not the only form of luxury goods recovered at the calpanería. During excavations in the midden, one single complete bottle turned up that would have once held perfume (fig. 8.5). Though it is easy to think of the life of hacienda workers as one of unmitigated toil,

Figure 8.5. Perfume bottle.

sadness, and exploitation, in fact there were surely moments of basic human joy. The calpanería's rooms housed people who were more than just workers. Labor at the Hacienda Acocotla gave workers access to disposable income, some of which was spent on pieces of jewelry or a small bottle of perfume. Perhaps these items represent some of those happy moments common to people around the world (regardless of economic standing): a man's attempt to begin a flirtation with a pretty girl, a young woman's desire to make herself pretty in the eyes of her parents, her children, or her boyfriend, or a husband's loving birthday gift.

While it is easy to assume that the owner of a found earring or ring was a woman, I am being unfair in assigning religious items, prayer, and worry about children to women while leaving money and tools in the hands of men. Men worshipped and worried, too, just as women went out into the fields and managed household finances. Still, many of these assignments that I make here are made in La Soledad Morelos today, and the expectations I perpetuate here are mirrored by the expectations of the descendant community. If thousands of years of history are to be believed, though, some artifacts almost certainly belong in the hands of women. Such objects were all things that would have been used for textile work and include artifacts that might be categorized as both European and indigenous.

Rafaela rubbed her aching temples. Embroidery was hard work by the light of a fire, but now that her pregnancy was so advanced, it was the only work she could do that would bring in money—even the mayordomo recognized the inadvisability of sending her out into the fields at the moment. She looked up and caught her husband watching her from across the fire with a worried frown. Nicolás was supposed to be relaxing with the other men, but his mind was clearly not on what his friends were saying. She nodded at him reassuringly, breaking their shared gaze as she felt the weight of a hand resting gently on her shoulder.

Turning, she met the understanding eyes of Hipólita. Gently, the older woman tried to hand her the familiar and well-worn drop spindle. "Let me finish the fine work for you, these old eyes don't even have to see to follow this pattern anymore. You finish spinning the cotton. My fingers are just about worn out."

Rafaela laughed at the thought of Hipólita's toughened hands wearing out on cotton fibers, but she also knew well the folly of disagreeing with the older woman. Hipólita had been winning battles of will since before Rafaela learned to speak her first word. Rafaela dropped the embroidery into Hipólita's lap. She felt a slight twinge of guilt at her sense of relief. Hipólita's old eyes would not be up to tracing the pattern in the dim and flickering light. Rafaela suspected that Hipólita would toss and turn all night because of the headache she would get, but she knew if she didn't agree to the trade in tasks, the older woman would toss and turn from worry instead. Sighing quietly, she decided that at least one of them might get a good night's sleep.

Shifting out of her cross-legged position and on to her knees, Rafaela wound the completed thread around the spindle Hipólita had handed her. As the thread ran through her fingers, she admired the evenness of Hipólita's spinning. Though women in the valley had been spinning cotton for more decades than anyone could count, it was difficult and skilled work, work that Rafaela just didn't have the patience for. But, as with many things, spinning was a task that Hipólita excelled at. As she set the spindle dancing and drew the next bit of fiber out, Rafaela hoped she wasn't ruining her friend's work. Regardless, it wouldn't be up to Hipólita's standards. Little ever was.

Three clay spindle whorls were recovered at Acocotla, one Prehispanic and the other two dating to the historic period (fig. 8.6b). Spindle whorls are the part of drop spindles that preserve in the archaeological record and are a common artifact found throughout Mesoamerica. The small size of the spindle whorls we found in our excavations indicates that they were used in spinning cotton thread, unsurprising given that the region was one that cultivated the crop prior to the arrival of the Spanish.[18] Throughout the world, women living in agricultural communities are skilled spinners, most working with nothing more than a weight (like the ceramic whorls we found) and a stick, or spindle, of some sort. Women often carry spindles out into the fields, or even spin on a long bus ride, and it seems likely that women living in the calpanería would have been no different, keeping a drop spindle in the pocket of an apron ready for idle moments.

In communities around the world, the production of cloth is a defining aspect of femininity in much the same way that the production of tortillas is and was definitional in central Mexico. The women of Atlixco had produced cotton thread since long before the Spanish arrived, just as they had produced tortillas for their families.[19] But during the nineteenth century, spinning may have become a casualty of the new world order in which women were pried from their homes and thrust into the fields, a transformation that may have been accelerated by the proliferation of "modern" textile mills.[20] Spinning might have been easily compatible with their new role and a form of production that the hacendado valued, but more likely, skill with the spindle slipped through a woman's fingertips as she was forced to spend her time in the fields.

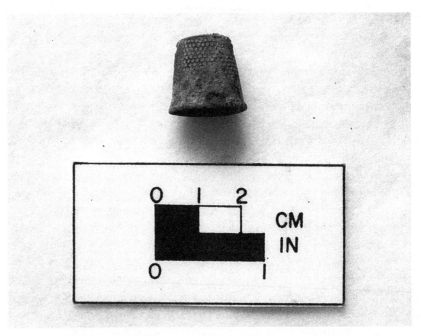

Figure 8.6a. Sewing/fabric production at Acocotla: copper or bronze thimble.

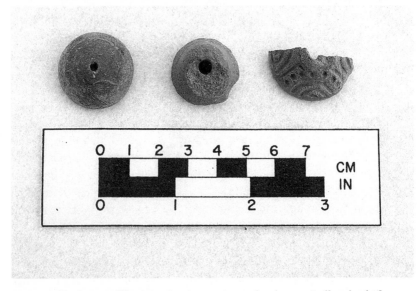

Figure 8.6b. Sewing/fabric production at Acocotla: three spindle whorls for producing cotton thread.

The presence of spindle whorls and thimbles (fig. 8.6a) indicates that spinning and sewing were regular activities for women living in Acocotla's calpanería. Oral history tells us that women worked in the fields next to their husbands, twelve hours a day, six days a week, so perhaps they took spindle whorls into the fields with them. Rafaela may have carried a thimble or spindle around in her pocket so she could produce thread or needlework for sale or for her family at lunchtime or sitting around a fire with her neighbors at the end of a long day. She and her friends would have had to balance the competing demands of being laborers, wives, and mothers in a world where culture and social classes narrowly defined traditional roles. It would have been a complex world in which to raise a child.

Martín, his face screwed up in disgust, watched with satisfaction as his mother dosed Petra. The medicine tasted awful, making his throat burn and his eyes water, and it looked as if Petra wasn't enjoying their mother's attention any more than he had. She was fighting Rafaela, but he knew his mother would win. She was well practiced in administering the medicines that the hacendado's doctor left for them. He couldn't wait until the new baby came. Martín hoped she would leave him and his siblings in peace when she had someone new and weak to worry about.

Rafael shouted for him, and Martín ran back to the game his mother had interrupted. The sun was setting, and they wouldn't have enough light to finish if he didn't hurry. He returned to the group of boys huddled around the circle drawn in the earth. It was his turn, and he fingered the marble in his pocket uneasily. The pretty, blue glass marble had been hard won, and he was nervous about risking it now.

As he knelt down to take his shot, he felt a hand tugging on his shirt and heard a whine in his ear. Angry, he whipped around. The baby had nearly cost him his favorite marble. "What?" he snarled at Petra, the bitter taste of the medicine in his mouth making him nastier than he might otherwise have been. She began to cry; she always did. He fumbled in his pockets, searching for something to keep her quiet. If his father caught them fighting, he'd be punished. His friends were already nudging each other, whispering and giggling. He didn't know what would be worse, the jokes they would make or his father's punishment.

His fingers found the arrowhead he'd picked up in the fields that day. . . . No, that he wanted to keep. Besides, she might cut herself on it. What else did he have? He reached into his other pocket and found the clay horse his father had made for him years before. He hesitated briefly and then pulled it reluctantly from his pocket. Petra's face lit up when she saw it, her tears stopping immediately. She coveted the little clay horse, but he'd always been afraid of letting her handle it. His father didn't have much time for fun, and the horse represented a rare Sunday afternoon of companionship. Martín remembered watching his father's deft fingers quickly form the little horse while he told stories of his own childhood.

He glanced back at his group of friends, thinking about his pretty blue marble, and then looking at the marbles still in the circle, calculating his potential winnings. Shrugging his shoulders, he handed his little sister the horse, warning her to be extra careful with it. She smiled at him, hugging the horse to her chest and promising to treat it well. Shrugging his shoulders again, Martín turned back to his group of friends and pulled the precious blue marble from his pocket.

On Being a Child

According to archival records, twenty-one of the fifty-six people living in the Hacienda Acocotla's calpanería in 1893 were children,[21] but the presence of these children is nearly impossible to discern in the archaeological record. In part, this is probably because when poor children have toys, they are most often quickly made out of materials that do not survive in the archaeological record and, in part, because children in the calpanería probably spent more time working than playing.[22] We know from oral histories that children as young as ten were employed twelve hours a day six days a week. It is easy to imagine that younger children, when not "officially" employed (or paid), were encouraged to help their parents rather than attend school or spend time with playthings.[23]

During the mid-nineteenth century, the Mexican government passed a law requiring all men between the ages of sixteen and sixty to pay a tax called the *Chicontepec*. The tax was intended to fund public schools that would replace schools run by the Catholic Church during the colonial period.[24] Thanks to this tax, twelve indigenous children in the village of La Mojonera were able to attend school, where, it is reported, they learned reading, writing, and religion.[25] At Acocotla, however, only the mayordomo's children were sent to school.[26] The workers made repeated attempts to get out of paying the tax because, they complained, they were unable to take advantage of it. Acocotla's workers claimed they couldn't send their children to school because they needed their labor to support the family, and even if they could afford to send them, the roads were too dangerous for children to travel unaccompanied.[27] In one particularly poignant plea, the valley's workers requested that the government reassign monies collected through the Chicontepec to build cemeteries instead of funding schools—the schools were of no use, but the rural poor were in desperate need of more places to bury their dead.[28]

This does not mean that life at the calpanería was unusually hard on children. As discussed in chapter 3, life would have been hard on children in the villages as well. Death records tell us that children regularly died in great numbers and were especially susceptible to the epidemics, such as smallpox, that swept the countryside every few years. Children in the calpanería may have had a small advantage when it came to injuries and illness. Though we may doubt the efficacy of nineteenth-century medicine, people living in the calpanería would have had greater access to it than their compatriots in the villages, a competitive advantage recognized even today.[29] While we were collecting oral history in the descendant community, one of the women and former hacienda workers told us that while the work was hard, life was not as bad as people today think it was. She asked us, "Today if you get sick, who takes care of you? Who pays for the doctor now?"

In the archaeological record, "health care" appears in the form of the remains of patent medicine bottles. During excavations, we found numerous bottle fragments, including seventeen bottle rims. Six of those rims belonged to nineteenth-century patent medicine bottles. Additionally, one base was identified as being from a medicine bottle and had embossed lettering reading "—RICAN APOTHECA—//SA—." Though we can only guess at the full text, it is clearly a bottle from an apothecary. It was common for the hacendado on large haciendas to provide free medical care to the peones working for him.[30] The medicine bottles found archaeologically suggest that this was also the case at Acocotla, though of course the value of these "cures" is questionable.

Rafaela and her neighbors did not put all their trust in the medicines provided by the hacendado. They may have resorted to alternative methods of protection and healing for themselves and their children. At the bottom of the midden, along with the coin dating to 1864, we found a single tooth from a ringtail (*Bassariscus astutus*). As mentioned in chapter 7, these animals are used today in shamanistic rituals. The Nahua peoples of central Mexico practice these rituals to heal illnesses that cannot be cured with Western medicines.[31]

The natives of the New World were not the only people to introduce magico-religious items into the material record. While digging in the midden, we came across a bronze figa, or higa (fig. 8.7). Figas are most

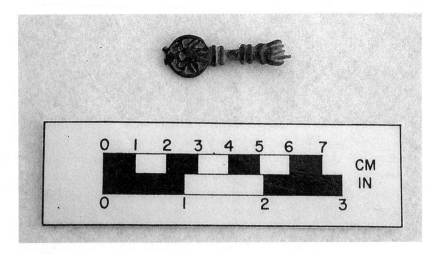

Figure 8.7. A figa (or higa).

commonly used to protect children from the evil eye and bad health, though they were considered generally useful for maintaining good health for all ages.[32] The figa recovered at Acocotla was certainly a mass-produced item. An identical figa was recovered from an undated unit during excavations at St. Augustine in Florida, suggesting that these items must have been traded widely throughout Spanish America.[33]

The figa is an object that underscores our often-made assumptions about ritual objects found in archaeological contexts. On seeing a figa, some people assume that it is associated with Africans or indigenous peoples (primarily because it is a charm still used in parts of the Caribbean and Brazil), but the figa's origins lie in Europe, and jet figas are still produced at Santiago de Compestela.[34] Though, through our own prejudices, we often assume that Europeans brought Western, "rational" practices to the New World while less rational magical beliefs were introduced by African and indigenous inhabitants, in fact Europeans had their own magico-religious belief system.[35] The figa is no less European than the rosaries imported in great numbers from Catholic Spain. The charm we found in Acocotla's midden is a symbol that has a long history in Europe, dating at least to Roman Italy and becoming common in Spain in the years following the *reconquista*.[36] These charms were brought to both Africa and the New World by Spanish and Portuguese explorers and colonizers throughout the colonial period and were imported from Europe in bulk, as is evidenced by shipping manifests of the period.[37] They remain in common use today in the circum-Caribbean region. While assisting me with artifact analysis in the laboratory, one of my Mexican students told me that his parents had a figa made for his little brother who had been sickly as a child.

Children who survived the dangers of childhood illness were expected to take on adult responsibilities at an early age. In chapter 3, we met María Catarina and Luis Tlalpanco, who were battling over the rights to her six-year-old son's labor. Tlalpanco took María Catarina's son to pay his recently deceased father's debt. María Catarina used the legal channels available to her to object to Tlalpanco's actions because, she said, she needed her six-year-old son to support her three daughters and herself. Given this evidence, it seems reasonable to assume that María Catarina's son was not the only six-year-old engaged in wage labor at the Hacienda Acocotla. Though Rafaela's youngest children would have been exempt, children as young as her youngest son, the seven-year-old Martín, would have spent their days working in the fields.

The children would have spent much if not most of their time working, but Martín, Petra, their siblings, and their friends would surely have had time for play. Seeing those moments of a "normal" childhood in the archaeological record is almost impossible. The only items we can recognize as toys with certainty are five marbles that were recovered during excavations. The game of marbles was played by children throughout Europe as early as Roman times, and it grew in popularity in the Spanish colonies during the seventeenth century.[38] The majority of marbles recovered on sites throughout the Americas are stone or ceramic, probably due to the early dates of most of the sites excavated in the Spanish Americas thus far. At Acocotla, all of the marbles recovered are made out of glass, probably because they were manufactured and used during the second half of the nineteenth century (though some German manufacturers were producing glass marbles as early as the early years of the eighteenth century).[39] Other possible toys were recovered in the form of forty-one figurines found during our excavations. Some were clearly from the Prehispanic period, and others had been produced in the historic period. While some of these figurine parts may have been used as toys, it is equally possible that some represent parts of household saints used for worship. One figurine looked like an image of Santa Claus (as the men from the village who found it immediately insisted it was). Would this small find be part of a religious display, a toy, or both? It is a question that is impossible to answer.

While excavating, we found a number of Prehispanic items along with the more expected nineteenth-century trash. Acocotla sits near a large

Preclassic site, and, once upon a time, its fields hosted the Aztec Flowery Wars. There is nothing surprising about the fact that we turned up arrowheads and ear spools mixed in with whitewares and patent medicine bottles while digging in the midden and households. These artifacts littered the ground waiting to be picked up by a inquisitive child in the nineteenth century just as they do now. Children and their parents may have picked up objects that sparked their interest. We can imagine that Martín had the same curiosity that most of the children we know today have in spite of the fact that he had to adopt the responsibilities of an adult.

Of the Prehispanic ceramic items we found, the ear spool was the most common; we collected six in varying sizes. Perhaps these made convenient gaming pieces. We also found stone tools at Acocotla, including 204 worked fragments of chert and an additional thirty-three fragments of obsidian. The majority are easily identified as Prehispanic items that were introduced to the site, either intentionally or unintentionally, long after their initial manufacture and use. How could Martín have resisted bringing a blade like the one in figure 8.8 home from the fields? It was not the

Figure 8.8. Chert biface.

only item introduced long after human hands had first shaped it. The eleven prismatic obsidian blades we recovered found their way into the hands of the calpanería's inhabitants many generations after they had been discarded or lost by someone else. Martín's parents may have brought still-sharp blades like these to the calpanería to use as handy cutting tools. In Puebla, and throughout Mesoamerica, Prehispanic items are often believed to be imbued with special powers from one's ancient ancestors, so it is even possible that the presence of these items carried a less utilitarian significance for the possessor.[40]

Sometimes, we make strange assumptions about the break between the historic and Prehispanic period, a dynamic seen in my investigation of the "coarse thin orange" amphora described in chapter 7.[41] When we find well-made, unglazed ceramics that echo traditions seen on Prehispanic sites, we assume that those ceramics are Prehispanic, possibly wrongly. We also cannot assume that all stone tools are Prehispanic. Some of the flaked lithics found at Acocotla may have been produced during the nineteenth century, and there is precedent for historic-period stone-tool making at other nineteenth-century sites.[42] Most of the flaked chert recovered during our excavations at the hacienda came in the form of cores, flakes, and what we identified as scrapers (large flakes with rough finishing along one edge). The inhabitants of the calpanería may have made some of these stone tools. During excavations in room 21, we found a chert core, scraper, and three flakes sitting on the lower floor in the southeast corner of the room. The placement of these items, all five of which appeared to be of the same material, suggests that the inhabitant of room 21 was making stone tools well into the second half of the nineteenth century. Three fragments of olive-green bottle glass (a substance not unlike obsidian) that we found during excavations also exhibited what appeared to be intentional flaking along one edge, suggesting that stone-knapping skills continued long after the arrival of the Spanish.

* * *

I glared at the hunk of metal in my hand. It was too big to be dismissed as nothing. I was going to have to figure out what it was. I dropped it on the table, ignoring its clunk of protest, and tried not to hate the inoffensive artifact. All archaeologists have certain classes of artifacts for which they feel the most affinity. For me, bones and ceramics were the most appealing. Metals were right at the bottom of my list, but this piece looked like it might prove interesting.

Admitting defeat, I stood up and squinted at the books lining the shelves in my lab. I quickly found my facsimile of the 1897 Sears Roebuck catalog, an invaluable resource for historical archaeologists trying to identify household goods from the nineteenth century. I pulled it off the shelf while I thought about what "department" to search through. "Hmmm," I thought, "farming implements?" I looked back at the metal. "Nope, not quite the right size or shape for something that industrial." I started flipping through the pages of household goods, stopping now and again to look more closely at the bit of metal on the lab table. Focusing on the sort of sprocket in the middle of the metal, I realized I might be holding the base of an oil or kerosene lamp. Looking in the index, I flipped to the section on lamps and found a reasonably close match to the twisted metal sitting in front of me. Suddenly, the hunk I'd been so unenthusiastic about identifying was more interesting.

✻   ✻   ✻

I began this chapter by explaining that the most unglamorous bits of people's trash are often what intrigue the archaeologist most. As I stood in the lab that day identifying what would be one of just two lamps discovered at Acocotla (fig. 8.9), I found myself thinking about the experience of inhabiting one of those rooms in the calpanería. We found only two lamp fragments and very few candlesticks (most of which seemed designed for family altars). People must have tied the rhythms of their days to the rising and setting sun, as agricultural people have around the world for centuries. At Acocotla, though, the workers would have had little if any control over their schedules. Oral history tells us that the hacienda's workers were employed in the fields from sunrise to sunset. Personal and family time would have been after dusk. With so little evidence for any sort of lighting, one imagines that the peones' activities were severely restricted. Would Rafaela have been able to spin and embroider in the evenings? Perhaps she was skilled enough with the drop spindle that light was of minimal importance. How much time would Martín and his friends have had for games of marbles? Maybe they found time to play only on Sundays. The small finds in this chapter are the archaeological remains of some of the most intimate aspects of people's lives—buttons on a shirt worn with pride or lost with shame, marbles hoarded in pockets, earrings worn every day or guarded for a special occasion. These items are the things with which we surround ourselves, the things that follow us throughout our lives, connecting us to friends and family, allowing us to establish to the outside world, and to ourselves, who, exactly, we are.

Figure 8.9. Part of an oil lamp.

Rafaela rolled over stiffly on her petate. She sat up slowly and started to massage her sore elbows. She smiled slightly as she remembered early mornings when this room was still full of her family. She had thought the room too small then, but now it felt too large and so lonely. Out of habit, she reached up to touch her gold earrings, but even these were gone. She'd lost one in the field and, upset, had foolishly thrown the other away. She wished she had it now; maybe it would bring her husband closer.

She shook her head, trying to chase away the lonely thoughts that plagued her these days. She had to get to work. Not in the fields, of course, she was too old to be of any use there now. When her husband died the month before, the manager had come to her with his account book. Of course she couldn't read it, but he read it to her, telling her that her husband had run up a debt of eighty pesos—an impossible sum. He told her it was her debt now and gave Rafaela two choices. Either she could pay it and leave or she could work in the kitchen. She was trapped. Even if she had the money to rid herself of this debt, where would she go? With the exception of Petra, all her children were gone. They had convinced hacendados at other haciendas to buy their debts, and they had left. They were all married now. She saw them and her grandchildren on Sundays, but they had no room for her. Even if they did, who would buy the debt of an old woman?

The manager made it clear he was doing her a favor, allowing her to pre-pare tortillas for the midday meal so she could pay off her dead husband's debt while continuing to live in the calpanería. She supposed he was, but by rights, she shouldn't be preparing food for anybody anymore. She was too old for the work. Her daughters-in-law should be bringing her tortillas, but they worked in the fields just as she had. They didn't have time to take care of an old woman. The manager seemed to think it was a kindness to put her to work in the kitchen. Clearly, he didn't understand the labor involved. Within the first hour in front of the metate, Rafaela's toes, ankles, knees, back, shoulders, and elbows were all on fire with a pain that didn't stop until she managed to fall asleep at night.

She sighed and got up, slowly and in pain. Straightening her clothes, she made her way to the door. She spotted Petra as she stepped out into the field in front of her room. Nobody else was up yet, but Petra always got up to check on her mother. She had been a sweet little girl, and she'd grown into a sweet woman. She knew that Petra felt guilty that she had to work, that she couldn't take care of her aging mother. There was nothing to be done about it, though; it was just hacienda life. Everyone in the calpanería had so much hope when the wars began, but that was many, many years ago.

Repressing a groan, Rafaela stepped into the warm sun and made her way to the kitchen. As she crossed the field, she heard one of the other peones shout. She turned to look in the direction he was pointing. Though she was having trouble seeing things close up recently, Rafaela had no trouble dis-cerning the approaching soldiers far across the fields. She easily counted about a dozen men riding toward Acocotla. All around her, chaos erupted. The women snatched up their children and ran for the casco's main en-trance. She breathed a bit easier as she saw Petra make it to the safety of the walls. The girl was too pretty for her own good. The men followed close be-hind the women. It didn't really matter what faction the soldiers represented; their arrival was certain to represent danger to everybody. Rafaela started to follow the others toward the casco's entrance before stopping and turning angrily back. She was fed up with these disruptions, with this war. She stood, indecisive for only a moment, before starting back toward the kitchen. The tortillas needed to be made, regardless of national politics or the aches and pains in her back and toes, and she was going to go on with her day.

Conclusion

"Un Platito de Frijoles"

*   *   *

I was squatting on one of the household's few chairs. The chair reminded me of my days as a preschool teacher. It was so small that I could have comfortably rested my chin on my knees had I wanted to. The chair balanced somewhat precariously next to the small table, and Karime perched just as precariously on a second chair next to me. Don Andrés's daughter Christina sat across the table from us on the last of the chairs. The three of us sipped room-temperature soft drinks from plastic cups.

Christina had recently returned from New Jersey, where she had lived with her husband and three children for seven years. She told us that she worked in the kitchen at a national fast-food chain. Her husband, Eduardo, standing in a dim corner of the room, proudly added that when the family decided to return to Mexico, the restaurant owner had told him that he "wouldn't know what he'd do without Christina, she was such a hard worker." We asked a bit more about what the work was like. Christina explained that she had worked in the kitchen from seven in the morning until midnight every day of the year. "But on Christmas, her boss let her go home at six in the evening to have dinner with us because she was such a good employee," Eduardo boasted. Christina shrugged ambivalently. Yes, the work was good and the money was more than was available in La Soledad Morelos.

Karime asked why she had decided to come home. Christina looked embarrassed. "I know. It's crazy, right? Everybody says I was crazy. The money was good, so much better than I could make here. But I missed my family. Most days, I didn't see my children. I was so lonely. In the United States, you can have meat at every meal if you want, but you eat that meat alone. Here all I can eat is a small plate of beans, but I eat those beans with my entire family."

It was a tough adjustment for her family. They were living in a second house owned by her father. Though he had built it with the money she and her husband had sent home, don Andrés never tired of reminding his son-in-law, in front of family, friends, and even perfect strangers, that he had been generous enough to give Eduardo a home. It was a reminder that clearly rankled, but Eduardo was too respectful of his elders to complain or contradict. The children, who had gone to the United States when they were still quite young, found themselves living in the foreign land of their birth. The small, poor farming village was a world away from suburban New Jersey. It wasn't just daily life in the village that required an adjustment. Christina's children had grown up with American futures and American ideas about social mobility. Her eldest son had dreams of going to college, something unheard of in La Soledad Morelos. He wanted to become a hydraulic engineer. I looked around the little cinder block room wondering silently how Miguel was going to achieve his goal from here.

The children had to adjust, but so did the parents. One day, Christina confided that the women in the village thought her husband was strange and maybe crazy. "Why?" I asked in confusion. He struck me as intelligent, kind, and unfailingly cheerful. Christina explained in whispered, shamed tones that he liked to cook. She said that he would disappear into the kitchen for hours, causing scandalized whispering among her friends and relatives. The worst of it was that he liked to cook Italian food. When they lived in New Jersey, Christina's husband had worked at an Italian restaurant in New York City. He'd developed a love of not only the food but also the cooking. Her husband was the only person in the village who enjoyed eating pasta. The fact that he was in the kitchen cooking it only made the situation worse.

The family, as a family, was trapped. One day, Eduardo, who was assisting in our excavations at Acocotla, approached me. He nodded at my truck and asked offhandedly, "Are you driving back to the United States in that?" I answered, somewhat cautiously, that I was. "My wife and I have been talking," he said. "Yes?" I prompted. "If I go back to the United States by myself and work for two years, we will be able to afford to send Miguel to college. He'll become an engineer and have a life that his mother and I can't have. He could help the whole family then." I nodded, worried about the dangers he faced crossing the border and working illegally in the United States, saddened by the family breakup I was hearing about, hopeful that Miguel would get his education and become an engineer against all odds.

He looked at my truck again. "Will you drive me?" he asked, casual and hopeful all at once. I looked at my feet, ashamed of my inability to help the family who had given me so much. Ethically, I couldn't break the law and involve myself in potentially endangering him, but I didn't know how to explain the niceties of my profession. "I can't drive you back. It is very complicated and dangerous, and I don't know the safe ways for you to travel," I tried to explain helplessly. He said, "No, it's very easy! I will travel as your servant. You can tell them at the border that I am nothing more than your servant. The coyotes will charge $5,000 this year. I will pay you the money, I promise. I have it! But I think it will be safer to travel with you."

Eduardo called me "patrona" as he pleaded for my help. Technically the word means "boss" or "ma'am," but it has subtle undertones of ownership. It was what the peones would have called the hacendada. Most days he called me "niña bonita," pretty little girl. I tried again to explain that if I could take him across the border to earn the money for his son's college education I would, for free, but that the journey was beyond my abilities. I was overwhelmed by shame, sadness, and fear. We walked away from each other, both feeling equally awful, but for very different reasons. I wondered if he would ever laughingly call me "niña bonita" again.

"Un platito de frijoles" ("A little plate of beans"). Christina had said those words to us to explain why she was happier in Mexico. The little plate of beans, and the meat she'd left behind, symbolized not just nutrition but the entire package she'd abandoned. Money, food, her children's educational futures, all had been traded in for a meal with her family each day. She wasn't afraid of hard work, but she was afraid of her children growing up without their mother sitting across from them at the dinner table, a not unreasonable fear that blossomed out of working conditions that most Americans would consider unacceptable. "A little plate of beans." Her words haunt me. Will Miguel's future hold more than a little plate of beans?

*　　*　　*

How did Christina and her family end up in this situation? One hundred years earlier, Emiliano Zapata had called for agrarian reform with the

Figure C.1. Planting the fields. (Photo by Isaac Guzmán.)

publication of his Plan de Ayala. Throughout his life, he watched the rural people of Mexico struggle to survive. He witnessed the oppression created by the hacienda system. Christina's grandparents answered Zapata's call and fought for agrarian reform. They had won the battle. So why was Christina trading hunger for loneliness now? Why was her husband leaving the family and making the dangerous border crossing alone? Why would it be so hard for Miguel to realize his dream of becoming an engineer? Most important, in the face of all of this hardship, why aren't Christina and her neighbors rebelling once again?

Researchers have suggested that the origins of the rural revolt during the Revolution (and during the War of Independence a century earlier) may lie in threats to rural men's patriarchal identity during the decades leading up to both wars.[1] During the last quarter of the nineteenth century, President Porfirio Díaz's program of modernization created national economic growth at the cost of local, rural jobs. Historians have linked this decline in available wage labor combined with restricted access to community lands to increased violence at the family and community level.[2] They argue that this increase in violence is the result of rural men no longer being able to assume the expected role of patriarch and that, when offered the outlet of rural revolt, their anger turned outward.

This book has been about daily life in nineteenth-century Mexico. The connections among ruined homes, fragments of cooking pots, children's marbles, and the origins of the Mexican Revolution may not be immediately obvious, but in fact, understanding how people lived their daily lives is necessary if we are to understand why people chose to rebel when they did. The historians cited in the previous paragraph posit that profound transformations were taking place within households, and they interpret these as transformations of male patriarchy and threats to male identity, threats that radicalized rural men, pushing them into the abyss of revolution. Of course, these historians are working with documents written almost exclusively by men. The anthropological and archaeological research I have presented in the preceding chapters suggests that patriarchs were not the only family members under attack and that the lives of women and children mattered, too.

We cannot know with certainty how the peones living in Acocotla's calpanería felt about Zapata's call for agrarian reforms. Zapata's General Fortino Ayaquica chose the Hacienda San Miguel Acocotla for his meeting with the opposition leaders one April morning in 1917. His choice hints that some of the inhabitants of the calpanería may have been sympathetic to his cause; others, like the elderly Rafaela, may simply have wished for an end to the chaos. Regardless of their individual sympathies, understanding their lives matters. They are part of a web of rural labor organization that drove many, if not all, of Puebla's rural poor to Zapata's side.

The story told in the last three chapters suggests that we ought to expect that the calpanería's peones were not particularly sympathetic to Zapata's struggle.[3] The archaeological and ethnohistorical data I collected catalog many of the perks enjoyed by the hacienda's resident laborers. They had houses that were nicer than those in the villages in which they were born. Their homes in the calpanería contained objects they otherwise would not have had, things like majolica tableware and gold earrings. They had reliable access to food, including luxuries like meat. When they were sick, somebody provided medicine and possibly even a doctor's care. They enjoyed the protection of Acocotla's walls in troubled times. While we were collecting oral histories, one woman suggested that Acocotla's resident peones had lived lives that were much better and more secure than she enjoyed today. The data do not contradict her.

In the fictional narratives embedded in the last chapters, we met Feliciana, a woman from a nearby village who came to cook for Acocotla's peones. Her jealousy and anger highlight the dissatisfaction that many villagers may have felt about the unequal access to goods and housing created by the hacienda system. Feliciana, her neighbors, and people like them would have been prime recruiting targets for Zapata's forces. The reasons are obvious. At the Hacienda Acocotla, people like Rafaela and her family did not just have nicer residences and access to goods that had previously been considered "elite"; they also had jobs—an entrée into the cash economy. Steady employment and credit at the hacienda store meant that the men of the families lucky enough to have regular work at the hacienda would have been able to maintain the patriarchal identity that historians have suggested is so important.

But what about the women? This study suggests that the ways in which labor was organized may have had a profound effect on the level of happiness, and thus willingness to revolt, among Acocotla's laborers. As we saw in chapter 4, Rafaela's descendants have maintained social practices and family organization dating to the Prehispanic period. In chapters 6–8, we saw how the hacendado and mayordomo reorganized living space and, by extension, family organization. During the second half of the nineteenth century, the hacendado, deliberately or unconsciously, forced inhabitants of the calpanería to abandon their traditional social roles in favor of those dictated by wage labor. For Mexico's upper classes, traditional and especially "indigenous" ways of life impeded social progress. Patriarchy was not the only component of family identity that was under attack.

The commodification of family labor across gender lines and in defiance of ancient social structures likely created personal, family, and community tensions. As we have seen, a Nahua woman's identity, or habitus, had long been defined by her skill in the kitchen, an area that was, quite literally, her own special territory—her "woman house." Rafaela and her female compatriots had to abandon their place in front of the metate and comal, making the journey out to the fields every day to work next to their husbands. Some women may have been uncomfortable finding themselves filling roles that they had been raised to think they were not intended to fulfill. Some husbands may have been equally uncomfortable as expectations for wife, child, family, and household were dismantled, either out of necessity or through force. This was not only an attack on patriarchy; it was also an attack on the very definition of "family."[4] The stresses and emotional contradictions experienced by Rafaela as she made her way through a day at the Hacienda San Miguel Acocotla in chapters 6–8 represent my imaginings of how a woman and her family might have experienced the conflict created by this situation.

I opened these concluding remarks by recounting a series of interactions I had with Christina and her family, and their experiences illustrate family labor dynamics. Christina and her family abandoned the financial gain of a working life in the United States in favor of family structure. Christina's husband was proud of the work she had done outside of the home—he bragged about Christina's boss's dependence on her—he had even come to love cooking for the family himself. He did not seem to feel that any of this threatened to his role as patriarch. Christina, on the other hand, could not bear the thought of eating dinner away from her family (and she was humiliated by her husband's desire to spend time in the kitchen). Though the family's experiences might easily be interpreted as a threat to Eduardo's patriarchal identity, it was Christina's discomfort that drove the family back to Mexico. Ultimately, Eduardo returned to the United States alone, accepting his patriarchal, and lonely, responsibility to earn the money necessary to send his son to college; however, it was Christina's decisions, her needs, and her understanding of her responsibilities as a woman and mother that drove him to do so. Their decisions were the result of an identity inherited from innumerable ancestors.

Until more work like that presented in this study is done, we cannot know with any certainty if labor organization and the transformation of gender roles contributed to the decision of rural peones to join in Zapata's uprising, because the transformation of gender roles is largely invisible in the documentary record. Regardless of the reasons, many of the peones did join, and those who joined were not just men protecting their patriarchal identity. The fact that many of Zapata's soldiers were female hints that rural women were among those who were deeply unhappy and who saw the need for the transformations he called for.[5] Furthermore, Zapata's reform program included provisions for the equality of women and to "humanize divorce."[6] Perhaps a woman's unhappiness had something to do with the way a rapidly modernizing Mexico was transforming not only her husband's but also her own social role, as well as her need to have a say in the shape a woman's life could take.

Today, a new rural, agrarian uprising in Chiapas, driven by people who have taken Zapata's name as their own in the struggle, offers some insight into the role of Revolutionary women who are caught between tradition and the modernizing forces of industrial capitalism. In January 1994, the Zapatistas came to the forefront of international news when they rose in rebellion against the Mexican government—a rebellion that was timed to coincide with the implementation of the North American Free Trade Agreement. Women and women's rights have been central to the rebellion since the beginning of the movement.[7] Western feminists have criticized the demands of Zapatista women as being "not feminist enough," but in fact, like all feminists, Zapatista women are calling for autonomy on their terms, an autonomy that they want to define rather than have imposed on them from the outside.[8] The attitude some hold toward wage labor is perhaps most telling for our story here. When defining the difference between working in the household for family versus working outside the house for money, Zapatista women have said that work in the house is more valuable to them because it benefits their families, whereas wage labor benefits their bosses.[9] One can imagine that Rafaela may have felt the same way.

Perhaps Rafaela felt that the fact that she was not in her own kitchen space preparing meals for her family was a problem. Perhaps Feliciana resented the fact that though she labored as hard as the men in the fields, she was compensated at a significantly lower pay rate and had to live without the security enjoyed by the peones in the calpanería. We can oversimplify this dynamic, see it as nothing more than women wanting their kitchens back (perhaps a reactionary and anti-feminist interpretation to our Western ears), but the conflict identified here is in fact a question of a woman's autonomy—Rafaela may have wanted to be able to choose to be in the kitchen, and Feliciana may have wanted to be fairly compensated for her choice of selling her labor. The dramatic changes we see in labor management and organization at Acocotla during the second half of the nineteenth century are significant; they undermined traditional roles while narrowing a woman's options. Industrialization did not bring women the opportunity to engage with wage labor—it pulled them into a web of exploitation.

With his 1911 issuance of the Plan de Ayala, Zapata articulated the anger and frustration of tens of thousands of central Mexico's peones, and his call to arms resulted in nearly a decade of fighting. In spite of Zapata's 1919 assassination, Mexico's ruling classes were eventually forced to acknowledge and address the demands of central Mexico's rural poor. In large part, this acknowledgment happened because Mexico was fragmented following the Revolution. The federal government was faced with the task of weaving a coherent national identity out of the many threads that had been spun into individual and separate identities during the Revolutionary period.[10] As had been the case when Madero took control of Mexico during the Revolution's early years, factions that had been fighting for their own agendas needed some of their demands met. The post-Revolutionary government had to find a way to convince the populace to become invested in the new government or risk the rapid devolution that had brought an end to Madero's rule. Because Zapata's calls for land reform were of central importance throughout the Revolutionary period and after, agrarian reforms provided the government with the necessary tools of incorporation.

Mexico's Constitution of 1917 included an article addressing the issue of agrarian reform. It proposed to return communal lands taken from rural communities under Díaz's regime and gave the government the right to confiscate and redistribute land that was not being used in a way that served the public interest. Though land redistribution was slow to start, President Lázaro Cárdenas accelerated the reforms during his presidency. Between 1934 and 1940, Cárdenas was responsible for the redistribution of more than forty-nine million acres of land, a figure that was more than double the cumulative totals of the six presidents that had ruled during the seventeen years preceding him.[11] Under Cárdenas's rule, the government confiscated the Hacienda Acocotla and parceled the land out to the people of La Soledad Morelos and neighboring villages.[12] In many communities, the land redistribution achieved what had proved impossible during the nineteenth century. The redistributions, along with government-instituted public education, allowed Mexico to finally turn many of its indigenous communities into "modern Mexicans." In La Soledad Morelos, people told me that until the Mexican Revolution, everybody who lived in the village was an Indian, but today, they say with pride, they are mestizos.

For many living in rural Mexico, the land redistribution did exactly what it was intended to do: it built substantial support for Mexico's ruling party, the Partido Revolucionario Institucional, and the PRI would return to this source of support throughout the twentieth century.[13] In the village, the reforms are still acknowledged with pride, gratitude, and honor today. During our interviews in La Soledad Morelos, people spoke in almost awestruck tones when they described receiving their due in the form of a plot of land to farm—enough land to support their families. In modern terms, it would be almost like the US government deciding to confiscate every bank-owned property and award each and every family in the country one home in restitution for the 2008 economic collapse. Initially, this would work beautifully, as the agrarian reforms did. But ultimately we might find ourselves with the same problem of Mexico's rural poor today. We would all have a resource intended to support a single family, but, for those who had more than one or two children, the resource would quickly prove insufficient. In Mexico, the growing population and static resources meant that by 1960, just twenty years after Cárdenas had finished his distribution of more than forty-nine million acres, 84 percent of all land-holdings in Mexico were insufficient to support the basic subsistence needs of the families who had received the plots.[14]

In spite of the poverty and hardship created by this situation, people like Christina and Eduardo do not turn to armed rebellion to solve their problems. It seems that poverty is not what drives rebellion but, rather, the ability to order their family lives and fulfill their own and their community's expectations (their moral economy) for who they should be.[15] Instead, individuals and entire families in rural Mexico close the economic gap left by diminishing land and resources by migrating either seasonally or permanently to nearby cities or the United States. If a family is to survive, they need an influx of cash that can only come from wage labor. People who migrate develop new economic needs, both good and bad, ranging from electronics purchased in a suburban superstore to a college education. The result is an ever-expanding spiral of need and financial opportunity, with the family and community waiting in the ever more distant center. It is estimated that by 2009, one out of every ten people born in Mexico had migrated to the United States, legally or illegally, in order to find the work (and money) their families and communities back home need simply to meet basic subsistence needs.[16] This is the heritage of Díaz's reforms and Zapata's revolution.

✳   ✳   ✳

I stood at the front of the lecture hall watching my students file in and find their favorite seats. I hadn't figured out exactly what I was going to say during lecture today. This was the lecture that would wrap up the course and, I hoped, leave the students thinking about the past and present a bit differently. Though I rarely use class time to lecture about my own research, the students had asked me to, and the topic was pertinent to the course. The course, Peoples of Latin America, had been my usual blend of archaeology, cultural anthropology, and history. As I stood there watching my students chat and take a last look at text messages, I tried to figure out how to make them understand that the past matters today, that my quirky blend of materials hadn't been at all quirky.

I thought about my drive to work that morning. I live in a rural part of Long Island dotted with vineyards and organic farms. Leaving my apartment, I had driven past a neighboring farm. A rusting mobile home sits tucked behind the barn. It has no running water, no electricity. Five men, refugees from Guatemala's civil war, share the space. They work on the farm by day for less than minimum wage and a place to live. In the evenings and on weekends, they cultivate their own small plot of land allotted to them. In the late summer, they sell me tomatoes at half the price of the local farm stands. We chat in Spanish about their families back home while my dog drools longingly at their chickens in the beautiful, golden, late-afternoon light. They split the proceeds from the purchases made by me and my neighbors. Some of the money gets sent back home to their families. The money-grams are often their only connection with wives, children, mothers, and brothers. At the end of a long, hot workday, one of the men picks up a bike and rides the mile and a half to the closest gas station. He uses the rest of the cash to buy food and beer for the guys. The local gas stations carry an impressive selection of Latin American beers and few expensive microbrews.

I mull this over on my way to work. I pass the neighborhood convenience store. For a block and a half, men are standing four deep along the curb. They are ostensibly waiting for the bus, but the bus passes and nobody gets on. In fact, they are waiting and hoping for work. As I drive by, their faces become alert, eyes hopefully watching my pickup pass. My truck looks like it belongs to a contractor, and I wait for the eager rush when I stop at a red light. When they see a woman driving, a woman who is avoiding making eye contact, they turn away again, but not before I see the disappointment in their eyes out of the corner of mine. Before the 2008 economic collapse, there were fewer than half this many men standing on the sidewalk hoping for casual day labor each morning. Today, men who can't afford to return to Mexico wait in hopes of a few hours of work for even more substandard wages than those who have regular employment. The Guatemalans around the corner from my apartment are the lucky ones.

Ironically, almost all the men on the street waiting for work at the "bus stop" come from the small village of San Jerónimo Coyula, one of the villages I've written about in this book. The men I drove past that morning on my way to lecture were the sons, grandsons, and great-grandsons of the men and women about whom I had to lecture that day. Once upon a time, their recent ancestors trudged a few miles from their village to work at the Hacienda San Miguel Acocotla. Today, thanks to failed or incompletely implemented agrarian reforms, the young men of San Jerónimo Coyula travel many thousands of miles to Long Island's elite Hamptons to do the same work, for the same poor pay, and to live in conditions like those their ancestors experienced at Acocotla. In large part, these men are still peones — they are just farther from home and even more alienated from their families and communities. And so, even in the Hamptons, I found it impossible to escape the history I was studying. The past wasn't in the past; we have globalized the hacienda system, making it an invisible part of our daily lives.

That was what I had to explain in lecture that day. The students came in prepared to listen to an academic lecture about something that mattered only in that it would fulfill an "international diversity requirement" on their long checklist of graduation requirements. They had to pass to graduate, so they would listen and take notes. I had to explain that what seemed required, impersonal, distant, and even romantically exotic was, in fact, just down the street waiting for the bus.

*   *   *

Appendix

Cast of Characters

These characters appear in the fictional sections of the text. They are listed here in alphabetical order with a brief explanation of who they are to help orient the reader.

Adriana. Chapter 6. Adriana is the "lazy" cook who sleeps in the sun and to whom Feliciana must go and ask for comales. Her character has no basis in the historical record; her name was chosen at random. We do not know whether she, or someone like her, existed. Her story highlights the fact that the hacendado and his family would likely have been in residence only rarely, and it also draws notice to the fact that the hacienda's workers were not a homogeneous social group.

Bonafacio. Chapter 7. Bonafacio is the husband of Rosa, the potter who makes ceramics that eventually find their way into the calpanería. His name was also chosen at random, and we don't know that he existed. Readers who are interested in pottery making and want to know more of Bonafacio and Rosa's story, however, may want to look at Louana Lackey's *The Pottery of Acatlán* (1982). Pottery from Acatlán probably found its way into Acocotla's calpanería. Pieces purchased in Acatlán today are indistinguishable from many of those found in the archaeological record at Acocotla.

Catalina. Chapter 3. Catalina de Malpica Sosa y Guzman is the daughter of Francisco Esteban de Malpica Ponce de León and his first wife. We know she was born in 1698 and that she was the second of nine children. Her mother died when she was seven, and she became a nun when she was sixteen. She appears as a supporting character in the documents that sketch an outline of her life (documents like her father's will). Her story is included to highlight the ways in which even elite women are often shadowy figures in the historical record.

Doña Ana. Chapter 6. Doña Ana Cristina Treviño de Ruelas purchased Acocotla in 1860 for 31,010 pesos. We do not know anything else about her, including whether or not she was responsible for the renovations of Acocotla's casco. We do, however, know from archaeological and archival data that those renovations took place after her purchase. Some might find doña Ana spoiled, and indeed she is. Contemporary accounts describe women like doña Ana as quite spoiled, while others written during the later Revolutionary period highlight the strength, heroism, and even victimization of hacendadas.[1] I chose to model doña Ana on the former accounts rather than the latter because as a spoiled, rich woman, she provides a neat foil for the cook Feliciana, who also appears in chapter 6.

Feliciana. Chapters 6 and 7. Feliciana is the cook who works in Acocotla's calpanería to produce food for its inhabitants and who babysits the sick Petra. Feliciana's story is based on an oral history collected during ethnographic research in La Soledad Morelos. To protect the privacy of the families we interviewed, all the names were changed, and so Feliciana's name wasn't actually Feliciana, but her story is based on the memories of the hacienda cook's descendants. Feliciana took the job at Acocotla because she needed to support her family due to her husband's drinking problem. Feliciana's bitterness, jealousy, and anger are my own interpretation of how a woman in her position might have felt.

Fortino Ayaquica (the General). Chapter 1. The General is a known historical figure who served in Emiliano Zapata's Liberation Army of the South and signed the amended Plan of Ayala in 1914. He was born in a village quite close to Acocotla, and he was employed as a textile worker prior to joining Zapata's forces.[2] He directed Zapata's forces in his hometown of Tochimilco, where, under his leadership, a committee to integrate rural villages into the national reform program as envisioned by Zapata was established; these committees have been described as the "true guardians of the revolution."[3] He was known as a strict disciplinarian, having taken the initiative to order any soldier abusing the local people or their rights to be shot on the spot.[4] We also know that he was at the Hacienda Acocotla one day in April thanks to correspondence he sent to Zapata regarding his meeting with the opposing forces. The narrative that appears in the text is based only on the fact that he was at the hacienda that day. His thoughts and personality are inferred.

Francisco Esteben de Malpica Ponce de León. Chapter 3. De Malpica Ponce de León was the eleventh owner of the Hacienda San Miguel Acocotla and Catalina's father. He is someone about whom we have extensive archival evidence; de Malpica Ponce de León was a pillar of the community, as well as a slave owner and someone who had trouble with money. He is the quintessential colonial-period hacendado.

Hipólita. Chapters 6–8. Like Rafaela and her family, Hipólita's name appears on the 1893 census. The document tells us that she was sixty and a widow. Her role in the goings on in the calpanería's community and her relationship to Rafaela are imagined but are based on patterns seen in the modern community in which older women are accorded a great deal of respect and authority. Her role in the story illustrates how the calpanería's residents may have functioned as a normal community in spite of the fact that they were not living as members of traditional villages.

Lucas Pérez Maldonado. Chapter 3. The infamous founder of the Hacienda San Miguel Acocotla, Lucas Pérez Maldonado is well known for his exploitation of indigenous communities. The story of his dealings in the Valley of Atlixco is based on both primary and secondary sources. Though some readers might be shocked at his referring to the indigenous peoples with whom he was dealing as "half-naked savages," it seems reasonable to assume that someone who was regularly charged with manipulating land deals with excessive quantities of liquor would think about people in just this way.

Luis Tlalpanco. Chapter 3. Tlalpanco, the mid-nineteenth-century manager (or mayordomo) of Acocotla, is something of a villain. He appears in our story and in the historic record when he confiscates María Catarina's six-year-old son to pay her dead husband's debt. He emphasizes the power that (often indigenous) hacienda managers had over the hacienda's workers and inhabitants of nearby villages.

María Catarina. Chapter 3. María Catarina was an indigenous woman who lived in the village of San Jerónimo Coyula during the third quarter of the nineteenth century. Her story comes to our notice in a single document: a complaint filed on her behalf by the mayor of her village against the mayordomo at the Hacienda Acocotla. The mayordomo, she alleged, had taken her six-year-old son to work off his deceased father's debt. Her story highlights the ways in which the actual experiences of debt peonage were not as benign as some scholars have suggested and also illuminates aspects of the relationship between villages and haciendas.

Martín. Chapter 8. Martín is Rafaela's son. We know from the 1893 census that he was seven years old, and that he had four older siblings (three brothers and a sister) and a younger sister, Petra, who appears in the story with him. Though he is not described in the census as being employed by the hacienda, oral history suggests that children his age were working in the fields with their families. He reminds us that though children had to work, they must also have found time to be children. The stone tool he has in his pocket suggests that children were sometimes creators of the archaeological record in unexpected, unintended, and difficult to interpret ways.

Miguel. Chapter 7. Miguel is another completely fictional character with a made-up name. He is an itinerant peddler who buys ceramics from Rosa in her village and brings them to Acocotla, where he sells them to Feliciana. In part, his character was created for the convenience of getting the ceramics from Rosa to Feliciana, but peddlers are common in Mexico and have been for many centuries. Today, they bring items like ceramic comales to the village of La Soledad Morelos and sell them on street corners. Miguel is modeled after one such man we met during our research.

Nicolás. Chapter 8. Nicolás is Rafaela's husband and Petra's and Martín's father. Like that of his wife and six children, Nicolás's story is recorded only in the 1893 census that tells us about the rest of his family. His story highlights the ways in which all members of a family were experiencing the stresses and tensions of hacienda life and labor. His journey from the nearby metropolis of Atlixco back to his family at Acocotla's calpanería also foreshadows the dangerous and lonely trip that many men make today as they cross the border for economic gain.

Petra. Chapters 6–8. Petra is Rafaela's youngest child. Her name appears on the 1893 census, which tells us she was two years old at the time. As discussed in chapter 3, infant mortality was high during this period, and so Petra's illness and her mother's seeming overreaction to it are meant to capture the precariousness of a young child's life.

Rafaela. Chapters 1, 6–8. Rafaela is the closest character to a protagonist in this book. Her historical existence is summed up in one line of a single census made of workers living at the Hacienda Acocotla in 1893. The names of her family members were all also taken from this document, including her husband, Nicolás, daughter Petra, son Martín, and four other children. Some of her thoughts are based on stories collected from the descendant community. For example, many of the older inhabitants of La Soledad Morelos claim the hacendado had made a pact with the devil because "nobody could be that cruel without the devil's help." Rafaela's role in this book is to illustrate the conflicting experiences of rural women during the latter half of the nineteenth and early twentieth centuries.

Rosa. Chapter 7. Rosa's life is based purely in imagination. We do not know that she existed, but, like that of her husband, Bonafacio, Rosa's story is based on ethnoarchaeological and ethnographic studies of modern potters. Again, readers who are interested in pottery making and would like to know more of Bonafacio and Rosa's story should consult Louana Lackey's *The Pottery of Acatlán* (1982). Other ethnoarchaeological ceramics studies of interest include Michael Deal's 1998 study of a Highland Maya community in Chiapas, *Pottery Ethnoarchaeology in the Central Maya Highlands*; George Foster's 1967 ethnographic study of a Tarascan village in West Mexico, *Tzintzuntzan: Mexican Peasants in a Changing World*; or Raymond Thompson's classic 1958 study of pottery making in a Yucatec Maya community, *Modern Yucatecan Maya Pottery Making*. A particularly fascinating account of pottery making that was made in a period contemporary with Rosa's life (though in Yucatan) may be found in Edward Thompson's unpublished 1900 manuscript, *The Maya Potter of Yucatan*, on file at the Peabody Museum, Harvard University.

Notes

Introduction

1. The "master" narrative is just that. The Mexican government issues free text-books to all public schools that emphasize the version of Mexican history recounted in the next chapter. See, e.g., Dennis Gilbert, "Rewriting History: Salinas, Zedillo and the 1992 Textbook Controversy," *Mexican Studies/Estudios Mexicanos* 13, no. 2 (1997); Dennis Gilbert, "Emiliano Zapata: Textbook Hero," *Mexican Studies/Estudios Mexicanos* 19, no. 1 (2003); Matthais vom Hau, "Unpacking the School: Textbooks, Teachers, and the Construction of Nationhood in Mexico, Argentina, and Peru," *Latin American Research Review* 44, no. 3 (2010).

2. Though race/ethnicity is a complex issue in Latin America, I have chosen to refer to the inhabitants of the *calpanería*, or workers' quarters, and members of the neigh-boring villages of San Jerónimo Coyula and La Soledad Morelos as "indigenous" be-cause that is how the historical record identifies them. Today, the people of the village of La Soledad Morelos self-identify as mestizo, though they explain that this is a devel-opment that has taken place only since the Mexican Revolution. In the neighboring San Jerónimo Coyula, villagers self-identify as indigenous, and Nahuatl is still com-monly heard in the streets. See Archivo General de la Nación, hereafter AGN Tierras, 1713, vol. 299, exp. 2, ff. 1–126; AGN, Tierras, 1784, vol. 1110, expediente, hereafter exp. 6, ff. 1–33; AGN, Tierras, 1805, vol. 1110, exp. 6, ff. 16–18; Archivo Historico del Municipio de Atlixco, hereafter AHMA, Gobierno, 1814, caja 2, exp. 3 (839); AHMA, Gobierno, 1839 caja 24, exp. 2 (1430); AHMA, Gobierno, 1842, caja 42, exp. 4 (1924); AHMA, 1848, Gobierno, caja 84, exp. 2, ff. 1–1v; AHMA, Gobierno, 1853, caja 73, exp. 3 (3053); AHMA, Gobierno, 1853, caja 74, exp. 1 (3068); AHMA, 1853, Gobi-erno, caja 92, exp. 1, ff. 1–30v; AHMA, Gobierno, 1865, caja 98, exp. 1 (4332); AHMA, Gobierno, 1867, caja 106, exp. 2 (4629); AHMA, Gobierno, 1893, caja 309, exp. 5 (12890); Archivo de las Notarias de Puebla, hereafter ANP, Notaria de Atlixco, 1738, ff. 87–92v. For discussions of the ways in which New Spain's (and Mexico's) racial

categories may be understood, see, e.g., Gonzalo Aguirre Beltrán, *La Población Negra de México, 1519–1810; Estudio Etno-Histórico* (Mexico City: Ediciones Fuente Cultural, 1946); R. Jovita Baber, "Categories, Self-Representation and the Construction of the *Indios*," *Journal of Spanish Cultural Studies* 10, no. 1 (2009); R. Douglas Cope, *The Limits of Racial Domination: Plebeian Society in Colonial Mexico City, 1660–1720* (Madison: University of Wisconsin Press, 1994); Jake Frederick, "Without Impediment: Crossing Racial Boundaries in Colonial Mexico," *Americas* 67, no. 4 (2011); María Elena Martínez, *Genealogical Fictions: Limpieza de Sangre, Religion, and Gender in Colonial Mexico* (Stanford, CA: Stanford University Press, 2008).

3. Centro de Estudios de Historia de México CARSO, hereafter CEHM-CARSO 1686, fondo 765, Mercedes, f. 50.

Chapter 1

1. AGN, Emiliano Zapata, caja 13, exp. 11, paginas, hereafter ps. 9–10, comunicados April 11–16, 1917; AGN, Emiliano Zapata, caja 13, exp. 12, ps. 10–13, informe April 17, 1917.

2. E.g. David A. Brading, *Haciendas and Ranchos in the Mexican Bajío, León, 1700–1860*, Cambridge Latin American Studies (Cambridge: Cambridge University Press, 1978); John K. Chance, "Haciendas, Ranchos, and Indian Towns: A Case Study from the Late Colonial Valley of Puebla," *Ethnohistory* 50, no. 1 (2003); François Chevalier, *Land and Society in Colonial Mexico: The Great Hacienda* (Berkeley: University of California Press, 1963); Isabel González Sánchez, *Haciendas, Tumultos y Trabajadores Puebla-Tlaxcala: 1778–1798*, Serie Manuales (Mexico City: Instituto Nacional de Antropología e Historia, 1997); María Teresa Jarquín, ed., *Origen y Evolución de la Hacienda en México, Siglos XVI al XX: Memorias del Simposio Realizado del 27 al 30 de Septiembre de 1989* (Zinacantepec, México: Colegio Mexiquense; Universidad Iberoamericana; Instituto Nacional de Antropología e Historia, 1990); María de Lourdes Herrera Feria, "Trabajadores Prófugos y Enduedados en la Región de Atlixco, Durante la Segunda Mitad del Siglo XIX," in Jarquín, *Orígen y Evolución de la Hacienda en México*; Magnus Mörner, "The Spanish American Hacienda: A Survey of Recent Research and Debate," *Hispanic American Historical Review* 53, no. 2 (1973); Herbert J. Nickel, *Morfología Social de la Hacienda Mexicana* (Mexico City: Fondo de Cultura Económica, 1988); Herbert J. Nickel, *Relaciones de Trabajo en las Haciendas de Puebla y Tlaxcala (1740–1914): Cuatro Análisis Sobre Reclutamiento, Peonaje y Remuneración* (Mexico City: Universidad Iberoamericana, 1987); William B. Taylor, *Landlord and Peasant in Colonial Oaxaca* (Stanford, CA: Stanford University Press, 1972); Eric Van Young, "Mexican Rural History Since Chevalier: The Historiography of the Colonial Hacienda," *Latin American Research Review* 18, no. 3 (1983); Eric Van Young, *Hacienda and Market in Eighteenth-Century Mexico: The Rural Economy of the Guadalajara Region, 1675–1820*, 2nd ed., Latin American Silhouettes (Lanham, MD: Rowman and Littlefield, 2006); Gisela Wobeser, *La Formación de la Hacienda en la Época Colonial. El Uso de la Tierra y el Agua* (Mexico City: Universidad Nacional Autónoma de México, 1989).

3. Eric R. Wolf and Sydney Mintz, "Haciendas and Plantations in Middle America and the Antilles," *Social and Economic Studies* 6 (1957): 380.

4. Van Young, *Hacienda and Market*, 112.

5. Chevalier, *Land and Society*.

6. Ibid.; Woodrow Wilson Borah, *New Spain's Century of Depression* (Berkeley: University of California Press, 1951); Silvio Zavala, "Orígenes Históricos del Peonaje en México," *Trimestre Económico* 10 (1944).

7. Peter J. Bakewell, *Silver Mining and Society in Colonial Mexico: Zacatecas, 1546–1700* (Cambridge: Cambridge University Press, 1971); Jonathan Irvine Israel, *Race, Class, and Politics in Colonial Mexico, 1610–1670*, Oxford Historical Monographs (London: Oxford University Press, 1975); John J. TePaske and Herbert S. Klein, "The Seventeenth-Century Crisis in New Spain: Myth or Reality?," *Past and Present* 90 (1981).

8. Charles Gibson, *The Aztecs Under Spanish Rule: A History of the Indians of the Valley of Mexico 1519–1810* (Stanford, CA: Stanford University Press, 1964); Wolf and Mintz, "Haciendas and Plantations"; Eric R. Wolf, *Peasant Wars of the Twentieth Century* (New York: Harper and Row, 1969).

9. Thomas H. Charlton, "Socioeconomic Dimensions of Urban-Rural Relations in the Colonial Period Basin of Mexico," in *Supplement to the Handbook of Middle American Indians*, vol. 4, *Ethnohistory*, ed. Ronald Spores (Austin: University of Texas Press, 1986), 129; Israel, *Race, Class, and Politics*, 270–71; Alan Knight, *Mexico: The Colonial Era* (Cambridge: Cambridge University Press, 2002), 96–97.

10. Charlton, "Socioeconomic Dimensions"; David Jones, "Nineteenth Century Haciendas and Ranchos of Otumba and Apan" (PhD diss., University of London, 1978).

11. Robert W. Patch, "Agrarian Change in Eighteenth-Century Yucatán," *Hispanic American Historical Review* 65, no. 1 (1985): 22.

12. Van Young, "Mexican Rural History," 15.

13. Knight, *Mexico*, 77–78.

14. Chevalier, *Land and Society*, 265.

15. Ibid.; Gibson, *Aztecs Under Spanish Rule*; Zavala, "Orígenes Históricos." The authors note, however, that in places like Central Mexico populations remained high enough that wage labor predominated.

16. Pedro Bracamonte y Sosa, *Amos y Sirvientes: Las Haciendas de Yucatán, 1789–1860* (Merida: Universidad Autónoma de Yucatán, 1993); Thomas Brass, "The Latin American Enganche System: Some Revisionist Reinterpretations Revisited," *Slavery and Abolition* 11, no. 1 (1990); Chevalier, *Land and Society*; González Sánchez, *Haciendas, Tumultos y Trabajadores*; Allan D. Meyers and David L. Carlson, "Peonage, Power Relations and the Built Environment at Hacienda Tabi, Yucatán, Mexico," *International Journal of Historical Archaeology* 6, no. 4 (2002); John Tutino, *From Insurrection to Revolution in Mexico: Social Bases of Agrarian Violence, 1750–1940* (Princeton, NJ: Princeton University Press, 1986); Zavala, "Orígenes Históricos."

17. Lee J. Alston, Shannan Mattiace, and Tomas Nonnenmacher, "Coercion, Culture, and Contracts: Labor and Debt on Henequen Haciendas in Yucatán, Mexico, 1870–1915," *Journal of Economic History* 69, no. 1 (2009); Arnold J. Bauer, "Rural Workers in Spanish America: Problems of Peonage and Oppression," *Hispanic American Historical Review* 59, no. 1 (1979); Gibson, *Aztecs Under Spanish Rule*; Alan Knight, "Mexican Peonage: What Was It and Why Was It?," *Journal of Latin American Studies* 18, no. 1 (1986); Knight, *Mexico*; Herbert J. Nickel, *El Peonaje en las*

Haciendas Mexicanas: Interpretaciones, Fuentes, Hallazgos (Mexico City: Universidad Iberoamericana, 1997).

18. Knight, *Mexico*, 98.

19. Ibid., 84–97.

20. Chance, "Haciendas, Ranchos, and Indian Towns."

21. Friedrich Katz, "Labor Conditions on Haciendas in Porfirian Mexico: Some Trends and Tendencies," *Hispanic American Historical Review* 54, no. 1 (1974).

22. AGN, 1754, Tierras vol. 789, exp. 1, f. 25.

23. Rani T. Alexander, "Introduction: Haciendas and Agrarian Change in Rural Mesoamerica," *Ethnohistory* 50, no. 1 (2003); Willem Assies, "Land Tenure and Tenure Regimes in Mexico: An Overview," *Journal of Agrarian Change* 8, no. 1 (2008); Thomas H. Charlton, "On Agrarian Landholdings in Post-conquest Rural Mesoamerica," *Ethnohistory* 50, no. 1 (2003); Deborah Ellen Kanter, *Hijos del Pueblo: Gender, Family, and Community in Rural Mexico, 1730–1850* (Austin: University of Texas Press, 2008); Deborah Ellen Kanter, "Native Female Land Tenure and Its Decline in Mexico, 1750–1900," *Ethnohistory* 42, no. 4 (1995); Christopher M. Nichols, "Solares in Tekax: The Impact of the Sugar Industry on a Nineteenth-Century Yucatecan Town," *Ethnohistory* 50, no. 1 (2003).

24. Chevalier, *Land and Society*, 187–88, 309.

25. Frederico Fernández Christlieb and Pedro Sergio Urquijo Torres, "Los Espacios del Pueblo de Indios Tras el Proceso de Congregación, 1550–1625," *Investigaciones Geográficas* 60 (2006); Mauricio Herrera Rodriguez, "Social Change and Land Tenure Regimes in Mexico," *GeoJournal* 70, no. 5 (2011); Ethelia Ruiz Medrano, *Mexico's Indigenous Communities: Their Lands and Histories 1500–2010*, ed. David Carrasco and Eduardo Matos Moctezuma, trans. Russ Davidson, Mesoamerican Worlds (Boulder: University Press of Colorado, 2010).

26. Assies, "Land Tenure," 35–36.

27. Charlton, "Agrarian Landholdings," 59.

28. Ibid.; Alexander, "Introduction"; Nichols, "Solares in Tekax"; Ruiz Medrano, *Mexico's Indigenous Communities*.

29. Kanter, *Hijos del Pueblo*; Kanter, "Native Female Land Tenure."

30. Eric Van Young, "Moving Toward Revolt: Agrarian Origins of the Hidalgo Rebellion in the Guadalajara Region," in *Riot, Rebellion, and Revolution: Rural Social Conflict in Mexico*, ed. Friedrich Katz (Princeton, NJ: Princeton University Press, 1988), 132.

31. Timothy J. Henderson, *The Mexican Wars for Independence* (New York: Hill and Wang, 2009), 8.

32. Virginia Guedea, "The Process of Mexican Independence," *American Historical Review* 105, no. 1 (2000).

33. Eric Van Young, "Islands in the Storm: Quiet Cities and Violent Countrysides in the Mexican Independence Era," *Past and Present*, no. 118 (1988): 176.

34. Kanter, *Hijos del Pueblo*; Jean A. Meyer, *Problemas Campesinos y Revueltas Agrarias (1821–1910)* (Mexico City: Secretaría de Educación Pública, 1973); Leticia Reina, *Las Rebeliones Campesinas en México, 1819–1906* (Mexico City: Siglo Veintiuno, 1980); Tutino, *From Insurrection to Revolution*; John Tutino, "From Involution to Revolution in Mexico: Liberal Development, Patriarchy, and Social Violence in the Central Highlands, 1870–1915," *History Compass* 6, no. 3 (2008); Van Young, "Islands in the Storm."

35. Charlton, "Agrarian Landholdings,"; Wolf, *Peasant Wars,* 13.

36. Tutino, "From Involution to Revolution"; Tutino, *From Insurrection to Revolution.*

37. Ruiz Medrano, *Mexico's Indigenous Communities.*

38. AGN 1754, Tierras, vol. 789, exp. 1, f. 25; AGN 1755, Tierras, vol. 818, exp. 4, ff. 1–66; AGN 1784, Tierras, vol. 1110, exp. 6, ff. 1–33; AHMA 1826, Gobierno, caja 6, exp. 5 (1000); AHMA 1837, Justicia, caja 18, exp. 2 (2731); AHMA 1839, Gobierno, caja 26, exp. 2 (1504); AHMA 1859, Gobierno, caja 87, exp. 4 (3916); AHMA 1864, Gobierno, caja 96, exp. 3 (4300); AHMA 1865, Gobierno, caja 99, exp. 3 (4397); AHMA 1889a, Gobierno, caja 268, exp. 1 (11886); AHMA 1889b, Gobierno, caja 268, exp. 1 (11886).

39. Assies, "Land Tenure," 38; Margarita Menegus Bornemann, "Ocoyoacac: Una Comunidad Agraria en el Siglo XIX," *Historia Mexicana* 30, no. 1 (1980); Ruiz Medrano, *Mexico's Indigenous Communities.*

40. Assies, "Land Tenure," 38.

41. Ibid.; Ruiz Medrano, *Mexico's Indigenous Communities.*

42. Brading, *Haciendas and Ranchos*; Andrés Lira González, *Comunidades Indígenas Frente a La Ciudad de México: Tenochtitlan y Tlatelolco, Sus Pueblos y Barrios, 1812–1919* (Zamora: Colegio de México; Colegio de Michoacán, 1983); Reina, *Rebeliones Campesinas*; John Tutino, "The Revolution in Mexican Independence: Insurgency and the Renegotiation of Property, Production, and Patriarchy in the Bajío, 1800–1855," *Hispanic American Historical Review* 78, no. 3 (1998); John Tutino, "Hacienda Social Relations in Mexico: The Chalco Region in the Era of Independence," *Hispanic American Historical Review* 55, no. 3 (1975); Paul J. Vanderwood, *Disorder and Progress: Bandits, Police, and Mexican Development,* rev. enl. ed., Latin American Silhouettes (Wilmington, DE: SR Books, 1992); Mark Wasserman, *Everyday Life and Politics in Nineteenth Century Mexico: Men, Women, and War* (Albuquerque: University of New Mexico Press, 2000).

43. Tutino, *From Insurrection to Revolution,* 277–325.

44. Jan Bazant, "Industria Algodonera Poblana de 1800–1843 en Números," *Historia Mexicana* 14, no. 1 (1964); Jeffrey Bortz, "The Revolution, the Labor Regime and Conditions of Work in the Cotton Textile Industry in Mexico," *Journal of Latin American Studies* 32 (2000); Gregory S. Crider, "Material Struggles: Workers' Strategies During the 'Institutionalization of the Revolution' in Atlixco, Puebla, Mexico, 1930–1942" (PhD diss., University of Wisconsin, 1996).

45. John Womack, *Zapata and the Mexican Revolution* (New York: Knopf, 1969), 81.

46. Assies, "Land Tenure"; Robert J. Knowlton and Lucrecia Orensanz, "El Ejido Mexicano en el Siglo XIX," *Historia Mexicana* 48, no. 1 (1998); Ruiz Medrano, *Mexico's Indigenous Communities*; Tutino, "From Involution to Revolution"; Tutino, *From Insurrection to Revolution*; Womack, *Zapata.*

47. Emilio Kourí, "Interpreting the Expropriation of Indian Pueblo Lands in Porfirian Mexico: The Unexamined Legacies of Andrés Molina Enríquez," *Hispanic American Historical Review* 82, no. 1 (2002): 85.

48. Tutino, *From Insurrection to Revolution*; Tutino, "From Involution to Revolution"; Womack, *Zapata.*

49. Tutino, *From Insurrection to Revolution,* 362.

50. Alan Knight, *The Mexican Revolution*, vol. 1 (Lincoln: University of Nebraska Press, 1990), 172–75.

51. Josefina Zoraida Vázquez, "La Revolución Mexicana," *Revista Iberoamericana* 55, no. 148 (2009): 696.

52. Arturo Warman, "The Political Project of Zapatismo," in Katz, *Riot, Rebellion, and Revolution*, 326.

53. Gilbert M. Joseph and Timothy J. Henderson, *The Mexico Reader: History, Culture, Politics* (Durham, NC: Duke University Press, 2002), 339–43.

54. Womack, *Zapata*.

55. Lourdes Arizpe, "The Rural Exodus in Mexico and Mexican Migration to the United States," *International Migration Review* 15, no. 4 (1981): 629; Cynthia Hewitt de Alcántara, *Anthropological Perspectives on Rural Mexico*, International Library of Anthropology (London: Routledge, 1984), 126.

Chapter 2

1. Chevalier, *Land and Society*, 64.

2. Patricia Plunket, "Arqueología y Etnohistoria en el Valle de Atlixco," *Notas Mesoamericanas* 12 (1990): 5–6.

3. Peter Gerhard, *A Guide to the Historical Geography of New Spain*, rev. ed. (Norman: University of Oklahoma Press, 1993), 56.

4. Carlos Paredes, *La Región de Atlixco, Huaquechula y Tochimilco. La Sociedad y la Agricultura en el Siglo XVI* (Mexico City: Centro de Investigaciones y Estudios Superiores en Antropología Social, Fondo de Cultura Económica, Gobierno del Estado de Puebla, 1991).

5. AHMA, 1785, Gobierno, caja 6, exp. 17 (517); AHMA, 1857, Gobierno, caja 85, exp. 1 (3754); AHMA, 1864, Hacienda, caja 97, exp. 4 (7236); AHMA, 1865, Hacienda, caja 99, exp. 1 (7258); AHMA, 1867, Gobierno, caja 106, exp. 2 (4644); AHMA 1876, Gobierno, caja 152, exp. 3 (5912); ANP 719, ff. 102v–6v; ANP 1860, ff. 218v–20v. See also María del Carmen Romano Soriano, "San Miguel Acocotla, Atlixco: Las Voces y la Historia de una Hacienda Triguera" (tesis licenciatura, Universidad de las Américas, Puebla, 2005).

6. James Deetz, "Archaeological Evidence of Sixteenth- and Seventeenth-Century Encounters," in *Historical Archaeology in Global Perspective*, ed. Lisa Falk (Washington, DC: Smithsonian Institution Press, 1991), 1.

7. Tutino, "From Involution to Revolution"; Tutino, *From Insurrection to Revolution*.

8. Patricia Fournier and Fernando A. Miranda-Flores, "Historic Sites Archaeology in Mexico," *Historical Archaeology* 26 (1992); Eduardo Noguera, "Estudio de la Cerámica Encontrada en el Sitio Donde Estaba el Templo Mayor de México," *Anales del Museo Nacional de Arqueología, Historia y Etnografía*, 5, no. 2 (1934).

9. John M. Goggin, *Spanish Majolica in the New World: Types of the Sixteenth to Eighteenth Centuries* (New Haven, CT: Department of Anthropology, Yale University, 1968); Florence Lister and Robert Lister, "The Potters' Quarter of Colonial Puebla, Mexico," *Historical Archaeology* 18, no. 1 (1984); Gonzalo López Cervantes, *Cerámica Colonial en la Ciudad de México*, Colección Científica 38, Serie Arqueología (Mexico

City: Instituto Nacional de Antropología e Historia, 1976); Florencia Müller, *Estudio de la Cerámica Hispánica y Moderna de Tlaxcala-Puebla*, Colección Científica 103 (Mexico City: Instituto Nacional de Antropología e Historia, 1981).

10. Thomas H. Charlton, "Ethnohistory and Archaeology: Post-conquest Aztec Sites," *American Antiquity* 34, no. 3 (1969).

11. Patricia Fournier, "Historical Archaeology in Mexico: A Reappraisal," *SAA Archaeological Record* 3, no. 4 (2003); Fournier and Miranda-Flores, "Historic Sites Archaeology."

12. Rani T. Alexander, "Prohibido Tocar Este Cenote: The Archaeological Basis for the Titles of Ebtun," *International Journal of Historical Archaeology* 16, no. 1 (2012); Rani T. Alexander, *Yaxcabá and the Caste War of Yucatán: An Archaeological Perspective* (Albuquerque: University of New Mexico Press, 2004); Anthony P. Andrews, Rafael Burgos Villanueva, and Luis Millet Cámara, "The Historic Port of el Real de Salinas in Campeche, and the Role of Coastal Resources in the Emergence of Capitalism in Yucatán, México," *International Journal of Historical Archaeology* 10, no. 2 (2006); Charlton, "Agrarian Landholdings"; Thomas H. Charlton, "Sociocultural Implications of House Types in the Teotihuacán Valley, Mexico," *Journal of the Society of Architectural Historians* 28, no. 4 (1969); Charlton, "Ethnohistory and Archaeology"; Janine Gasco, Greg Charles Smith, and Patricia Fournier-Garcia, eds., *Approaches to the Historical Archaeology of Mexico, Central, and South America* (Los Angeles: Institute of Archaeology, University of California, 1997); Patricia Fournier-Garcia, "Tendencias de Consumo en México Durante los Períodios Colonial e Independiente," in Gasco, Smith, and Fournier-Garcia, *Approaches to the Historical Archaeology of Mexico*; Patricia Fournier, *Evidencias Arqueológicas de la Importación de Cerámica en México, con Base en los Materiales del Ex-Convento de San Jerónimo*, Colección Científica no. 213, Serie Arqueología (Mexico City: Instituto Nacional de Antropología e Historia, 1990); Susan Kepecs and Rani T. Alexander, eds., *The Postclassic to Spanish-Era Transition in Mesoamerica: Archaeological Perspectives* (Albuquerque: University of New Mexico Press, 2005); David Jones, *The Archaeology of Nineteenth Century Haciendas and Ranchos of Otumba and Apan, Basin of Mexico* (Iowa City: University of Iowa, Department of Anthropology Mesoamerican Research Colloquium, 1980); Joel W. Palka, *Unconquered Lacandon Maya: Ethnohistory and Archaeology of Indigenous Culture Change, Maya Studies* (Gainesville: University Press of Florida, 2005); Judith Francis Zeitlin, *Cultural Politics in Colonial Tehuantepec: Community and State Among the Isthmus Zapotec, 1500–1750* (Stanford, CA: Stanford University Press, 2005).

13. Alexander, *Yaxcabá*; Alexander, "Introduction"; Rani T. Alexander, "Mesoamerican House Lots and Archaeological Site Structure: Problems of Inference in Yaxcabá, Yucatán, Mexico, 1750–1847," in *The Archaeology of Household Activities*, ed. Penelope M. Allison (New York: Routledge, 1999); Rani T. Alexander, "Settlement Patterns of the Late Colonial Period in Yaxcabá Parish, Yucatán, Mexico: Implications for the Distribution of Land and Population before the Caste War," in Gasco, Smith, and Fournier-Garcia, *Approaches to the Historical Archaeology of Mexico*; Antonio Benavides Castillo, "Notas Sobre la Arquelología Histórica de la Hacienda Tabi, Yucatán," *Revista Mexicana de Estudios Antropológicos* 31 (1985); Patricia Fournier-Garcia and Lourdes Mondragon, "Haciendas, Ranchos, and the Otomi Way of Life in the Mezquital Valley, Hidalgo, Mexico," *Ethnohistory* 50, no. 1 (2003); David Jones, "The

Importance of the Hacienda in 19th Century Otumba and Apan, Basin of Mexico," *Historical Archaeology* 15, no. 2 (1981); Jones, "Nineteenth Century Haciendas and Ranchos"; Harold Juli, "Perspectives on Mexican Hacienda Archaeology," *SAA Archaeological Record* 3, no. 4 (2003); Allan D. Meyers, "Material Expressions of Social Inequality on a Porfirian Sugar Hacienda in Yucatán, Mexico," *Historical Archaeology* 39, no. 4 (2005); Allan D. Meyers, *Outside the Hacienda Walls: The Archaeology of Plantation Peonage in Nineteenth-Century Yucatán*, Archaeology of Colonialism in Native North America (Tucson: University of Arizona Press, 2012); Meyers and Carlson, "Peonage, Power Relations and the Built Environment"; Allan D. Meyers, Allison S. Harvey, and Sarah A. Levithol, "Houselot Refuse Disposal and Geochemistry at a Late 19th Century Hacienda Village in Yucatán, Mexico," *Journal of Field Archaeology* 33, no. 4 (2008); Elizabeth Terese Newman, "San Miguel Acocotla: The History and Archaeology of a Central Mexican Hacienda" (PhD diss., Yale University, 2008); Elizabeth Terese Newman, "Butchers and Shamans: Zooarchaeology at a Central Mexican Hacienda," *Historical Archaeology* 44, no. 2 (2010); Elizabeth Terese Newman, "From Prison to Home: Coercion and Cooption in 19th Century Mexico," *Ethnohistory* 60, no. 4 (2013), Samuel Randles Sweitz, "On the Periphery of the Periphery: Household Archaeology at Hacienda Tabi, Yucatan, Mexico" (PhD diss., Texas A&M University, 2005).

14. Alexander, "Settlement Patterns"; Alexander, "Mesoamerican House Lots"; Alexander, "Introduction"; Alexander, *Yaxcabá*; Alexander, "Prohibido Tocar."

15. Meyers, "Material Expressions"; Meyers, *Outside the Hacienda Walls*; Meyers and Carlson, "Peonage, Power Relations, and the Built Environment"; Meyers, Harvey, and Levithol, "Houselot Refuse Disposal."

16. Juli, "Perspectives."

17. AHMA 1853, Gobierno, caja 92, exp. 1, ff. 1–30v.

18. Romano Soriano, "San Miguel Acocotla, Atlixco."

19. Alexander, "Mesoamerican House Lots"; Philip J. Arnold, *Domestic Ceramic Production and Spatial Organization: A Mexican Case Study in Ethnoarchaeology*, New Studies in Archaeology (Cambridge: Cambridge University Press, 1991); Luis Barba and Agustin Ortiz, "Análisis Químico de Pisos de Ocupación: Un Caso Etnográfico en Tlaxcala, Mexico," *Latin American Antiquity* 3, no. 1 (1992); David M. Carballo, "Advances in the Household Archaeology of Highland Mesoamerica," *Journal of Archaeological Research* 19, no. 2 (2011); Maria Elisa Christie, *Kitchenspace: Women, Fiestas, and Everyday Life in Central Mexico*, Joe R. and Teresa Lozano Long Series in Latin American and Latino Art and Culture (Austin: University of Texas Press, 2008); Guadalupe Corro, María Eugenia Pastor, and Nancy Ojeda Macías, "Recientes Investigaciones Etnográficas en San Juan Tejupa, Puebla," *Notas Mesoamericanas* 13 (1991); Kenneth Hirth, "The Household as an Analytical Unit: Problems in Method and Theory," in *Prehispanic Domestic Units in Western Mesoamerica: Studies of the Household, Compound, and Residence*, ed. Robert S. Santley and Kenneth G. Hirth (Boca Raton, FL: CRC Press, 1993); Scott R. Hutson et al., "Beyond the Buildings: Formation Processes of Ancient Maya Houselots and Methods for the Study of Non-architectural Space," *Journal of Anthropological Archaeology* 26, no. 3 (2007); Thomas W. Killion, "Residential Ethnoarchaeology and Ancient Site Structure: Contemporary Farming and Preshistoric Settlement Agriculture at Matacapan, Veracruz, Mexico," in *Gardens of Prehistory: The Archaeology of Settlement Agriculture in Greater*

Mesoamerica, ed. Thomas W. Killion (Tuscaloosa: University of Alabama Press, 1992); Stacie M. King, "The Spatial Organization of Food Sharing in Early Postclassic Households: An Application of Soil Chemistry in Ancient Oaxaca, Mexico," *Journal of Archaeological Science* 35, no. 5 (2008); Meyers, Harvey, and Levithol, "Houselot Refuse Disposal"; Lynette Norr, "The Excavation of a Postclassic House at Tetla," in *Ancient Chalcatzingo*, ed. David Grove (Austin: University of Texas Press, 1987); Michael E. Smith, "Houses and the Settlement Hierarchy in Late Postclassic Morelos: A Comparison of Archaeology and Ethnohistory," in Santley and Hirth, *Prehispanic Domestic Units in Western Mesoamerica*; Livingston D. Sutro and Theodore E. Downing, "A Step Toward a Grammar of Space: Domestic Space Use in Zapotec Villages," in *Household and Community in the Mesoamerican Past*, ed. Richard R. Wilk and Wendy Ashmore (Albuquerque: University of New Mexico Press, 1988); Richard Wilk and William L. Rathje, "Household Archaeology," *American Behavioral Scientist* 25 (1982); Richard R. Wilk, "Little House in the Jungle: The Causes of Variation in House Size Among Modern Kekchi Maya," *Journal of Anthropological Archaeology* 2, no. 2 (1983); Richard R. Wilk, *Household Ecology: Economic Change and Domestic Life Among the Kekchi Maya in Belize*, Arizona Studies in Human Ecology (Tucson: University of Arizona Press, 1991).

20. David L. Frye, *Indians into Mexicans: History and Identity in a Mexican Town* (Austin: University of Texas Press, 1996), 9.

21. Steve J. Stern, *The Secret History of Gender: Women, Men, and Power in Late Colonial Mexico* (Chapel Hill: University of North Carolina Press, 1995), 11–13; Tutino, *From Insurrection to Revolution*; Tutino, "From Involution to Revolution."

22. Kanter, *Hijos del Pueblo*; Meyer, *Problemas Campesinos*; Reina, *Rebeliones Campesinas*; Tutino, *From Insurrection to Revolution*; Tutino, "From Involution to Revolution"; Van Young, "Islands in the Storm."

23. Wolf, *Peasant Wars*.

24. Anthony Giddens, *The Class Structure of the Advanced Societies* (London: Hutchinson, 1973), 213.

25. Edward P. Thompson, *The Making of the English Working Class* (Harmondsworth, UK: Penguin, 1968).

26. Ibid.; Edward P. Thompson, "The Moral Economy of the English Crowd in the Eighteenth Century," *Past and Present* 50 (1971).

27. James C. Scott, *The Moral Economy of the Peasant: Rebellion and Subsistence in Southeast Asia* (New Haven, CT: Yale University Press, 1976).

28. Frye, *Indians into Mexicans*.

29. Tutino, *From Insurrection to Revolution*, 3–11.

30. Mörner, "Spanish American Hacienda"; Van Young, "Mexican Rural History."

Chapter 3

1. Plunket, "Arqueología y Etnohistoria"; Ursula Dyckerhoff, "La Región del Alto Atoyac en la Historia: La Época Prehispánica," in *Milpa y Hacienda: Tenencia de la Tierra Indígena y Española en la Cuenca del Alto Atoyac, Puebla, México (1520–1650)*, ed. Hans J. Prem (Puebla: Centro de Investigaciones y Estudios Superiores en Antropología Social, 1988).

2. Sherburne Friend Cook and Lesley Byrd Simpson, *The Population of Central Mexico in the Sixteenth Century*, (Berkeley: University of California Press, 1948), 45–46.

3. Paredes, *Región de Atlixco*; Romano Soriano, "San Miguel Acocotla, Atlixco."

4. Paredes, *Región de Atlixco*, 67. Illegal purchases and sales were not just a problem of the early years. As late as 1788, complaints were being filed regarding the illegal purchase and sale of indigenous lands in Atlixco. AHMA 1788, Gobierno, caja 7, exp. 3 (537).

5. Romano Soriano, "San Miguel Acocotla, Atlixco."

6. CEHM-CARSO 1602, Mercedes, fondo 765, f. 613.

7. Gerhard, *Guide to the Historical Geography*, 56–57.

8. Rodolfo Acuna-Soto et al., "Megadrought and Megadeath in 16th Century Mexico," *Emerging Infectious Diseases* 8, no. 4 (2002).

9. Knight, *Mexico*, 77.

10. Chevalier, *Land and Society*, 64.

11. Ibid. Each fanega of wheat equals anywhere from one to two bushels.

12. Romano Soriano, "San Miguel Acocotla, Atlixco," 39–40.

13. *Telenovelas* are soap operas popular in Mexico and throughout Latin America. Many of these television shows are set in purportedly colonial haciendas.

14. Charlton, "Socioeconomic Dimensions," 221–22; Jones, "Nineteenth Century Haciendas and Ranchos"; Herman W. Konrad, *A Jesuit Hacienda in Colonial Mexico: Santa Lucía, 1576–1767* (Stanford, CA: Stanford University Press, 1980), 313.

15. CEHM-CARSO 1686, Mercedes, fondo 765, f. 623.

16. CEHM-CARSO 1632, Mercedes, fondo 765, f. 50. Though the Spanish Crown prohibited the mention of indigenous laborers in bills of sale in 1601 and again in 1609, this decree was often ignored. Chevalier, *Land and Society*, 281–82.

17. Alexander, "Introduction," 5.

18. Alexander, "Prohibido Tocar"; Chance, "Haciendas, Ranchos, and Indian Towns"; Jean Meyer, "Haciendas y Ranchos, Peones y Campesinos en el Porfiriato. Algunas Falacias e Estadísticas," *Historia Mexicana* 35, no. 3 (1986); Van Young, *Hacienda and Market*.

19. AHMA 1785, Gobierno, caja 6, exp. 17 (517); AHMA 1841, Gobierno, caja 34, exp. 5 (1712); AHMA 1848, Gobierno, caja 84, exp. 2, ff. 1–1v; AHMA 1865, Hacienda, caja 99, exp. 4 (7258); AHMA 1867, Gobierno, caja 106, exp. 2 (4644).

20. ANP 1711, Atlixco, caja 54, ff. 32v–34v; ANP 1714, Atlixco, ff. 117v–18; ANP 1715, Atlixco, ff. 131v–36; ANP 1717, Atlixco, ff. 117v–18.

21. ANP 1714, Atlixco, ff. 117v–18.

22. ANP 1704, Atlixco, f. 22; ANP 1711, Atlixco, caja 54, ff. 32v–34v; ANP 1715, Atlixco, ff. 39v–42v; ANP 1719, Atlixco, ff. 102v–6v.

23. Woodrow Wilson Borah and Sherburne Friend Cook, *Price Trends of Some Basic Commodities in Central Mexico, 1531–1570*, Ibero-Americana 40 (Berkeley: University of California Press, 1958); Chevalier, *Land and Society*; Richard L. Garner, "Price Trends in Eighteenth-Century Mexico," *Hispanic American Historical Review* 65, no. 2 (1985); Knight, *Mexico*.

24. ANP 1706, Atlixco, ff. 84v–85; ANP 1707, Atlixco, ff. 48v–49; AGN 1712, Tierras, vol. 2797-2, exp. 7, f. 11v; ANP 1713, Atlixco, ff. 90v–91. Enrique Florescano

and Margarita Menegus, "La Época de las Reformas Borbónicas y el Crecimiento Económico (1750–1808)," in *Historia General de México: Versión 2000* (Mexico City: Colegio de México, Centro de Estudios Históricos de México, 2000), 421; Nickel, *Morfología Social*, 70; Enrique Semo, "Introducción," in *Siete Ensayos Sobre la Hacienda Mexicana*, ed. Enrique Semo (Mexico City: Instituto Nacional de Antropología e Historia, 1977), 11; Gisela Wobeser, "El Crédito y la Banca en México: Siglos XVI al XIX," *Estudios Mexicanos* 4, no. 1 (1988): 166; Wobeser, *Formación de la Hacienda*, 65.

25. Newman, "San Miguel Acocotla," 35; Romano Soriano, "San Miguel Acocotla, Atlixco," table 3.

26. ANP 1707, Atlixco, ff. 48v–49.

27. ANP 1705, Atlixco, ff. 207v–8v; ANP 1706, Atlixco, ff. 118v–19v; ANP 1707, Atlixco, ff. 51v–52; ANP 1707, Atlixco, ff. 127–28; ANP 1709, Atlixco, ff. 31v–32v; ANP 1709, Atlixco, ff. 40–41; ANP 1714, Atlixco, ff. 94v–95v; ANP 1714, Atlixco, ff. 113v–14v; ANP 1715, Atlixco, ff. 20–21; ANP 1715, Atlixco, ff. 39v–42v; ANP 1718, Atlixco, ff. 14v–15v.

28. George Reid Andrews, *Afro-Latin America, 1800–2000* (Oxford: Oxford University Press, 2004); Herman L. Bennett, *Colonial Blackness: A History of Afro-Mexico*, Blacks in the Diaspora (Bloomington: Indiana University Press, 2010); Patrick James Carroll, *Blacks in Colonial Veracruz: Race, Ethnicity, and Regional Development* (Austin: University of Texas Press, 1991); Marco Polo Hernández Cuevas, *African Mexicans and the Discourse on Modern Nation* (Lanham, MD: University Press of America, 2004); Ben Vinson and Matthew Restall, *Black Mexico: Race and Society from Colonial to Modern Times*, Diálogos (Albuquerque: University of New Mexico Press, 2009).

29. José Vasconcelos, *La Raza Cosmica: Mision de la Raza Iberoamericana* (Mexico City: Espasa-Calpe Mexicana, 1966).

30. Hernández Cuevas, *African Mexicans*, ix.

31. Frances Calderón de la Barca, *Life in Mexico* (Berkeley: University of California Press, 1982); Rosalie Caden Evans and Daisy Pettus, *The Rosalie Evans Letters from Mexico* (Indianapolis, IN: Bobbs-Merrill, 1926).

32. AHMA 1826, Gobierno, caja 6, exp. 5 (1000).

33. AHMA, 1826, Gobierno, caja 6, exp. 5 (997).

34. AHMA, 1864, Gobierno, caja 96, exp. 3 (4300).

35. In some documents, the mayordomo and his family are listed as being "de razon," meaning that the manager and his family behaved "with reason" like the European conquerors. Workers are, without exception, described as indigenous. AGN 1792, Padrones, vol. 25, ff. 1–45. In spite of the slave purchases and sales discussed earlier, a general census of the Valley of Atlixco conducted in 1792 is the only document that identifies an individual of African descent at Acocotla. A fifty-year-old servant named Manuel Toledo, identified as a "pardo" (a free person of African descent) from Atlixco, is said to be living at the hacienda with his twenty-five-year-old daughter and his three-year-old granddaughter.

36. Chevalier, *Land and Society*, 281–82.

37. CEHM-CARSO 1632, Mercedes, fondo 765, f. 50.

38. Charlton, "Socioeconomic Dimensions"; Jones, "Nineteenth Century Haciendas and Ranchos"; Konrad, *Jesuit Hacienda*; José Antonio Terán Bonilla, *La Construcción de las Haciendas de Tlaxcala* (Mexico City: Instituto Nacional de Antropología e

Historia, 1996); Wolfgang Trautmann, *Las Transformaciones en el Paisaje Cultural de Tlaxcala Durante la Época Colonial: Una Contribución a la Historia de México Bajo Especial Consideración de Aspectos Geográfico-Económicos y Sociales* (Wiesbaden: F. Steiner, 1981).

39. Alston, Mattiace, and Nonnenmacher, "Coercion, Culture, and Contracts"; Bauer, "Rural Workers"; Brass, "Latin American Enganche System"; Chevalier, *Land and Society*; Harry E. Cross, "Debt Peonage Reconsidered: A Case Study in Nineteenth-Century Zacatecas, Mexico," *Business History Review* 53 (1979); González Sánchez, *Haciendas, Tumultos y Trabajadores*; Knight, *Mexico*; Meyers and Carlson, "Peonage, Power Relations, and the Built Environment"; Nickel, *Peonaje en las Haciendas Mexicanas*; Tutino, *From Insurrection to Revolution*; Zavala, "Orígenes Históricos."

40. Herrera Feria, "Trabajadores Prófugos," 147–49.

41. AHMA 1855, Gobierno, caja 78, exp. 1 (3240).

42. Nickel, *Relaciones de Trabajo*, 55; Romano Soriano, "San Miguel Acocotla, Atlixco," 78–79. AHMA 1860, Gobierno, caja 87, exp. 4 (3916).

43. AHMA 1839, Gobierno, caja 26, exp. 2 (1504).

44. AHMA 1837, Justicia, caja 18, exp. 2 (2731).

45. AHMA 1865, Gobierno, caja 99, exp. 3 (4397).

46. AHMA 1837, Gobierno, caja 35, exp. 5, ff. 1–1v; AHMA 1841, Gobierno, caja 34, exp. 5 (1712); AHMA 1842, Gobierno, caja 42, exp. 4 (1924); AHMA 1844, Gobierno, caja 56, exp. 5 (2245); AHMA 1853, Gobierno, caja 73, exp. 3 (3053); AHMA 1854, Gobierno, caja 56, exp. 5 (2245); AHMA 1854, Gobierno, caja 95, exp. 1, ff. 1–2; AHMA 1857, Gobernación, caja 82, exp. 2 (3540); AHMA 1867, Gobierno, caja 106, exp. 2 (4629); AHMA 1868, Gobierno, caja 110, exp. 3 (4857); AHMA 1870, Gobierno, caja 115, exp. 2 (4971); AHMA 1871, Gobierno, caja 118, exp. 2 (5001); AHMA 1871, Gobierno, caja 123, exp. 4 (5206); AHMA 1872, Gobernación, caja 123, exp. 4 (5174); AHMA 1873, Gobierno, caja 133, exp. 3 (5565); AHMA 1884, Hacienda Pública, caja 221, exp. 5 (15318); AHMA 1889, Gobierno, caja 263, exp. 2 (11532); AHMA 1893, Gobernación, caja 309, exp. 5 (12890).

47. See also Bauer, "Rural Workers"; Cross, "Debt Peonage Reconsidered"; Mörner, "Spanish American Hacienda"; Van Young, "Mexican Rural History."

48. I limit the calculations to adult males (fourteen or more years of age) because women and children appear on only half of the censuses.

49. Romano Soriano, "San Miguel Acocotla, Atlixco." The reason behind the name of "Rancho la Mojonera" is unclear. As discussed earlier, a rancho is usually a small agricultural establishment. The record for La Mojonera indicates that it was an indigenous village. Documentary evidence from Coyula suggests that, at least in the Valley of Atlixco, a "rancho" was some sort of independent settlement associated with an operating hacienda. For example, an 1840 electoral census mentions, as one of the neighborhoods, "the rancho in front of the hacienda." Nine years later, four of the five men listed as inhabitants of the rancho in 1840 are listed as being inhabitants of the hacienda itself, suggesting a shift in settlement definition rather than a shift in domicile. It seems possible that the Rancho la Mojonera was established on former hacienda lands as a town for the workers. AHMA 1840, Gobernación, caja 30 exp. 2 (1581); AHMA 1849, Gobierno, caja 65, exp. 1 (2439).

50. AHMA 1872, Justicia, caja 130, exp. 3 (8233).

51. Antonio Peñafiel, "División Territorial de la República Mexicana," in *Censo y*

División Territorial del Estado de Puebla (Mexico City: Secretaria de Fomento, Colonización e Industria, 1903), 22.

52. Meyers, *Outside the Hacienda Walls* (see also n. 49 for a discussion of the available evidence).

53. AGN 1754, Tierras, vol. 789, exp. 1, f. 25.

54. Sonya Lipsett-Rivera, "Indigenous Communities and Water Rights in Colonial Puebla: Patterns of Resistance," *Americas* 48, no. 4 (1992); Sonya Lipsett-Rivera, *To Defend Our Water with the Blood of Our Veins: The Struggle for Resources in Colonial Puebla* (Albuquerque: University of New Mexico Press, 1999).

55. AGN 1784, Tierras, vol. 1110, exp. 6, ff. 1–33. Disputes over water were common throughout the history of the valley, not only between village and hacienda but among hacienda owners. See, e.g., AGN 1712 Tierras, vol. 2797-2, f. 11v; AGN 1713 Tierras, vol. 299, exp. 2, ff. 1–126; AGN 1713 Tierras, vol. 2797-2, exp. 7, ff. 1–19; AGN 1755 Tierras, vol. 818, exp. 4, ff. 1–66; AHMA 1872, Justicia, caja 130, exp. 3 (8233); AHMA 1889a, Gobierno, caja 268, exp. 1 (11886); AHMA 1889b, Gobierno, caja 268, exp. 1 (11886); ANP 1721 Atlixco, ff. 60–62. See also Rocío Castañeda González, *Las Aguas de Atlixco. Estado, Haciendas, Fábricas y Pueblos, 1880–1920* (Mexico City: El Colegio de Mexico, 2005); Lipsett-Rivera, "Indigenous Communities"; Lipsett-Rivera, *To Defend Our Water*; Gisela Wobeser, "El uso del agua en la region de Cuernavaca, Cuatla durante la epoca colonial," *Historia Mexicana* 32, no. 4 (1983).

56. AHMA 1841, caja 34, exp. 5 (1713); AHMA 1842, Gobierno, caja 43, exp. 4 (1925); AHMA 1842, Gobierno, caja 43, exp. 4 (1928).

57. AHMA 1842, Gobierno, caja 40, exp. 1 (1852); AHMA 1843, Gobierno, caja 48, exp. 2 (2030); AHMA 1843, Gobierno, caja 54, exp. 5 (2176); AHMA 1855, Gobierno, caja 78, exp. 2 (3293).

58. AHMA 1840, Gobierno, caja 30, exp. 1 (1576); AHMA 1840, Gobierno, caja 30, exp. 2 (1581); AHMA 1849, Gobierno, caja 65, exp. 1 (2439); AHMA 1852, Gobierno, caja 71, exp. 1 (2979); AHMA 1855, Gobierno, caja 78, exp. 2 (3293).

59. Archivo General del Estado de Puebla, hereafter AGEP, Registro Civil, Actas de Defunciones de la Municipalidad de Atlixco, libro 3, 1870; libro 3, 1871; libro 4, 1872; libro 4, vols. 1 and 2, 1873.

Chapter 4

1. INEGI, "Conteo de Población y Vivienda 2005," in *Información Estadística* (Mexico City: Instituto Nacional de Estadística y Geográfica), http://www.inegi.org.mx/est/contenidos/proyectos/ccpv/cpv2005/default.aspx, accessed September 24, 2013.

2. Ibid.

3. Ibid.

4. Akesha Baron, "'I'm a Woman but I Know God Leads My Way': Agency and Tzotzil Evangelical Discourse," *Language in Society* 33, no. 2 (2004); Christie, *Kitchenspace*, 76; Alan R. Sandstrom, "Conclusion: Anthropological Perspectives on Protestant Conversion in Mesoamerica," in *Holy Saints and Fiery Preachers: The Anthropology of Protestantism in Mexico and Central America*, ed. James W. Dow and Alan R. Sandstrom (Westport, CT: Praeger, 2001), 275–76.

5. Sandstrom, "Conclusion," 278; Yanna Yannakakis, *The Art of Being In-Between:*

Native Intermediaries, Indian Identity, and Local Rule in Colonial Oaxaca (Durham, NC: Duke University Press, 2008), xii–xiii.

6. Tobias Hecht, *At Home in the Street: Street Children of Northeast Brazil* (Cambridge: Cambridge University Press, 1998).

7. INEGI, "Conteo de Población y Vivienda 2005."

8. Fernando Armstrong-Fumero, "Before There Was Culture Here: Vernacular Discourse on Modernity in Yucatan, Mexico" (PhD diss., Stanford University, 2007); Paul K. Eiss, *In the Name of el Pueblo: Place, Community, and the Politics of History in Yucatán* (Durham, NC: Duke University Press, 2010); Barry J. Lyons, *Remembering the Hacienda: Religion, Authority, and Social Change in Highland Ecuador* (Austin: University of Texas Press, 2006).

9. This is not an unusual dynamic in Mesoamerica. See, e.g., Leigh Binford, "Migrant Remittances and (Under)Development in Mexico," *Critique of Anthropology* 23, no. 3 (2003); Jeffrey H. Cohen and Leila Rodriguez, "Remittance Outcomes in Rural Oaxaca, Mexico: Challenges, Options and Opportunities for Migrant Households," *Population, Space and Place* 11, no. 1 (2005); Sutro and Downing, "Step Toward a Grammar of Space," 39.

10. The typology was developed by Dr. Harold Juli (unpublished data) during the initial phase of research.

11. Barba and Ortiz, "Análisis Químico de Pisos"; Corro, Pastor, and Ojeda Macías, "Recientes Investigaciones Etnográficas"; William D. Middleton and T. Douglas Price, "Identification of Activity Areas by Multi-element Characterization of Sediments from Modern and Archaeological House Floors Using Inductively Coupled Plasma-Atomic Emission Spectroscopy," *Journal of Archaeological Science* 23 (1996); Sutro and Downing, "Step Toward a Grammar of Space."

12. For diagrams of layouts, see Newman, "San Miguel Acocotla," chap. 3.

13. Multiple kitchens for nuclear families are not unusual in Mesoamerica. Richard R. Wilk, "Households in Process: Agricultural Change and Domestic Transformation Among the Kekchi Maya of Belize," in *Households: Comparative and Historical Studies of the Domestic Group*, ed. Robert M. Netting, Richard R. Wilk, and Eric J. Arnould (Berkeley: University of California Press, 1984), 225.

14. Marshall Joseph Becker, "Houselots at Tikal Guatemala: It's What's Out Back That Counts," in *Reconstruyendo la Ciudad Maya: El Urbanismo en las Sociedades Antiguas*, ed. A. Cuidad Ruiz, M. J. Iglesias Ponce de León, and M. C. Martínez Martínez (Madrid: Sociedad Española de Estudios Mayas, 2001); Marion Cutting, "More Than One Way to Study a Building: Approaches to Prehistoric Household and Settlement Space," *Oxford Journal of Archaeology* 25, no. 3 (2006); Hutson et al., "Beyond the Buildings"; Kevin J. Johnston and Nancy Gonlin, "What Do Houses Mean? Approaches to the Analysis of Classic Maya Commoner Residences," in *Function and Meaning in Classic Maya Architecture*, ed. Stephen D. Houston (Washington, DC: Dumbarton Oaks, 1998); Kathryn A. Kamp, "Towards an Archaeology of Architecture: Clues from a Modern Syrian Village," *Journal of Anthropological Research* 49, no. 4 (1993); Kathryn A. Kamp, "From Village to Tell: Household Ethnoarchaeology in Syria," *Near Eastern Archaeology* 14 (2000); Killion, "Residential Ethnoarchaeology"; Carol Kramer, "An Archaeological View of a Contemporary Kurdish Village: Domestic Architecture, Household Size, and Wealth," in *Ethnoarchaeology: Implications of Ethnography for Archaeology*, ed. Carol Kramer (New York: Columbia University

Press, 1979); Lynn Meskell, "An Archaeology of Social Relations in an Egyptian Village," *Journal of Archaeological Method and Theory* 5 (1988); Cynthia Robin, "Outside of Houses," *Journal of Social Archaeology* 2, no. 2 (2002); Cynthia Robin, "New Directions in Classic Maya Household Archaeology," *Journal of Archaeological Research* 11, no. 4 (2003); Michael P. Smyth, Christopher D. Dore, and Nicholas P. Dunning, "Interpreting Prehistoric Settlement Patterns: Lessons from the Maya Center of Sayil, Yucatan," *Journal of Field Archaeology* 22, no. 3 (1995); Delwen Samuel, "Bread Making and Social Interactions at the Amarna Workmen's Village, Egypt," *World Archaeology* 31 (1999).

15. Alexander, "Mesoamerican House Lots"; Arnold, *Domestic Ceramic Production*; Philip J. Arnold, "The Organization of Refuse Disposal and Ceramic Production Within Contemporary Mexican Houselots," *American Anthropologist* 92, no. 4 (1990); Michael Deal, *Pottery Ethnoarchaeology in the Central Maya Highlands*, Foundations of Archaeological Inquiry (Salt Lake City: University of Utah Press, 1998); Brian Hayden and Aubrey Cannon, "Where the Garbage Goes: Refuse Disposal in the Maya Highlands," *Journal of Anthropological Archaeology* 2 (1983); Hutson et al., "Beyond the Buildings"; Thomas W. Killion, "Cultivation Intensity and Residential Site Structure: An Ethnoarchaeological Examination of Peasant Agriculture in the Sierra de los Tuxtlas, Veracruz, Mexico," *Latin American Antiquity* 1, no. 3 (1990); Meyers, Harvey, and Levithol, "Houselot Refuse Disposal."

16. Brian F. Byrd, "Households in Transition: Neolithic Social Organization Within Southwest Asia," in *Life in Neolithic Farming Communities: Social Organization, Identity and Differentiation*, ed. Ian Kuijt (New York/London: Springer, 2000); Samuel E. Casselberry, "Further Refinement for Formulae for Determining Population from Floor Area," *World Archaeology* 6 (1974); Cutting, "More Than One Way"; Kent V. Flannery, "The Cultural Evolution of Civilizations," *Annual Review of Ecology and Systematics* 3 (1972); Charles C. Kolb et al., "Demographic Estimates in Archaeology: Contributions from Ethnoarchaeology on Mesoamerican Peasants [and Comments and Reply]," *Current Anthropology* 26, no. 5 (1985).

17. King, "Spatial Organization of Food Sharing," 1224.

18. Arnold J. Bauer, *Goods, Power, History: Latin America's Material Culture*, New Approaches to the Americas (Cambridge: Cambridge University Press, 2001); Arnold J. Bauer, "Millers and Grinders: Technology and Household Economy in Meso-America," *Agricultural History* 64, no. 1 (1990); Louise M. Burkhart, "Mexica Women on the Home Front: Housework and Religion in Aztec Mexico," in *Indian Women of Early Mexico*, ed. Susan Schroeder, Stephanie Wood, and Robert Hasket (Norman: University of Oklahoma Press, 1997); Susan Kellogg, "The Woman's Room: Some Aspects of Gender Relations in Tenochtitlan in the Late-Prehispanic Period," *Ethnohistory* 42, no. 4 (1995); King, "Spatial Organization of Food Sharing"; Norr, "Excavation of a Postclassic House"; Jacques Soustelle, *The Daily Life of the Aztecs: On the Eve of the Spanish Conquest*, trans. Patrick O'Brian, Daily Life Series (New York: Macmillan, 1962); Susan Kellogg, *Law and the Transformation of Aztec Culture, 1500–1700* (Norman: University of Oklahoma Press, 1995).

19. Fray Bernardino de Sahagún, *Florentine Codex*, qtd. in Kellogg, "Woman's Room," 570.

20. Burkhart, "Mexica Women," 41–42.

21. James Lockhart, *The Nahuas After the Conquest: A Social and Cultural History*

of the Indians of Central Mexico, Sixteenth through Eighteenth Centuries (Stanford, CA: Stanford University Press, 1992), 66–67; also see Susan Kellogg, "The Social Organization of Households among the Tenochca Mexica Before and After the Conquest," in Santley and Hirth, *Prehispanic Domestic Units in Western Mesoamerica*, 210.

22. Lockhart, *Nahuas After the Conquest*, 66.

23. Kellogg, "Social Organization of Households," 218; Norr, "Excavation of a Postclassic House."

24. Whether or not people's answers reflect the hard facts is debatable. Cement blocks may be more durable or easier to come by—the Mexican government even has housing programs that deliver blocks to poor communities (though this program has not reached La Soledad)—and the practical reason for their use may have to do with these factors. The ways people understand, interpret, and represent their decisions is significant—people here believe adobe is the better building material and that cement block is "modern."

25. Lockhart, *Nahuas After the Conquest*, 59–93.

26. Ibid., 63–65.

27. Barba and Ortiz, "Análisis Químico de Pisos"; Kamp, "Archaeology of Architecture"; Kamp, "From Village to Tell"; Kellogg, "Social Organization of Households," fig. 2; Soustelle, *Daily Life*; Sutro and Downing, "Step Toward a Grammar of Space."

28. Sutro and Downing, "Step Toward a Grammar of Space," 35.

29. Wilk, *Household Ecology*, 167.

30. Though ostentatious displays of wealth are unusual in many Mesoamerican communities, scholars working in some have been able to connect architectural elaboration with status. See, e.g., Richard E. Blanton, *Houses and Households: A Comparative Study*, Interdisciplinary Contributions to Archaeology (New York: Plenum Press, 1994); Carballo, "Advances in the Household Archaeology"; Sutro and Downing, "Step Toward a Grammar of Space"; Wilk, *Household Ecology*; Wilk and Rathje, "Household Archaeology."

31. Wilk, "Little House in the Jungle," 167.

32. See also Arnold, *Domestic Ceramic Production*; Cutting, "More Than One Way"; Johnston and Gonlin, "What Do Houses Mean?"; Laura J. Levi, "An Institutional Perspective on Prehispanic Maya Residential Variation: Settlement and Community at San Estevan, Belize," *Journal of Anthropological Archaeology* 21, no. 2 (2002); Kamp, "Archaeology of Architecture"; Kamp, "From Village to Tell"; Kramer, "Archaeological View"; Meskell, "Archaeology of Social Relations"; Samuel, "Bread Making."

33. Alexander, "Mesoamerican House Lots"; Arnold, *Domestic Ceramic Production*; Hirth, "Household as an Analytical Unit"; Michael E. Smith, "Braudel's Temporal Rhythms and Chronology Theory in Archaeology," in *Archaeology, Annales, and Ethnohistory*, ed. A. Bernard Knapp (Cambridge: Cambridge University Press, 1992).

Chapter 5

1. CEHM-CARSO 1686, Mercedes, fondo 765, ff. 623–30.

2. Numbers in the text correlate with locations on the hacienda map (fig. 5.1); letters represent areas that were unidentified by our informants.

3. AHMA 1842, Gobierno, caja 42, exp. 4 (1924).

4. Romano Soriano, "San Miguel Acocotla, Atlixco," 107.

5. Calderón de la Barca, *Life in Mexico*, 147.

6. Puddled adobe is a wet adobe that has been poured between wooden frames and left to dry, after which the frames are removed.

7. Julia A. King and Henry Miller, "The View from the Midden: An Analysis of Midden Distribution and Composition at the Van Sweringen Site, St. Mary's City, Maryland," *Historical Archaeology* 21, no. 2 (1987); Thomas F. King, *The Archeological Survey: Methods and Uses* (Washington, DC: Heritage Conservation and Recreation Service, US Department of the Interior, 1978); Henry Miller, *Discovering Maryland's First City: A Summary Report on the 1981–1984 Archaeological Excavations in St. Mary's City, Maryland*, St. Mary's City Archaeology Series 2 (St. Mary's City, MD: St. Mary's City Commission, 1986).

Chapter 6

1. AHMA 1893, Gobierno, caja 309, exp. 5 (12890).

2. Stern, *Secret History of Gender*, 91–92.

3. See, e.g., Jane Eva Baxter, "The Paradox of a Capitalist Utopia: Visionary Ideals and Lived Experience in the Pullman Community 1880–1900," *International Journal of Historical Archaeology* 16, no. 4 (2012); Mary C. Beaudry, "The Lowell Boott Mills Complex and Its Housing: Material Expressions of Corporate Ideology," *Historical Archaeology* 23, no. 1 (1989); James Deetz, *In Small Things Forgotten: The Archaeology of Early American Life* (Garden City, NY: Doubleday, 1977); Henry H. Glassie, *Folk Housing in Middle Virginia: A Structural Analysis of Historic Artifacts* (Knoxville: University of Tennessee Press, 1975); Ross W. Jamieson, *Domestic Architecture and Power: The Historical Archaeology of Colonial Ecuador*, Contributions to Global Historical Archaeology (New York: Kluwer Academic/Plenum Publishers, 2000); Matthew Johnson, *An Archaeology of Capitalism*, Social Archaeology (Oxford: Blackwell Publishers, 1996); Mark P. Leone, "The Georgian Order as the Order of Merchant Capitalism in Annapolis, MD," in *The Recovery of Meaning: Historical Archaeology in the Eastern United States*, ed. Mark P. Leone and Parker B. Potter Jr. (Washington, DC: Smithsonian Institution Press, 1988); Meyers, "Material Expressions"; Meyers, *Outside the Hacienda Walls*; Theresa A. Singleton, "Slavery and Spatial Dialectics on Cuban Coffee Plantations," *World Archaeology* 33, no. 1 (2001); John Michael Vlach, *Back of the Big House: The Architecture of Plantation Slavery* (Chapel Hill: University of North Carolina Press, 1993).

4. Stephen A. Mrozowski, "Interdisciplinary Perspectives on the Production of Urban Industrial Space," in *Old and New Worlds*, ed. Geoff Egan and Ronald L. Michael (Oxford: Oxbow Books, 1999).

5. Improvements to the casco's structure, such as the construction of a neat and orderly row of worker housing, would also improve the value of the property.

6. ANP 1860, Atlixco, ff. 198–243v.

7. Ibid., ff. 218v–20v.

8. Kanter, *Hijos del Pueblo*; Tutino, *From Insurrection to Revolution*; Tutino, "From Involution to Revolution."

9. AHMA 1814, Gobierno, caja 2, exp. 3 (839).

10. For details on attracting and maintaining a consistent worker population, see chapter 3 and Newman, "Prison to Home."

11. Michel Foucault, *Discipline and Punish: The Birth of the Prison* (New York: Vintage Books, 1979); Anthony Giddens, *The Constitution of Society: Outline of the Theory of Structuration* (Cambridge: Polity Press, 1984); Henri Lefebvre, *The Production of Space* (Oxford: Blackwell, 1991); Mark P. Leone, "A Historical Archaeology of Capitalism," *American Anthropologist* 97, no. 2 (1995); Amos Rapoport, *House Form and Culture*, Foundations of Cultural Geography Series (Englewood Cliffs, NJ: Prentice-Hall, 1969).

12. Leone, "Historical Archaeology of Capitalism," 255; see also Edmund N. Bacon, *Design of Cities* (New York: Viking Press, 1967); Foucault, *Discipline and Punish*; Lefebvre, *Production of Space*.

13. Baxter, "Paradox of a Capitalist Utopia"; Beaudry, "Lowell Boott Mills Complex"; William Chapman, "Slave Villages in the Danish West Indies: Changes of the Late Eighteenth and Early Nineteenth Centuries," *Perspectives in Vernacular Architecture* 4 (1991); James A. Delle, "Landscapes of Class Negotiation on Coffee Plantations in the Blue Mountains of Jamaica: 1790–1850," *Historical Archaeology* 33, no. 1 (1999); Terrence Epperson, "Race and the Disciplines of the Plantation," *Historical Archaeology* 24, no. 4 (1990); Pedro Paulo A. Funari and Andres Zarankin, "Social Archaeology of Housing from a Latin American Perspective," *Journal of Social Archaeology* 3, no. 1 (2003); Jamieson, *Domestic Architecture and Power*; Johnson, *Archaeology of Capitalism*; Joe W. Joseph, "White Columns and Black Hands: Class and Classification in the Plantation Ideology of the Georgia and South Carolina Low Country," *Historical Archaeology* 27, no. 3 (1993); Leone, "Historical Archaeology of Capitalism"; Mark P. Leone, "Interpreting Ideology in Historical Archaeology: Using the Rules of Perspective in the William Paca Garden in Annapolis, Maryland," in *Ideology, Power, and Prehistory*, ed. Daniel Miller and Christopher Tilley (Cambridge: Cambridge University Press, 1984); Henry Miller, "Baroque Cities in the Wilderness: Archaeology and Urban Development in the Colonial Chesapeake," *Historical Archaeology* 22, no. 2 (1988); Stephen A. Mrozowski, "Landscapes of Inequality," in *The Archaeology of Inequality*, ed. Randall H. McGuire and Robert Paynter (Oxford: Basil Blackwell, 1991); Stephen A. Mrozowski, "Managerial Capitalism and the Subtleties of Class Analysis in Historical Archaeology," in *Lines That Divide: The Archaeologies of Race, Class and Gender*, ed. James Delle, Stephen Mrozowski, and Robert Paynter (Knoxville: University of Tennessee Press, 2000); Stephen A. Mrozowski, Grace H. Ziesing, and Mary C. Beaudry, *Living on the Boott: Historical Archaeology at the Boott Mills Boardinghouses, Lowell, Massachusetts* (Amherst: University of Massachusetts Press, 1996).

14. Guadalupe de la Torre Villalpando, *Las Calpanerías de las Haciendas Tlaxcaltecas*, (Tlaxcala: Instituto Nacional de Antropología e Historia, 1988).

15. Francisco Javier Bravo Juárez and Arturo Córdova Durana, "Unidades de Producción de la Ciudad de Atlixco: Haciendas, Ranchos, y Molinos," in *Atlixco: Historia Patrimonio y Sociedad*, ed. Arturo Córdova Durana and Gustavo Mauleón Rodríguez (Atlixco, Mexico: L'Anxaneta Ediciones, 2007).

16. Giddens, *Constitution of Society*.

17. Foucault, *Discipline and Punish*; Leone, "Historical Archaeology of Capitalism."

18. Deetz, *In Small Things Forgotten*; Funari and Zarankin, "Social Archaeology of Housing"; Giddens, *Constitution of Society*; Henry H. Glassie, "Vernacular Architecture and Society," in *Mirror and Metaphor: Material and Social Constructions of Reality*, ed. Daniel W. Ingersoll and Gordon Bronitsky (Lanham, MD: University Press of America, 1987); Jamieson, *Domestic Architecture and Power*; Johnson, *Archaeology of Capitalism*.

19. Meyers and Carlson, "Peonage, Power Relations, and the Built Environment"; Meyers, *Outside the Hacienda Walls*.

20. The hacienda's workers were paid partly in cash and partly in food rations, most commonly maize. Romano Soriano, "San Miguel Acocotla, Atlixco."

21. AHMA, 1842, Gobierno, caja 42, exp. 4 (1924).

22. AHMA, 1893, Gobierno, caja 309, exp. 5 (12890).

23. Cutting, "More Than One Way"; Kamp, "Archaeology of Architecture"; Kamp, "From Village to Tell"; Kramer, "Archaeological View"; Meskell, "Archaeology of Social Relations"; Samuel, "Bread Making."

24. Hayden and Cannon, "Where the Garbage Goes."

25. This was suggested by Lewis R. Binford with his famous "drop toss" model. Binford, "Willow Smoke and Dogs' Tail: Hunter Gatherer Settlement Systems and Archaeological Site Formation," *American Antiquity* 45 (1980); Lewis R. Binford, *In Pursuit of the Past* (London: Thames and Hudson, 1983).

26. Kamp, "Archaeology of Architecture."

27. Ibid., 299.

28. Dan M. Healan, "Urbanism at Tula from the Perspective of Residential Archaeology," in Santley and Hirth, *Prehispanic Domestic Units in Western Mesoamerica*; Kellogg, "Social Organization of Households"; Kellogg, "Woman's Room"; Lockhart, *Nahuas After the Conquest*; Norr, "Excavation of a Postclassic House"; Soustelle, *Daily Life*; Burkhart, "Mexica Women."

29. Norr, "Excavation of a Postclassic House."

30. Soustelle, *Daily Life*, 121.

31. Healan, "Urbanism at Tula," 111.

32. King, "Spatial Organization of Food Sharing," 1224.

33. Lockhart, *Nahuas After the Conquest*, 66–67.

34. Kanter, *Hijos del Pueblo*; Newman, "San Miguel Acocotla"; Romano Soriano, "San Miguel Acocotla, Atlixco"; Tutino, *From Insurrection to Revolution*; Tutino, "From Involution to Revolution."

35. For an examination of the male, patriarchal side of the experience, see John Tutino, "From Involution to Revolution in Mexico: Liberal Development, Patriarchy, and Social Violence in the Central Highlands, 1870–1915," *History Compass* 6, no. 3 (2008).

36. Kamp, "Archaeology of Architecture," 310.

Chapter 7

1. Fernand Braudel, *Capitalism and Material Life, 1400–1800* (London: Fontana, 1974).

2. Ibid., 23–24.

3. Fernand Braudel, *On History* (Chicago: University of Chicago Press, 1980), 25–54.

4. Pierre Bourdieu, *The Logic of Practice* (Cambridge: Polity Press, 1990), 53.

5. Pierre Bourdieu, *Outline of a Theory of Practice*, Cambridge Studies in Social Anthropology 16 (Cambridge: Cambridge University Press, 1977), 85.

6. M. James Blackman, Patricia Fournier, and Ronald Bishop, "Complejidad e Interacción Social en México Colonial: La Producción, Intercambio y Consumo de Cerámicas Vidriadas y Esmaltadas con Base en Análisis de Activación Neutrónica," *Cuicuilco* 36 (2006); Thomas H. Charlton and Patricia Fournier, "Urban and Rural Dimensions of the Contact Period: Central Mexico, 1521–1620," in *Ethnohistory and Archaeology: Approaches to Postcontact Change in the Americas*, ed. J. Rogers and S. Wilson (New York: Plenum Press, 1993); Thomas H. Charlton, Patricia Fournier, and Cynthia Otis Charlton, "La Cerámica del Período Colonial Temprano en la Cuenca de México: Permanencia y Cambio en la Cultural Material," in *La Producción Alfarera en México Antiguo*, ed. Beatriz Leonor Merino Carrión and Angel García Cook (Mexico City: Instituto Nacional de Antropología e Historia, 2002); Thomas H. Charlton and Roberta Katz, "Tonalá Bruñida Ware, Past and Present," *Archaeology* 32, no. 1 (1979); Fournier-Garcia, "Tendencias de Consumo"; Patricia Fournier, *Evidencias Arqueológicas de la Importación de Cerámica en México, con Base en los Materialses del Ex-Convento de San Jerónimo*, Colección Científica No. 213, Serie Arqueologia (Mexico City: Instituto National de Antropología y Historia, 1990); Patricia Fournier, "La Cerámica Colonial del Templo Mayor," *Arqueología Mexicana* 31 (1998); F. Monroy-Guzman and Patricia Fournier, "Elemental Composition of the Mexican Colonial Majolica Using Inaa," in *Nuclear Analytical Techniques in Archaeological Investigations*, Technical Reports Series 416 (Vienna, Austria: International Atomic Energy Agency, 2003). Enrique Rodríguez-Alegría, "Eating like an Indian: Negotiating Social Relations in the Spanish Colonies," *Current Anthropology* 46, no. 4 (2005); Enrique Rodríguez-Alegría, Hector Neff, and Michael D. Glascock, "Indigenous Ware or Spanish Import? The Case of Indígena Ware and Approaches to Power in Colonial Mexico," *Latin American Antiquity* 14, no. 1 (2003).

7. For exceptions, see e.g. Fournier, Patricia. "The Mayolica of Guanajuato." In *Ceramica Y Cultura: The Story of Spanish and Mexican Mayolica*, ed. Robin Farwell Gavin, Donna Pierce and Alfonso Pleguezuelo, 296–313 (Albuquerque: University of New Mexico Press, 2003); Jones, "Importance of the Hacienda"; Donna Seifert, "Archaeological Majolicas of the Rural Teotihuacán Valley, Mexico" (PhD diss., University of Iowa, 1977); Velasquez Sánchez-Hidalgo, Verónica. *Lugar De Maravillas: Arqueología en Pacific City: Sedimentos y vestigios de un sueño utópico del Siglo XIX en el Norte de Sinaloa*. Mexico City: Axial, 2012.

8. Harold Juli, Elizabeth Terese Newman, and Martha Adriana Sáenz Serdio, "Arqueología Histórica en la Hacienda San Miguel Acocotla, Atlixco Puebla: Informe de la Primera Temporada de Excavaciones, 2005 y Propuesta para la Segunda Temporada, 2006," (Mexico City: Unpublished report to the Instituto Nacional de Antropología e Historia, 2006); Newman, "San Miguel Acocotla."

9. Kathleen A. Deagan, *Artifacts of the Spanish Colonies of Florida and the Caribbean, 1500–1800*, 2 vols. (Washington, DC: Smithsonian Institution Press, 1987), 1:96.

10. Florence Lister and Robert Lister, "Majolica in Colonial Spanish America,"

Historical Archaeology 8 (1974): 28–29; Florence Lister and Robert Lister, "The First Mexican Maiolicas: Imported and Locally Produced," *Historical Archaeology* 12 (1978): 10.

11. Lister and Lister, "Majolica in Colonial Spanish America," 29.

12. Deagan, *Artifacts of the Spanish Colonies*, 1:101.

13. Oliva Castro Morales, "La Fábrica de Loza Fina de Puebla," in *Cerámica Inglesa en México*, ed. Jones Barclay, Olivia, Oliva Castro Morales, and Ana Paulina Gámez (Mexico City: Museo Franz Mayer, Artes de México, British Council, 2003); Fournier, *La Importación de Cerámica*, 253–56.

14. Meyers, *Outside the Hacienda Walls*, 107.

15. Barbara E. Borg, "Archaeological Whitewares of the Teotihuacán Valley, Mexico" (master's thesis, University of Iowa, 1975), 43; Jones, "Nineteenth Century Haciendas and Ranchos," 154, 63.

16. Francisco Rafael Burgos Villanueva, "Materiales Históricos Recuperados en el Edificio del D.A.P., Campeche, Camp.," *Boletín de la Escuela de Cienceias Antropológicas de la Universidad de Yucatán* 19, no. 110–11 (1991); Francisco Rafael Burgos Villanueva, *El Olimpo: Un Predio Colonial en el Lado Poniente de la Plaza Mayor de Mérida, Yucatán, y Análisis Cerámico Comparativo* (Mexico City: Instituto Nacional de Antropología e Historia, 1995); Fournier-Garcia, "Tendencias de Consumo"; Meyers, "Material Expressions"; Meyers, *Outside the Hacienda Walls*; Sweitz, "On the Periphery of the Periphery."

17. Ivor Noël Hume, "An Indian Ware of the Colonial Period," *Quarterly Bulletin of the Archaeological Society of Virginia* 17, no. 1 (1962).

18. Leland G. Ferguson, *Uncommon Ground: Archaeology and Early African America, 1650–1800* (Washington, DC: Smithsonian Institution Press, 1992); Laura J. Galke, "Colonowhen, Colonowho, Colonowhere, Colonowhy: Exploring the Meaning Behind the Use of Colonoware Ceramics in Nineteenth-Century Manassas, Virginia," *International Journal of Historical Archaeology* 13, no. 3 (2009).

19. Though few studies explicitly connect Prehispanic and historic pottery *types*, a number of studies deal with ceramic manufacture in twentieth-century rural communities, especially among the Maya. These studies were conducted both as part of larger ethnographic studies and as more focused ethnoarchaeological studies of pottery production. See, e.g., Arnold, *Domestic Ceramic Production*; Deal, *Pottery Ethnoarchaeology*; George M. Foster, *Tzintzuntzan: Mexican Peasants in a Changing World*, (Boston: Little Brown, 1967); Louana M. Lackey, *The Pottery of Acatlán: A Changing Mexican Tradition* (Norman: University of Oklahoma Press, 1982); Raymond H. Thompson, *Modern Yucatecan Maya Pottery Making*, Memoirs of the Society for American Archaeology (Salt Lake City: Society for American Archaeology, 1958). For a particularly fascinating account of Maya pottery making that was made in a time period contemporary with the potters discussed here, see Edward H. Thompson *The Maya Potter of Yucatan* (Cambridge, MA. unpublished manuscript on file with the Peabody Museum Library, Harvard University, 1900).

20. Arnulfo Allende Carrera, "Informe Preliminar del Laboratorio de Análisis de Materiales Arqueológicos. Archivo Proyecto de Salvamento Arqueológico de Plan de Conservación y Ordenamiento Urbano y Arquitectónico del Paseo del Río de San Francisco, Puebla," (Puebla, 1997); López Cervantes, *Cerámica Colonial*, 38; Müller, *Estudio de la Cerámica*, 103.

21. López Cervantes, *Cerámica Colonial*, 38; Müller, *Estudio de la Cerámica*, 103.

22. Patricia Plunket and Gabriela Uruñuela, "Recent Research in Puebla Prehistory," *Journal of Archaeological Research* 13, no. 2 (2005); Patricia Plunket et al., "A Rural Perspective on Mesoamerican Integration During the Late and Terminal Formative," *New Perspectives on Formative Mesoamerican Cultures* (2005); Evelyn Childs Rattray, "Anaranjado Delgado: Cerámica de Comercio de Teotihuacán," in *Interacción Cultural En México Central*, ed. Evelyn Childs Rattray, Jaime Litvak King, and Clara Díaz Oyarzabal (Mexico City: Instituto de Investigaciones Antropológicas, Universidad Nacional Autónoma de México, 1981).

23. Evelyn Childs Rattray, "New Findings on the Origins of Thin Orange Ceramics," *Ancient Mesoamerica* 1, no. 2 (1990).

24. Lackey, *The Pottery of Acatlán*.

25. AHMA 1826, Gobierno, caja 6, exp. 5 (997).

26. Minimum vessel counts were calculated using rim sherds. Ceramic type, vessel form, rim diameter and surface treatment were taken into account.

27. Total number of vessels identified in each area were, for room 11, 23; room 18, 44; room 20, 81; room 21, 87; room 22, 62; midden, 612.

28. Sophie D. Coe, *America's First Cuisines* (Austin: University of Texas Press, 1994), 14–16.

29. Margaret Beck, "Archaeological Signatures of Corn Preparation in the U.S. Southwest," *Kiva* 67, no. 2 (2001); David Cheetham, "Corn, Colanders, and Cooking: Early Maize Processing in the Maya Lowlands and Its Implications," in *Pre-Columbian Foodways*, ed. John E. Staller and Michael Carrasco (New York: Springer, 2010).

30. Patricia S. Bridges, "Prehistoric Arthritis in the Americas," *Annual Review of Anthropology* 21 (1992); Vered Eshed et al., "Paleopathology and the Origin of Agriculture in the Levant," *American Journal of Physical Anthropology* 143, no. 1 (2010); Anne Fausto-Sterling, "The Bare Bones of Sex," in *Women, Science, and Technology: A Reader in Feminist Science Studies*, ed. Mary Wyer et al. (New York: Routledge, 2008); Theya Molleson, "Bone of Work at the Origins of Labor," in *Archaeology and Women: Ancient and Modern Issues*, ed. Sue Hamilton, Ruth D. Whitehouse, and Katherine I. Wright (Walnut Creek, CA: Left Coast Press, 2007); Theya Molleson, "The Eloquent Bones of Abu Hureyra," *Scientific American* 271, no. 2 (1994).

31. Charles F. Merbes, "The Pathology of a La Jollan Skeleton from Punta Minitas, Baja California," *Pacific Coast Archaeological Society Quarterly* 16 (1980).

32. Ross W. Jamieson, "The Market for Meat in Colonial Cuenca," *Historical Archaeology* 42, no. 4 (2008); David B. Landon, "Foodways in the Lowell Boardinghouses: The Historical and Zooarchaeological Evidence," in *Interdisciplinary Investigations of the Lowell Boott Mills, Lowell, Massachusetts*, Vol. 1, *Life in the Boardinghouses*, ed. Mary C. Beaudry and Stephen A. Mrozowski, Cultural Resources Management Study 18 (Boston: Department of the Interior, National Park Service, North Atlantic Regional Office, 1987); David B. Landon, "Domestic Ideology and the Economics of Boardinghouse Keeping," in *Interdisciplinary Investigations of the Boott Mills, Lowell, Massachusetts*, Vol. 3, *The Boardinghouse System as a Way of Life*, ed. Mary C. Beaudry and Stephen A. Mrozowski, Cultural Resource Management Study 21 (Boston: Department of the Interior, National Park Service, North Atlantic Regional Office, 1989); David B. Landon, "Zooarchaeology and Urban Foodways: A Case Study from Eastern Massachusetts" (PhD diss., Boston University, 1991); Stephen

A. Mrozowski et al., "Living on the Boott: Health and Well Being in a Boardinghouse Population," *World Archaeology* 21, no. 2 (1989); Newman, "Butchers and Shamans; Vincent C. Peloso, "Succulence and Sustenance: Region, Class, and Diet in Nineteenth-Century Peru," in *Food, Politics, and Society in Latin America*, ed. John C. Super and Thomas C. Wright (Lincoln: University of Nebraska Press, 1985); Elizabeth J. Reitz, "Spanish and British Subsistence Strategies at St. Augustine, Florida, and Frederica, Georgia, Between 1565 and 1733" (PhD diss., University of Florida, 1979); Elizabeth J. Reitz, "Vertebrate Fauna and Socioeconomic Status," in *Consumer Choice in Historical Archaeology*, ed. Suzanne M. Spencer-Wood (New York: Plenum Press, 1987); Elizabeth J. Reitz, "Animal Use and Culture Change in Spanish Florida," in *Animal Use and Culture Change*, ed. Pam J. Crabtree and Kathleen Ryan (Philadelphia: University Museum, University of Pennsylvania, 1991); Elizabeth J. Reitz, "Zooarchaeological Analysis of a Free African Community: Gracia Real de Santa Teresa de Mose," *Historical Archaeology* 28, no. 1 (1994); Elizabeth J. Reitz and Martha A. Zierden, "Cattle Bones and Status from Charleston, South Carolina," in *Beamers, Bobwhites, and Blue-Points: Tributes to the Career of Paul W. Parmalee*, ed. James R. Purdue, Walter E. Klippel, and Bonnie W. Styles (Springfield: Illinois State Museum, 1991); Schulz and Gust, "Faunal Remains and Social Status"; Elizabeth Scott, "Who Ate What? Archaeological Food Remains and Cultural Diversity," in *Case Studies in Environmental Archaeology*, ed. Elizabeth Jean Reitz, Lee A. Newsom, and Sylvia J. Scudder, Interdisciplinary Contributions to Archaeology (New York: Plenum Press, 1996).

33. Following Diane P. Gifford and Diana C. Crader, "A Computer Coding System for Archaeological Faunal Remains," *American Antiquity* 42, no. 2 (1977).

34. Following Anna K. Behrensmeyer, "Taphonomic and Ecologic Information from Bone Weathering," *Paleobiology* 4, no. 2 (1978).

35. Though people in the modern community do, on occasion, go fishing, fish is a negligible part of the diet. During a food survey in La Soledad Morelos in 2005, only one woman mentioned fish at all—as her least favorite food.

36. Timothy Knab, pers. comm.

37. Barnet Pavao-Zuckerman, "Rendering Economies: Native American Labor and Secondary Animal Products in the Eighteenth-Century Pimería Alta," *American Antiquity* 75, no. 1 (2011); Susan D. deFrance and Craig A. Hanson, "Labor, Population Movement, and Food in Sixteenth-Century Ek Balam, Yucatán," *Latin American Antiquity* 19, no. 3 (2008).

38. R. Lee Lyman, "Quantitative Units and Terminology in Zooarchaeology," *American Antiquity* 59, no. 1 (1994).

39. Lewis R. Binford, *Nunamuit Ethnoarchaeology* (New York: Academic Press, 1978); Walter E. Klippel, "Sugar Monoculture, Bovid Skeletal Part Frequencies, and Stable Carbon Isotopes: Interpreting Enslaved African Diet at Brimstone Hill, St Kitts, West Indies," *Journal of Archaeological Science* 28 (2001).

40. Schulz and Gust, "Faunal Remains and Social Status."

41. At the time, the US dollar was equal to about eleven Mexican pesos, and a kilo is equivalent to 2.21 pounds. Thus, a cut of meat that costs 170 pesos per kilo would be equivalent to about $7 a pound.

42. Schulz and Gust, "Faunal Remains and Social Status," 48; Lyman, "Quantitative Units"; Klippel, "Sugar Monoculture."

43. Elizabeth J. Reitz, "The Spanish Colonial Experience and Domestic Animals," *Historical Archaeology* 26, no. 1 (1992): 88–89; for an exception from Southern Peru, see Susan deFrance, "Iberian Foodways in the Moquegua and Torata Valleys of Southern Peru," *Historical Archaeology* 30 (1996).

44. Romano Soriano, "San Miguel Acocotla, Atlixco"; Zeitlin, *Cultural Politics.*

45. Judith Francis Zeitlin and Elizabeth Terese Newman, "Domestic Animals in Domestic Spaces: The Indigenization of Pastoral Economies in Colonial Mexico," paper presented at the annual conference of the Society for Historical Archaeology, York, England, 2005.

46. Fournier-Garcia, "Tendencias de Consumo"; Lister and Lister, "Potters' Quarter."

47. Charlton, "Socioeconomic Dimensions," 131.

48. Deagan, *Artifacts of the Spanish Colonies,* 1:87–88.

49. The nineteenth-century majolicas were characterized following the typology set forth in Seifert, "Archaeological Majolicas." Many of the patterns found at Acocotla are also identical to nineteenth-century sherds found at Puebla's pottery factories; see Lister and Lister, "Potters' Quarter."

50. Seifert, "Archaeological Majolicas," 201; Goggin, *Spanish Majolica.*

51. Ivor Noël Hume, *A Guide to the Artifacts of Colonial America* (New York: Alfred A. Knopf, 1970), 197–98.

52. Though people in the descendant community do not use hand-painted majolicas today, they are still available throughout Mexico and are popular with tourists.

Chapter 8

1. AHMA 1893, Gobierno, caja 309, exp. 5 (12890).

2. Prosser buttons are high-fired ceramic buttons produced after June of 1840. Roderick Sprague, "China or Prosser Button Identification and Dating," *Historical Archaeology* 36, no. 2 (2002).

3. Ibid., fig. 1g.

4. Herrera Feria, "Trabajadores Prófugos," 149.

5. An 1872 census of the workers at the Hacienda San Miguel Acocotla documents children's wages. Children ages ten to thirteen were paid twelve and a half centavos a day, compared with the twenty-five centavos a day their fathers received. During interviews in the descendant community, individuals said that they and their parents had worked on the hacienda as children for the same wages, suggesting that children's wages remained stagnant while adult's wages rose only slightly between 1872 and 1910. AHMA 1872, Gobierno, caja 123, exp. 4 (5206).

6. Meyers, *Outside the Hacienda Walls,* 44–45; Sweitz, "On the Periphery of the Periphery," 380–81; Alejandro Tortolero Villaseñor, *Notarios y Agricultores: Crecimiento y Atraso en el Campo Cexicano, 1780–1920: Propiedad, Crédito, Irrigación y Conflictos Sociales en el Agro Mexicano* (Mexico City: Universidad Autónoma Metropolitana Siglo Veintiuno Editores, 2008), 115–18. Though the traditionally held view is that prices of goods sold at the tiendas de raya were inflated, some scholars have found this to be untrue. See, e.g., William Bluestein, "The Class Relations of the

Hacienda and the Village in Prerevolutionary Morelos," *Latin American Perspectives* 9, no. 3 (1982): 16–17; Harry E. Cross, "Living Standards in Rural Nineteenth-Century Mexico: Zacatecas 1820–80," *Journal of Latin American Studies* 10, no. 1 (1978); Cross, "Debt Peonage Reconsidered," 478–79; Herrera Rodriguez, "Social Change," 6; Katz, "Labor Conditions," 9; Meyers, "Material Expressions"; Nickel, *Relaciones de Trabajo*, 167–72; Nickel, *Peonaje en las Haciendas Mexicanas*, 215–16; Wasserman, *Everyday Life*, 25. Others have suggested that while prices charged may have been no higher than at local stores, the tienda de raya, as the place where workers spent money and managers made a profit, was "the focus of nearly everything residents saw as wrong in their economic relations with the hacienda." David W. Walker, "Homegrown Revolution: The Hacienda Santa Catalina del Alamo y Anexas and Agrarian Protest in Eastern Durango, Mexico, 1897–1913," *Hispanic American Historical Review* 72, no. 2 (1992): 244.

7. Deagan, *Artifacts of the Spanish Colonies*, 1:52; Müller, *Estudio de la Cerámica*, 103, 38.

8. Müller, *Estudio de la Cerámica*, 103, 38.

9. Charlton and Katz, "Tonalá Bruñida Ware," 46.

10. Deagan, *Artifacts of the Spanish Colonies*, 1:44–46.

11. Ibid., 1:45.

12. Natacha Seseña "El búcaro de las Meninas" (1999) qtd. in María Concepción García Sáiz, "Mexican Ceramics in Spain," in *Cerámica y Cultura: The Story of Spanish and Mexican Mayólica*, ed. Robin Farwell Gavin, Donna Pierce, and Alfonso Pleguezuelo (Albuquerque: University of New Mexico Press, 2003), 190.

13. Peter W. Abrahams, "'Earth Eaters': Ancient and Modern Perspectives on Human Geophagy," *Soil and Culture* (2009); John M. Hunter and Renate de Kleine, "Geophagy in Central America," *Geographical Review* 74, no. 2 (1984); Ellen Simpson et al., "Pica During Pregnancy in Low-Income Women Born in Mexico," *Western Journal of Medicine* 173, no. 1 (2000).

14. Deagan, *Artifacts of the Spanish Colonies*, 2:66.

15. Ibid., 2:120.

16. Ibid., 2:90.

17. Ibid.

18. Mary H. Parsons, "Spindle Whorls from the Teotihuacán Valley, Mexico," in *Miscellaneous Studies in Mexican Prehistory*, ed. Michael V. Spence, Jeffery R. Parsons, and Mary H. Parsons (Ann Arbor: University of Michigan, 1972); Francis F. Berdan, "Cotton in Aztec Mexico: Production, Distribution and Uses," *Mexican Studies/Estudios Mexicanos* 3, no. 2 (1987); Michael E. Smith, *The Aztecs*, People of the Americas (Oxford: Wiley-Blackwell, 2003).

19. Smith, *Aztecs*, 84.

20. Bazant, "Industria Algodonera Poblana"; Crider, "Material Struggles."

21. AHMA 1893, Gobierno, caja 309, exp. 5 (12890).

22. Deagan, *Artifacts of the Spanish Colonies*, 2:298–301.

23. Mílada Bazant de Saldaña, *En Busca de la Modernidad: Procesos Educativos en el Estado de México, 1873–1912* (Zinacantepec, México: Colegio Mexiquense, Colegio de Michoacán, 2002); Kanter, *Hijos del Pueblo*; Tutino, "From Involution to Revolution."

24. Guy P. C. Thomson and David G. LaFrance, *Patriotism, Politics, and Popular Liberalism in Nineteenth-Century Mexico: Juan Francisco Lucas and the Puebla Sierra* (Wilmington, DE: Scholarly Resources, 2002).

25. AHMA 1865, Gobierno, caja 98, exp. 1 (4332).

26. AHMA 1870, Gobierno, caja 115, exp. 2 (4971); AHMA 1873, Gobierno, caja 133, exp. 3 (5565).

27. AHMA 1841, Gobierno, caja 34, exp. 5 (1714).

28. AHMA 1841, Gobierno, caja 36, exp. 2 (1770).

29. Bracamonte y Sosa, *Amos y Sirvientes*.

30. Allan D. Meyers, "Community Household and Status at Hacienda Tabi, Yucatan, Mexico" (PhD diss., Texas A&M University, 1998), 154.

31. Timothy J. H. Knab, *A War of Witches: A Journey into the Underworld of the Contemporary Aztecs* (San Francisco: Harper, 1995).

32. Deagan, *Artifacts of the Spanish Colonies*, 2:95.

33. K. Deagan, pers. comm., November 2007; pictured in Deagan, *Artifacts of the Spanish Colonies*, 2:103, fig. 5.16.

34. W. L. Hildburg, "Images of the Human Hand as Amulets in Spain," *Journal of the Warburg and Courtauld Institutes* 18, no. 1/2 (1955): 67.

35. James M. Davidson, "Rituals Captured in Context and Time: Charm Use in North Dallas Freedman's Town (1869–1907), Dallas, Texas," *Historical Archaeology* 38, no. 2 (2004): 26.

36. Hildburg, "Images of the Human Hand."

37. Deagan, *Artifacts of the Spanish Colonies*, 2:98–99, table 5.2.

38. Ibid., 300.

39. Ibid., 301.

40. Byron Hamann, "The Social Life of Pre-sunrise Things," *Current Anthropology* 43, no. 3 (2002); Timothy J. H. Knab, *The Dialogue of Earth and Sky: Dreams, Souls, Curing, and the Modern Aztec Underworld* (Tucson: University of Arizona Press, 2004).

41. Enrique Rodríguez-Alegría, "Narratives of Conquest, Colonialism, and Cutting Edge Technology," *American Anthropologist* 110, no. 1 (2008).

42. Stephen W. Silliman, *Lost Laborers in Colonial California: Native Americans and the Archaeology of Rancho Petaluma* (Tucson: University of Arizona Press, 2004); Palka, *Unconquered Lacandon Maya*.

Conclusion

1. Kanter, *Hijos del Pueblo*; Tutino, "From Involution to Revolution"; John Tutino, "The Revolutionary Capacity of Rural Communities: Ecological Autonomy and Its Demise," in *Cycles of Conflict, Centuries of Change: Crisis, Reform, and Revolution in Mexico*, ed. Elisa Servìn, Leticia Reina, and John Tutino (Durham, NC: Duke University Press, 2007); John Tutino, "Soberanìa Quebrada, Insurgencias Populares, y la Independence de México: La Guerra de Independencias, 1808–1821," *Historia Mexicana* 59, no. 1 (2009); Eric Van Young, "1810–1910: Semejanzas y Diferencias," *Historia Mexicana* 59, no. 1 (2009).

2. Kanter, *Hijos del Pueblo*; Tutino, "From Involution to Revolution."

3. Katz, "Labor Conditions."

4. It is worth noting that by employing the wives of the workers, the hacendado was further limiting the number of paying positions available to men from the villages.

5. Andrés Reséndez Fuentes, "Battleground Women: Soldaderas and Female Soldiers in the Mexican Revolution," *Americas* 51, no. 4 (1995); Elizabeth Salas, *Soldaderas in the Mexican Military: Myth and History* (Austin: University of Texas Press, 1990).

6. Warman, "Political Project," 327.

7. See, e.g., Christine Eber and Christine Kovic, *Women of Chiapas: Making History in Times of Struggle and Hope* (New York: Routledge, 2003); Shannon Speed, Rosalva Aída Hernández Castillo, and Lynn M. Stephen, eds., *Dissident Women: Gender and Cultural Politics in Chiapas*, Louann Atkins Temple Women and Culture Series (Austin: University of Texas Press, 2006); Rosalva Aída Hernández Castillo, *Histories and Stories from Chiapas: Border Identities in Southern Mexico* (Austin: University of Texas Press, 2001); Rosalva Aída Hernández Castillo, "Between Hope and Adversity: The Struggle of Organized Women in Chiapas Since the Zapatista Uprising," *Journal of Latin American Anthropology* 3, no. 1 (1997); Rosalva Aída Hernández Castillo, "Zapatismo and the Emergence of Indigenous Feminism," *NACLA Report on the Americas* 35, no. 6 (2002). The more recent but less studied uprising in Oaxaca shows similar trends for indigenous women's participation. See Lynn Stephen, "'We Are Brown, We Are Short, We Are Fat, We Are the Face of Oaxaca': Women Leaders in the Oaxaca Rebellion," *Socialism and Democracy* 21, no. 2 (2007).

8. Melissa M. Forbis, "Hacía la Autonomía: Zapatista Women Developing a New World," in Eber and Kovic, *Women of Chiapas*; Rosalva Aída Hernández Castillo, "Between Feminist Ethnocentricity and Ethnic Essentialism: The Zapatistas' Demands and the National Indigenous Women's Movement," in Speed, Hernández Castillo, and Stephen, *Dissident Women: Gender and Cultural Politics in Chiapas*.

9. Christine Kovic, "Demanding Their Dignity as Daughters of God: Catholic Women and Human Rights," in Eber and Kovic, *Women of Chiapas*, 143.

10. Samuel Brunk, *The Posthumous Career of Emiliano Zapata: Myth, Memory, and Mexico's Twentieth Century*, Joe R. and Teresa Lozano Long Series in Latin American and Latino Art and Culture (Austin: University of Texas Press, 2008), 65.

11. Michael C. Meyer, William L. Sherman, and Susan M. Deeds, *The Course of Mexican History*, 6th ed. (New York: Oxford University Press, 1999), 578.

12. Romano Soriano, "San Miguel Acocotla, Atlixco."

13. Brunk, *Posthumous Career*.

14. Hewitt de Alcántara, *Anthropological Perspectives*, 126.

15. Scott, *Moral Economy of the Peasant*; Thompson, *The Making of the English Working Class*; Thompson, "Moral Economy of the English Crowd."

16. Jeffrey S. Passel and D'Vera Cohn, *Mexican Immigrants: How Many Come? How Many Leave?* (Washington, DC: Pew Hispanic Center, 2009), i.

Appendix

1. Calderón de la Barca, *Life in Mexico*; Evans and Pettus, *Rosalie Evans Letters*.

2. Womack, *Zapata*, 81.

3. Ibid., 275–77.

4. Ibid., 267.

Glossary

alguacíl mayor. A sheriff or constable.

barranca. A ravine and/or dry stream.

barrio. Neighborhood.

bruja. A witch.

cacique. A native "chief," often the head of a village or community.

calpanería. Housing provided by a hacienda owner for his/her workers.

caporal(es). Higher status/more trusted workers allotted living space within the hacienda's walls.

casco. The architectural core of a hacienda property.

cazuela. Stewpot, traditionally ceramic but today can be purchased in aluminum alloys as well.

chinamite. Dried corn stalks used both to build structures and as animal feed.

comal(es). A round ceramic griddle used most commonly to prepare tortillas over an open fire.

compadre (comadre; compadres). Godfather (godmother; godparents). In Latin America, this relationship is not only or necessarily established at birth.

coyote. Person who guides migrants across the border.

dormitorio. Bedroom.

El Norte. Literally "the North," slang for the United States.

encomienda. Spanish colonial system used to regulate indigenous labor.

fiesta. A party.

hacendado(a). The owner of a hacienda.

hornos. Adobe ovens used for baking bread on Day of the Dead.

huesero. A healer, often self-trained or trained through apprenticeship to another huesero, whose focus is on setting bones and massage, though they may offer other cures to the community as needed.

informant. Interviewee.

lebrillo. An open bowl.

mano. Grinding stone/pestle often used with a metate.

mayordomo. Manager.

metate. Stone platform on which things, most often corn, are ground.

midden. Trash heap.

molcajete. A mortar, but here more specifically, a tripod bowl made out of stone or ceramic for grinding nuts, spices, etc.

mole. A spicy sauce. There are a number of different kinds of moles with a wide variety of ingredients. They are usually known by their colors, such as mole verde (green mole) and mole negra (black mole, which is made with chocolate).

Nahuatl. Indigenous language belonging to the Uto-Aztecan family spoken by the Nahua and, most famously, by the Aztecs.

nixtamal. Dried corn treated with lime and heat; not unlike hominy; used to make tortillas, pozole, tamales, and so on.

olla. A tall ceramic jar with a globular body, narrow neck, and wide mouth used for food/water storage and cooking.

peone. Worker.

presidencia ejidal. In effect, the mayor's office. The *ejido* refers to the shared, communal land received by the community during the agrarian reforms. The *presidente* is traditionally the head of this organization.

pulque. A mildly alcoholic beverage made from fermented maguey (or agave) sap.

strata. Layers of earth identified during excavation; may be identified as either natural and/or cultural.

telenovela. Soap opera.

telesecundaria. A secondary school for rural students. The schools generally have one or two teachers to supervise, but lessons are broadcast to the classrooms via satellite.

temascal. Sweat bath.

tepetate. Sterile soil found below archaeological deposits.

tienda de raya. A hacienda store, which would have sold a variety of foods, beverages, and household goods.

Selected Bibliography

The following list does not provide a comprehensive record of all works cited in this book but rather is composed of materials referenced in the endnotes that I felt were the most appropriate for offering the student or non-specialist insight into the major issues or historical periods discussed in the text. Interested scholars may consult the author's webpage, www.elizabethnewman.org for a complete bibliography of the primary and secondary works cited.

Alexander, Rani T. 2004. *Yaxcabá and the Caste War of Yucatán: An Archaeological Perspective*. Albuquerque: University of New Mexico Press.

Bauer, Arnold J. 2001. *Goods, Power, History: Latin America's Material Culture*. New Approaches to the Americas. Cambridge: Cambridge University Press.

Benavides Castillo, Antonio. 1985. "Notas Sobre la Arquelología Histórica de la Hacienda Tabi, Yucatán." *Revista Mexicana de Estudios Antropológicos* 31:45–58.

Bracamonte y Sosa, Pedro. 1993. *Amos y Sirvientes: las Haciendas de Yucatán, 1789–1860*. Merida: Universidad Autónoma de Yucatán.

Brading, David A. 1978. *Haciendas and Ranchos in the Mexican Bajío, León, 1700–1860*. Cambridge Latin American Studies. Cambridge: Cambridge University Press.

Castañeda González, Rocío. 2005. *Las Aguas de Atlixco. Estado, Haciendas, Fábricas y Pueblos, 1880–1920*. Mexico City: El Colegio de Mexico.

Chance, John K. 2003. "Haciendas, Ranchos, and Indian Towns: A Case Study from the Late Colonial Valley of Puebla." *Ethnohistory* 50(1):15–45.

Charlton, Thomas H. 1969. "Ethnohistory and Archaeology: Post-conquest Aztec Sites." *American Antiquity* 34(3):286–94.

———. 1986. "Socioeconomic Dimensions of Urban-Rural Relations in the Colonial Period Basin of Mexico." In *Supplement to the Handbook of Middle American*

Indians, Vol. 4, *Ethnohistory*, edited by Ronald Spores, 122–33. Austin: University of Texas Press.

Chevalier, François. 1963. *Land and Society in Colonial Mexico: The Great Hacienda.* Berkeley: University of California Press.

Christie, Maria Elisa. 2008. *Kitchenspace: Women, Fiestas, and Everyday Life in Central Mexico.* Joe R. and Teresa Lozano Long Series in Latin American and Latino Art and Culture. Austin: University of Texas Press.

Deagan, Kathleen A. 1987. *Artifacts of the Spanish Colonies of Florida and the Caribbean, 1500–1800.* 2 vols. Washington, DC: Smithsonian Institution Press.

Deal, Michael. 1998. *Pottery Ethnoarchaeology in the Central Maya Highlands.* Foundations of Archaeological Inquiry. Salt Lake City: University of Utah Press.

De la Torre Villalpando, Guadalupe. 1988. *Las Calpanerías de las Haciendas Tlaxcaltecas.* Tlaxcala, México: Instituto Nacional de Antropología e Historia.

Evans, Rosalie Caden, and Daisy Pettus. 1926. *The Rosalie Evans Letters from Mexico.* Indianapolis, IN: Bobbs-Merrill.

Fournier, Patricia. 2003. "Historical Archaeology in Mexico: A Reappraisal." *SAA Archaeological Record* 3(4):18–19.

Fournier-Garcia, Patricia, and Lourdes Mondragon. 2003. "Haciendas, Ranchos, and the Otomi Way of Life in the Mezquital Valley, Hidalgo, Mexico." *Ethnohistory* 50(1):47–68.

Gasco, Janine, Greg Charles Smith, and Patricia Fournier-Garcia, eds. 1997. *Approaches to the Historical Archaeology of Mexico, Central, and South America.* Los Angeles: Institute of Archaeology, University of California.

Gibson, Charles. 1964. *The Aztecs Under Spanish Rule: A History of the Indians of the Valley of Mexico 1519–1810.* Stanford, CA: Stanford University Press.

González Sánchez, Isabel. 1997. *Haciendas, Tumultos y Trabajadores Puebla-Tlaxcala: 1778–1798.* Serie Manuales. Mexico City: Instituto Nacional de Antropología e Historia.

Hewitt de Alcántara, Cynthia. 1984. *Anthropological Perspectives on Rural Mexico.* International Library of Anthropology. London: Routledge.

Jarquín, María Teresa, ed. 1990. *Origen y Evolución de la Hacienda en México, Siglos XVI al XX: Memorias del Simposio Realizado del 27 al 30 de Septiembre de 1989.* Zinacantepec, México: Colegio Mexiquense; Universidad Iberoamericana; Instituto Nacional de Antropología e Historia (Mexico).

Juli, Harold. 2003. "Perspectives on Mexican Hacienda Archaeology." *SAA Archaeological Record* 3(4):23–24.

Kanter, Deborah Ellen. 2008. *Hijos del Pueblo: Gender, Family, and Community in Rural Mexico, 1730–1850.* Austin: University of Texas Press.

Katz, Friedrich. 1974. "Labor Conditions on Haciendas in Porfirian Mexico: Some Trends and Tendencies." *Hispanic American Historical Review* 54(1):1–47.

Kepecs, Susan, and Rani T. Alexander, eds. 2005. *The Postclassic to Spanish-Era Transition in Mesoamerica: Archaeological Perspectives.* Albuquerque: University of New Mexico Press.

Knab, Timothy J. H. 1995. *A War of Witches: A Journey into the Underworld of the Contemporary Aztecs.* San Francisco: Harper.

Lackey, Louana M. 1982. *The Pottery of Acatlán: A Changing Mexican Tradition.* Norman: University of Oklahoma Press.

Lipsett-Rivera, Sonya. 1999. *To Defend Our Water with the Blood of Our Veins: The Struggle for Resources in Colonial Puebla*. Albuquerque: University of New Mexico Press.

Lockhart, James. 1992. *The Nahuas After the Conquest: a Social and Cultural History of the Indians of Central Mexico, Sixteenth Through Eighteenth Centuries*. Stanford, CA: Stanford University Press.

Meyers, Allan D. 2012. *Outside the Hacienda Walls: The Archaeology of Plantation Peonage in Nineteenth-Century Yucatán*. Archaeology of Colonialism in Native North America. Tucson: University of Arizona Press.

Newman, Elizabeth Terese. 2010. "Butchers and Shamans: Zooarchaeology at a Central Mexican Hacienda." *Historical Archaeology* 44(2):35–50.

———.2013. "From Prison to Home: Labor Relations and Social Control in Nineteenth Century Mexico." *Ethnohistory* 60(4): 663-692.

Nickel, Herbert J. 1997. *El Peonaje en las Haciendas Mexicanas: Interpretaciones, Fuentes, Hallazgos*. Mexico City: Universidad Iberoamericana.

Palka, Joel W. 2005. *Unconquered Lacandon Maya: Ethnohistory and Archaeology of Indigenous Culture Change*. Maya Studies. Gainesville: University Press of Florida.

Reina, Leticia. 1980. *Las Rebeliones Campesinas en México, 1819–1906*. Mexico City: Siglo Veintiuno.

Rodríguez-Alegría, Enrique. 2005. "Eating Like an Indian: Negotiating Social Relations in the Spanish Colonies." *Current Anthropology* 46(4):551–73.

Stern, Steve J. 1995. *The Secret History of Gender: Women, Men, and Power in Late Colonial Mexico*. Chapel Hill: University of North Carolina Press.

Terán Bonilla, José Antonio. 1996. *La Construcción de las Haciendas de Tlaxcala*. Mexico City: Instituto Nacional de Antropología e Historia.

Tutino, John. 1986. *From Insurrection to Revolution in Mexico: Social Bases of Agrarian Violence, 1750–1940*. Princeton, NJ: Princeton University Press.

Van Young, Eric. 1983. "Mexican Rural History Since Chevalier: The Historiography of the Colonial Hacienda." *Latin American Research Review* 18(3):5–61.

———. 2006. *Hacienda and Market in Eighteenth-Century Mexico: The Rural Economy of the Guadalajara Region, 1675–1820*. 2nd ed. Latin American Silhouettes. Lanham, MD: Rowman and Littlefield.

Wasserman, Mark. 2000. *Everyday Life and Politics in Nineteenth Century Mexico: Men, Women, and War*. Albuquerque: University of New Mexico Press.

Wobeser, Gisela. 1989. *La Formación de la Hacienda en la Época Colonial. El Uso de la Tierra y el Agua*. Mexico City: Universidad Nacional Autónoma de México.

Wolf, Eric R. 1969. *Peasant Wars of the Twentieth Century*. New York: Harper and Row.

Wolf, Eric R., and Sydney Mintz. 1957. "Haciendas and Plantations in Middle America and the Antilles." *Social and Economic Studies* 6:380–411.

Womack, John. 1968. *Zapata and the Mexican Revolution*. New York: Knopf.

Zeitlin, Judith Francis. 2005. *Cultural Politics in Colonial Tehuantepec: Community and State Among the Isthmus Zapotec, 1500–1750*. Stanford, CA: Stanford University Press.

Index

acculturation, 12, 13, 17, 207, 215n2. *See also* modernization

activity areas, 7, 27, 69–70, 71–74, 75, 76, 80, 81–82, 87, 90, 93–94, 109–11, 115, 122–23, 131–32, 134

agrarian reform, 4, 8, 17, 18–19, 25, 30, 57, 65–66, 83, 84, 115, 201–3, 207–8, 209

agriculture, 12, 13, 23–24, 36, 37–38, 42, 51, 63–64, 67, 119, 132, 173, 176. *See also* water, irrigation

alcohol, 36, 62, 87, 131, 165

Alexander, Rani, 26, 111

animal bones. *See* foodways

architecture, 78, 82–83, 110; and abandonment, 80–81, 83, 111; domestic, 66–67, 68–69, 70–73, 78–79, 81–83, 117–18, 122–23; and gender, 69–70, 76, 132–34, 137; hacienda, 37–38, 47, 84–90, 119–20, 125–27, 231n5; interior versus exterior space, 69, 71–73, 74–76, 81–82, 109–10, 122–23, 130–32; and power, 117–27, 131–32, 136–38; and status, 78–79, 110, 126–27, 137, 160, 176, 203, 204, 230n24, 230n30. *See also* households; calpanería

autonomy, 205–6

Ayaquica, Fortino, 10–11, 17, 21, 30, 203

beads, 115, 171, 182–84; and medicinal properties, 182

beef. *See* foodways, meat

bones. *See* foodways, meat

bottles, 94, 162, 165, 185–86, 191, 195

Bourbon Reforms, 14

Braudel, Fernand, 141

bullets, 173–74

butchering, 154–55, 156, 157–59

buttons, 171–72, 174–75, 196, 238n2

calpanería, 22–23, 27, 31, 47, 71, 74, 75, 86–87, 100, 109–11, 114, 125, 128–34, 150, 166, 168, 176, 196, 203; architecture, 86–87, 90–93, 95, 115, 117–18, 122–23, 125, 128–29, 137–38; calpanería, excavations of, 7, 98, 99, 100–106, 119

capitalism, 12, 17, 30–32, 125–27, 134, 136–37, 141, 156, 187, 202, 205–6

caporales, 88, 126

Caste War, 26

Catholic Church, 16, 37, 40–41, 47, 50, 61, 114, 171, 181, 190, 192–93; as bank, 34, 42

cattle. *See* livestock

About the Author

Elizabeth Terese Newman received a BA in history and archaeology from the University of Massachusetts, Boston in 2000 and PhD in anthropology from Yale University in 2008. This book, based on her doctoral dissertation, incorporates significant new research. Newman's research interests include Mesoamerican ethnohistory, historical archaeology, and environmental archaeology with a specialty in zooarchaeology. Since 2006, she has been directing an ongoing research project that examines the social and cultural origins of revolution in Puebla, Mexico, using the disciplines of ethnohistory, ethnography, and archaeology.

Newman is currently assistant professor of history at Stony Brook University. Prior to joining the history department, she taught environmental humanities and anthropology at Stony Brook's Southampton campus. While at Stony Brook Southampton, Newman was responsible for the creation and direction of a new interdisciplinary BA degree in environmental humanities, one of only a handful of programs of its kind in the country. She has also taught for the University of the Americas in Puebla, Mexico, and at Connecticut College. Outside of academia, Newman worked for the National Park Service and the Boston Museum of Science.